TOURING

CALIFORNIA AND NEVADA HOT SPRINGS

Help Us Keep This Guide Up to Date

Every effort has been made by the author and editors to make this guide as accurate and useful as possible. However, many things can change after a guide is published—establishments close, facilities come under new management, routes change, and so forth.

We would love to hear from you concerning your experiences with this guide and how you feel it could be improved and kept up to date. While we may not be able to respond to all comments and suggestions, we'll take them to heart and we'll also make certain to share them with the author. Please send your comments and suggestions to the following address:

The Globe Pequot Press
Reader Response/Editorial Department
P.O. Box 480
Guilford, CT 06437

Or you may e-mail us at:

editorial@GlobePequot.com

Thanks for your input, and happy travels!

TOURING

CALIFORNIA AND NEVADA HOT SPRINGS

SECOND EDITION

MATT C. BISCHOFF

FALCONGUIDES®

GUILFORD, CONNECTICUT
HELENA, MONTANA

AN IMPRINT OF THE GLOBE PEQUOT PRESS

FALCONGUIDES®

Previously published by Falcon Publishing, Inc. in 1997.

Maps by Tim Kissel © Morris Book Publishing, LLC.
Photos by Matt C. Bischoff

ISBN 978-0-7627-3641-6

Manufactured in the United States of America
Second Edition/Fourth Printing

The author and The Globe Pequot Press assume no liability for accidents happening to, or injuries sustained by, readers who engage in activities described in this book.

To Dr. James L. Bischoff, who first introduced me to hot springs and shared his enthusiasm for these geological wonders.

Touring California and Nevada Hot Springs

SCALE RF 1 : 8,260,000 — 0 50 100 150 200 km. / 0 50 100 150 mi. N

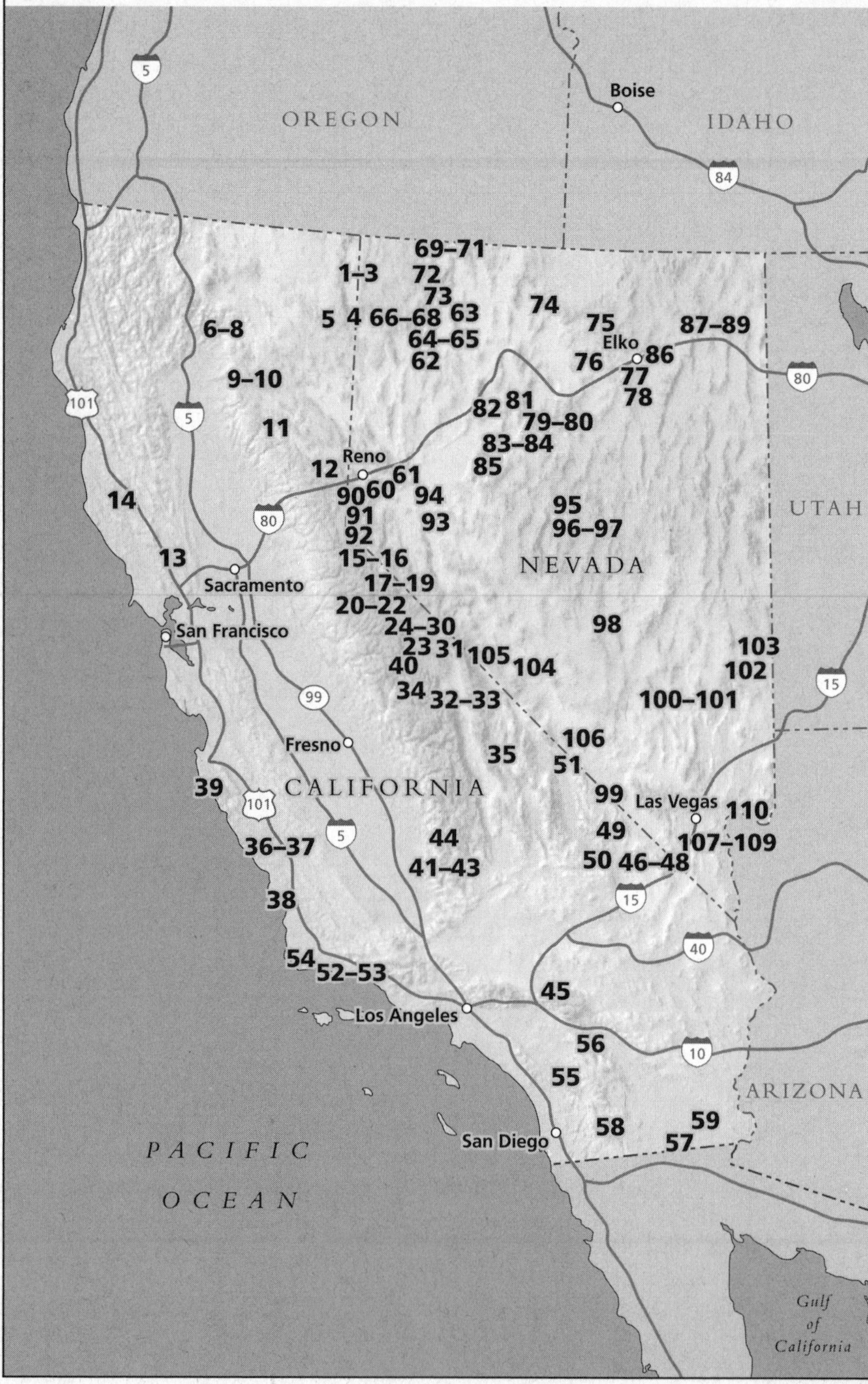

CONTENTS

ACKNOWLEDGMENTS

So many people helped in the production of this book. Thanks first go to my wife, Patty, who is literally an answered prayer. Thank you for all those late nights putting the maps together, as well as letting me drag you along on yet another hot springs trip. Thanks must also go to Mary Beth and James Bischoff, for encouraging me in this endeavor so many years ago. They are the best marketing staff anyone could ever hope for! I also want to thank the Russo family for all of their support these many years. The dedicated and talented staff at The Globe Pequot Press have made this effort far easier and made me look good through all of their hard work. Thanks also go to Bill Schneider and Dave Singleton, who have ably assisted in the many production and format issues related to such a large undertaking. None of this would have been possible without my Lord and my God, Jesus Christ, who sustains me and upholds me all the days of my life.

INTRODUCTION

Hot Springs in History

Hissing steam vents, erupting geysers, boiling mud pots, and bubbling springs of hot water issuing naturally from the earth are fascinating and mysterious things to behold. Peering into these springs, one gets the distinct feeling that one is viewing the interior of the earth. That, in fact, is not far from the truth.

Long before recorded history, ancient people used hot springs for bathing and food preparation. According to archaeological evidence, balneology, the utilization of natural mineral waters for the treatment of disease, has been practiced for over 5,000 years. Hot springs have been used in religious rites and ceremonies in both Egypt and the Middle East for thousands of years. The ancient Greeks and Romans were addicted to the pleasures of spas, and they built important communities around natural hot springs and harnessed and channeled the thermal waters into their elaborate buildings and colossal public baths. The Japanese have particularly enjoyed such a tradition continuously from their ancient past to the present, and a visit to a traditional Japanese hot spring resort today is a special experience and pleasure. The Victorian era in Europe saw a rebirth of the interest in spas, particularly for the medicinal benefits attributed to drinking the waters, though bathing was still an important activity. A visit to a spa became a fashionable pastime for Europe's wealthy, and centers of thermal waters that had earlier been exploited by the Romans were developed into elaborate resort-hotel complexes.

On this continent Native Americans for untold years have used hot springs as campsites, village locations, and sacred places. As illustrated in this book, the evidence of Native use of hot springs remains today. Soon after Europeans arrived in North America, hot springs were sought out, discovered, and exploited. The popularity of hot spring resorts in Europe eventually spilled over into America, and they were particularly popular from the 1880s through the turn of the century. Resorts were built at such locations as Hot Springs, Arkansas; Saratoga Springs, New York; Warm Springs, Georgia; and White Sulphur Springs, West Virginia. Because of the lower population and lack of governmental support, however, these resorts never became as extensive as their European counterparts. As people had used the natural hot spring pools and ponds for therapy for years, those in the Victorian age desired a more civilized way of bathing. Resorts and spas became the answer, allowing for private and controlled bathing in the medicinal waters.

Hot springs throughout the country began to be harnessed for use in resorts during the Victorian period, in the years near the beginning of the twentieth century. Remains at countless hot springs in the West attest to this boom time in commercial hot spring bathing. These resorts generally promised that their spring waters contained preventative and curative values. By the turn of the century, transportation had vastly improved in the West, allowing people to visit places in days that would have taken weeks otherwise. The arrival of the automobile also increased the mobility of Americans, allowing many people to visit the various hot spring resorts across the country.

The fashion waned by the outbreak of the First World War, but by that time all the major thermal areas of the eastern United States had been developed. In the West development of thermal waters was much less extensive because of a much smaller population density during the same period. Nevertheless, by the 1950s the boom in hot spring resorts had passed, and many closed down or were simply abandoned. Many of these resorts have never reopened. Today, an increased interest in hot springs has witnessed the reuse of previously abandoned springs, with varying results.

A tub at White Sulphur Springs Resort in California

Despite their decline in popularity, hot springs continue to be used for a variety of purposes. In many places around the world, particularly in Europe and Japan, hot springs are still used for medical purposes, and they are believed by millions to have preventative and treatment values for a variety of ailments. Today, there are an estimated 1,800 hot springs in the United States, the majority of which are in the West. Out of those hot springs, approximately 115 have been developed into extensive resorts or spas.

Geology of Hot Springs

Much is known about the geological setting of hot springs, the surface manifestation of what geologists term geothermal systems. Much is known because many of these systems have been tapped for the generation of electricity, a clean source of energy to replace fossil fuels. Hot springs on the surface of the earth can be no hotter than the boiling point at the earth's surface (100 degrees C, or 212 degrees F). Waters at depth, however, can reach temperatures as high as 400 degrees C, or 752 degrees F! Such super temperatures are possible because the boiling point is raised by the high hydrostatic pressure at great depth, and because of the nearness to subsurface molten rock (magma).

The earth's heat originates deep beneath the crust, through the decaying of natural radioactive elements such as uranium, thorium, and potassium. Hot springs generally occur where the earth's heat, in the form of hot or molten rock, exists at relatively shallow depths. Areas of recent or active volcanic activity (such as Lassen Volcanic National Park) are obvious locales. Though hot springs are abundant in these regions, the most prevalent and spectacular ones are on the sea floor, far from human view. These underwater springs occur along chains of active submarine volcanoes called spreading centers, the places where the earth's plates diverge. Hot springs can also occur in places where there is no obvious source for the heating of the water (far from volcanic areas, for example). These hot springs are formed either from magma bodies at depth with no surface manifestation, or the water itself has come from great depths where there is abundant heat, forced to the surface by some unexplained means.

Hot springs occur because of convection. Just as air above a radiator rises as it expands from being heated, water also rises as it is heated. Rocks are generally full of cracks and fractures, and these inevitably become filled with water as rainwater percolates downward to fill all the voids. This water is collected in the porous rocks and kept as groundwater (where well water comes from). In mountainous regions this water sometimes emerges again as springs, downhill from where the water first entered the fractured rocks, at times forced to the surface from some impermeable barrier. These natural cold-water springs occur because of simple gravity flow and differ from hot springs, which flow because of convective forcing.

The source of Crowley (Wild Willy's) Hot Spring in California

The convective process giving rise to hot springs can be visualized as follows: Groundwater near a recently injected molten body becomes very hot, even boiling. Such heated water (with associated steam) is less dense than the surrounding cold groundwater, so it rises toward the surface. As it does, cold groundwater instantaneously moves into the void around the magma to replace the rising water, and convection is initiated. The system functions like a coffee percolator. The heated water mixes with overlying water as it rises, and loses some of its heat to the rocks through which it passes, eventually discharging at the surface as a hot spring. The pathway of ascent is commonly along a fault because of ease of flow (see diagram on page 5).

Once such convection systems are set up, they can last for hundreds of years, as heat is slowly harvested from the magma, forcing it to cool and solidify. Water flow, temperatures, and the chemical composition of such hot spring waters often remain stable for long periods of time in spite of year-to-year variation in rainfall, suggesting the complex plumbing systems are very deep and large.

The chemical composition of the thermal waters is controlled by the rocks through which they pass. For example, some hot springs deposit calcium carbonate–rich travertine around their orifices, such as Travertine Hot Springs (described in this book) and Mammoth Hot Springs in Yellowstone National Park. Waters of these springs leach and dissolve calcium carbonate from limestone they traverse in the subsurface. When the thermal waters discharge at the surface, the water effervesces dissolved CO_2 gas in the same way soda pop effervesces when the bottle cap is removed. Loss of CO_2 results in the precipitation of calcium carbonate. Thus, hot springs with travertine are evidence of limestone down below.

In most volcanically active regions where limestone is not present, hot springs deposit siliceous sinter around their orifices, which has an entirely different character than travertine. Sinter is relatively pure silica, the same composition as quartz and the most common constituent of igneous rocks. At room temperature silica is almost insoluble, and we use it for glass. At the high temperatures at depth in the geothermal systems, however, silica is relatively soluble, so the thermal waters leach silica from the rocks. As the waters discharge, the silica becomes supersaturated upon the cooling of the spring, and the silica precipitates as sinter. These two types of chemical deposits, sinter and travertine, are quite different in character and tell us much about the subsurface geology through which the hot waters passed.

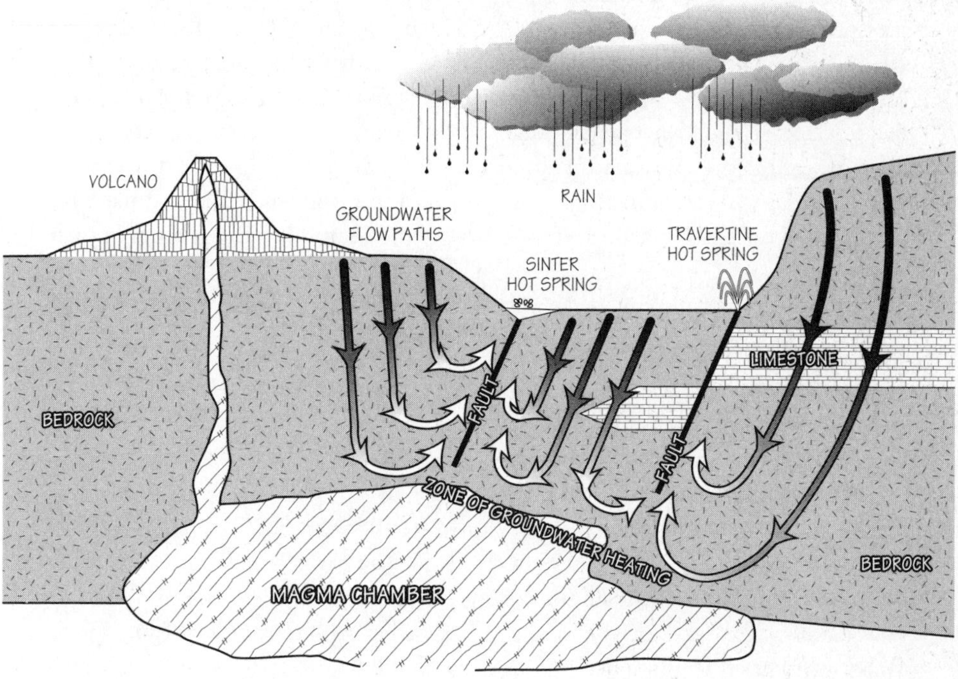

Microbes

A variety of microorganisms are known to live in hot springs. Recently, however, scientists have discovered a unique, previously unknown community of microbes living in particular hot springs in the West. These microbes appear to thrive in the geothermal environment, even without sunlight or oxygen. The one-celled organisms are called *Archaea,* and they live off hydrogen produced by the hot water when it interacts with bedrock as deep as 600 feet below the surface. In turn, the microbes produce a small amount of methane. These organisms have been found in hot springs in the Yellowstone area, though they could potentially exist in other locations as well. The ramifications of the discovery are limitless. Generally, life on Earth requires not only water, but also oxygen, sunlight, and organic carbon. Other planets in the solar system lack these conditions. If organisms can live in the hostile environment presented by deep hot springs, then the potential for their existence in other inhospitable locations, such as Mars, is also greater.

Precautions

As many hot springs are far from civilization, precautions should be taken. Be sure your vehicle is in sound shape and able to make a long trip. Check on all of the engine's fluids, including oil and coolant. Be sure that every tire has the necessary pressure, and that you have a spare (along with a jack and lug wrench). Be sure you know how to change a tire before you head out. By far the most common breakdown is a flat tire, and when driving on dirt roads, you will eventually get a flat. Rocks have a tendency to get caught in your treads, occasionally puncturing the fabric of the tire. Always plan ahead when considering gasoline. Be sure you know how far you are going, what your gas mileage is, and where the next place is that you can purchase gasoline. The location of the nearest services is given in each of the entries.

If you plan on camping, make a checklist of equipment needed before heading out. I recommend you bring at least the following:

- ☐ spare tire, jack, lug wrench
- ☐ basic tool kit for the car (screwdrivers, wrenches, hammer, etc.)
- ☐ shelter of some kind (e.g., tent)
- ☐ extra clothing (including wet-weather gear)
- ☐ sleeping bag, insulating pad, blankets
- ☐ food and water (more than you will need)
- ☐ stove or other means by which to cook food
- ☐ electrical tape
- ☐ rope
- ☐ shovel
- ☐ ax or small saw
- ☐ firewood
- ☐ candles
- ☐ matches
- ☐ flashlights, extra batteries
- ☐ knife
- ☐ first-aid kit

Once you have packed all this gear, be sure to notify someone of your trip and when you plan on returning. If you are planning on being out for the day only, it is not a bad idea to bring along most of this equipment, as you'll be glad you did if you do get stranded. Contact the land management agency for the area into which you are heading and ask about access, restrictions, and permit requirements. Be sure to keep a watch on the weather, and if storms threaten, stay off secondary dirt roads even if you have four-wheel drive, and all dirt roads if you have a passenger vehicle. A road may not be wet when you depart, but may become impassable during and following a storm. When in the desert portions of California and Nevada, be especially aware of thunderstorms and flash floods. Flash floods can occur even when it is not raining where you are. Desert washes can fill with no warning and become raging torrents. Do not under any circumstances make camp in a wash.

Heat

Visiting hot springs carries with it certain risks and inherent dangers. Hot springs, after all, can contain scalding water. Pay attention to all directions and descriptions given in this book. Most dangers are pointed out to the reader, but not all can be anticipated. Do not under any circumstances get into water without first testing it in some way. You will usually be able to tell how hot a spring is just by coming near the water. If you can feel the heat of the water from a few inches away, it's probably too hot. If the water is steaming even on a warm day, it's also probably too hot. If the water appears to be fine, put a finger or hand in the water to test it. If your hand can't stay submerged without hurting, don't put your body in. More importantly, if you cannot see the bottom of a spring in any way, don't get in. The water on the top of the spring may be fine, but deeper water may scald you. Be careful also around mud in hot springs, as it can often hide extremely hot water underneath. When in doubt, stay out.

Amoebae

Perhaps one of the most lethal dangers posed by certain hot springs is the presence of the amoeba *Naegleria fowleri*. This amoeba enters human hosts through mucus membranes via the nose, causing an infection resembling meningitis that is nearly always fatal. Just to be safe when visiting these springs, do not put your head under the water or let the water enter your nose or mouth.

Responsible Behavior

Visiting hot springs carries with it a sort of unspoken etiquette. As most of the hot springs described in this book are on public land, you will not be trespassing. A few of the springs are located on private land, in which case I tell you this and recommend that you do not trespass. In other cases the landowner has allowed people to visit the springs on his or her property. Either way, respect private

Concrete tubs above the Kern River at Remington Hot Spring in California

property. If there are NO TRESPASSING signs, obey them. This will not only prevent you from getting shot, but will also help to keep numerous hot springs open to the public. When on public land, also obey all signs. Overnight camping is often not permitted, and is usually so posted. Obey these signs, as there are usually campgrounds or other public lands that do not restrict camping nearby.

One of the biggest problems faced by hot spring enthusiasts is vandalism and trash. Most of the well-known hot springs have experienced some aspect of these activities. Graffiti, broken glass, trash, and off-road driving truly detract from the beauty these places hold. Be sure to pack out all trash, stay on established roads, and generally leave things as you found them (or better).

Several hot springs described in this book are quite popular. Do not be surprised (especially in California) when you find people already at your hot spring destination. People generally prefer privacy and will appreciate it if you let them finish their soak before you enjoy the water. This is especially true for families and couples. Others may enjoy your company, and a simple inquiry will let you know either way. Many locations offer several soaking opportunities, sometimes quite removed from the other pools.

Many people enjoy hot springs in a natural state. For those hot springs in remote locations, this is generally the norm. Most public bathing facilities or pools in public view generally require bathing suits, unless you have a private room. You will generally see the prevalent trend at most springs. Again, obey any and all signs posted and there should be no problem. In several localities nudity has become pervasive. The frequenters of these springs prefer to go clothesless for just about every activity. Some of the locations where nudity is more prevalent include Deep Creek, Saline Valley Hot Springs, and the Long Valley hot springs. Some of the resorts listed also allow visitors to remain nude in the pool areas. These locations include Sierraville Hot Springs and Tecopa. If nudity offends you, you may not want to visit these places, or you may wish to wait until you can have the locality to yourself.

AUTHOR'S FAVORITES

For an Isolated Experience

Black Rock Hot Springs. Located on the margins of an immense dry lake in northern Nevada, only accessible during a few dry months, Black Rock Hot Springs truly gives you a feeling of isolation. The large black rock formation from which the hot spring derives its name has long been a beacon for travelers. Native Americans used the spring as a campsite for generations. For emigrants to Oregon and California in the mid-nineteenth century, the black rock and its hot spring served as a milestone and campsite. Today, a historical marker, placed by an overland trails club, reminds visitors of the historical significance of the spot. A Bureau of Land Management sign also reminds one of the twentieth century. Otherwise, the landscape has changed little.

The hot spring can only be reached by traveling across the Black Rock Desert Playa, a worthy experience in itself. For only a short three months, the playa is generally safe to drive on, otherwise the mud becomes wet and undrivable. Occasionally, the mighty prehistoric lake actually becomes a lake again, giving one a glimpse back to the Pleistocene when large mammals roamed the same country. A mammoth was discovered on this very playa, dating to over 10,000 years old.

Hot Springs Near the City

Big Caliente and Little Caliente Hot Springs. The two Caliente hot springs lie in the rugged mountains above Santa Barbara. Although the road to the springs is long, windy, and dirt for much of its distance, the springs can easily be visited in a day from Santa Barbara. The best seasons in which to visit are fall and spring, as summer can be too hot to make bathing enjoyable, and winter's rains may make the road impassable.

Located within the Los Padres National Forest, Big and Little Caliente Hot Springs see a high volume of visitors throughout the year, particularly on weekends. There are several campgrounds and picnic areas within the national forest, along with countless trails for hiking and mountain biking. The best chance for seclusion is during the week.

Most Amazing Geologic Feature

Diana's Punch Bowl. This hot spring is the most visually spectacular in the book, and the most amazing one I've ever seen. A huge travertine hill marks the location of the spring from miles away. In the middle of this huge hill is a gigantic cavern, extending into the hill approximately 30 feet. At the bottom crystal clear hot spring water forms a large pool. You can then see another 10 to 20 feet down into the spring itself. The view feels like a window to the interior of the earth.

In addition to the spectacular nature of this spring, there are bathing opportunities to boot (don't even think of trying to get into the cavern). Along the flank of the hill are several small pools of varying temperature, offering a view of the beautiful Monitor Valley. This hot spring is near several other interesting sites, most notably the ghost town of Belmont to the west.

Most Popular Spring with Everyone Else

Travertine Hot Springs. Close to the highway and easy to reach, Travertine Hot Springs has seen a rapid increase in visitors the past few years. It is no wonder, however. The spring is another fascinating geologic feature, exhibiting a prominent ridge of travertine. The bathing opportunities are also fantastic at Travertine. The upper pool has been meticulously maintained by dedicated volunteers, and the lower ones offer a more natural bathing experience. The water temperature is also ideal, and the scenery is unparalleled, with a view of the Bridgeport Valley and the mighty Sierras beyond. U.S. Highway 395 is a well-traveled road, carrying skiers headed for Mammoth Lakes, sightseers going to Yosemite, and a wide variety of other tourists. Located less than 2 miles from the highway, Travertine is an easy stopover for a quick soak.

For the Family

Agua Caliente Hot Spring. Although a developed hot spring, Agua Caliente is a great place for a bath. The large indoor pool is reserved for adults, but the cooler outdoor pool is also open to children. Either one offers a great soaking opportunity in a great location. The spring is run by the County of San Diego, within the Anza Borrego Desert State Park in extreme southern California. The state park offers unlimited recreational opportunities for the family, including camping, hiking, biking, sightseeing, bird and other animal viewing, history, and archaeology. Plan on visiting the hot springs during the winter when temperatures moderate from the summer highs of 110 to 120 degrees F. The campground and springs are closed from June 1 to September 1.

HOW TO USE THIS BOOK

Book Organization

California and Nevada are the two largest producers of geothermal power in the country. California, in fact, produces more geothermal energy than anywhere else in the world. Despite the abundance of harnessed hot springs in these two states, there are plenty that are still in their natural form.

This guide does not pretend to be an exhaustive list of hot springs and hot spring resorts in California and Nevada. It is, instead, a guide to and description of some of the best hot springs in the West. Most of the springs you will find in this book are of the natural type. There are a few listings for hot spring resorts, but the focus is upon natural hot springs in natural settings. There are many hot spring resorts in California and Nevada, and I have included those that are particularly enjoyable, have natural pools on their property, or are in a particularly picturesque or historic setting. This book is also not strictly a guide to hot spring soaking. Though most of the springs described offer wonderful bathing experiences, there are several that are worth visiting simply for interest's sake or because they are located in a particularly important setting. Before you visit any of these springs, please read the precautions and etiquette sections in the introduction.

The book is organized geographically, to allow for the greatest ease in traveling from one hot spring to the next. Following a short introduction to the spring, all the pertinent information you will need for a visit is provided. Subjects such as location, best time of year, access, and nearest services are listed. Detailed directions are given for each spring, followed by a more in-depth discussion and description of the spring itself.

The book is divided into nine geographic regions. Each hot spring is placed within one of these regions. In some cases hot springs in one region may be closer to springs in another region than to those in its own. Bowers Mansion and Carson Hot Springs (Central Nevada) are far closer to Steamboat Villa Hot Springs Spa (Northern Nevada) than they are to any other spring in Central Nevada. The lines between the regions were drawn arbitrarily, simply for the sake of organization. To find out what other springs are in the area, check the overview map of California and Nevada.

The book is further divided into subregions. These subregions were also created arbitrarily, though they are designed to give the reader a sense of place when visiting a hot spring or series of hot springs. Generally, these subregions follow geographical, archaeological, or historical lines.

A short introduction is given for each region, as well as for most subregions, pointing out some of the more salient features of the area in which the reader finds him/herself. In several places historical vignettes are also included to add some flavor to the region, putting the reader far ahead of the casual tourist who generally knows nothing about the area he or she is visiting.

How to Follow the Directions and Maps

Each set of directions is designed to be used in conjunction with the maps provided. These directions have all been field checked and should get you to the spring with minimal confusion. The maps provided show the important features needed for reaching the spring, but the reader needs to pay close attention to the mileages given in the "Finding the spring" portion of the entry. These maps use shaded, or shadow, relief. Shadow relief does not represent elevation; it demonstrates slope or relative steepness. This gives an almost 3-D perspective of the physiography of a region and will help you see where ranges and valleys are.

A recommended topographic quadrangle map name is listed prior to "Finding the spring" under "Map." These maps can be ordered directly from the USGS for under ten bucks. They can also be found at many map stores and some specialty outdoor outlets. Topographic map software is also readily available; it provides digitized maps by state or region.

In several cases it is recommended that the reader obtain a Forest Service map for the region. The phone number for the pertinent national forest is given in the spring's description. It is also recommended that the reader contact the land management agency with jurisdiction over the hot spring to be visited. Important information such as up-to-date road conditions, access, permit requirements, and weather can usually be obtained from these offices. The numbers for most of these offices are also given in the springs' descriptions.

Map Legend

Transportation

Limited Access Freeway	
U.S. Highway	
State Highway	
Local Road	
Local Road (unpaved)	
Trail	
Railroad	
Old Railroad Grade	
Interstate Highway	25
U.S. Highway	85
State Highway	14
County Highway	58
Forest Road	558

Boundaries

National Park, National Forest, Large State or Local Park	PARK
Wilderness Area	PARK

Population

City	Reno
Town	Wells

Grids

Latitude / Longitude Number and Ticks	38° 53' N

Hydrology

Featured Spring	
Spring	
Reservoir or Lake	Lake
Alkali Lake	Lake
Intermittent Lake	Lake
River or Creek	Creek

Physiography

Terrain (Shaded Relief)

Mountain, Peak, or Butte

Valley

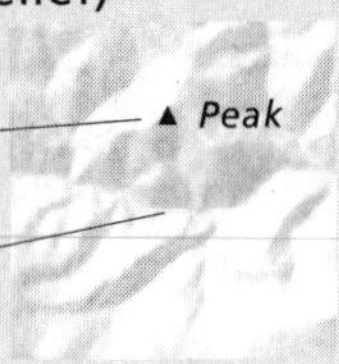

Symbols

Building or Structure	
Airport	
Ranger Station	
Point of Interest	
Campground	
Picnic Ground	
Church	
Trailhead	
Golf Course	
Gate	
Pass	

NORTHERN CALIFORNIA

Extending from Surprise Valley along the Nevada border in the east to the redwood country along U.S. Highway 101 in the west, northern California is a region of beauty and contrasts. Numerous mountain ranges cover the region, leaving most of the country high in elevation. In the north the Cascades cover a majority of the eastern part of the state, with an abundance of volcanic activity. The Cascades are met (at Lassen Volcanic National Park) by the Sierra Nevada, which covers the next two-thirds of the state to the south. In the west the state is dominated by the Trinity and Siskiyou mountains, providing rugged backcountry largely controlled by the USDA Forest Service. As the northern portion is the least developed of the state, many people forget that the majority of California is only lightly populated and offers outdoor recreation aplenty. Although the Surprise Valley region is relatively dry, the rest of northern California is much wetter than Nevada. Most of the springs described in this section are located in the high country, and therefore are better visited during the drier times of the year.

Indian Springs at Big Bend Hot Springs

SURPRISE VALLEY REGION

The Surprise Valley is topographically very similar to regions lying to the east, within the state of Nevada. Bounded on the west by the Warner Mountains, the valley largely lies within a rain shadow and therefore is rather dry. The largest town, Cedarville, is small but does offer some basic services (gas, food). For more complete services one must drive over the mountains into Alturas, approximately 23 miles away. The Surprise Valley is largely farming and cattle-raising country. The three lakes within the valley are generally dry, though in wetter years they will have a few feet of water in them. Numerous lakes and rivers abound in the surrounding mountains, offering fishing, hiking, and camping opportunities. Because of its relative lack of population and its out-of-the-way location, few people visit Surprise Valley. The county road through the valley is not a major thoroughfare, and aside from California Highway 299 to Alturas, the few roads in the area are largely unimproved. For these reasons you should have ample opportunity for seclusion in this region.

1 Leonard's Hot Spring

General description: A series of ponds created by the damming up of a creek of hot spring water in an isolated part of northeastern California. The remains of a hot spring resort, complete with empty swimming pool and collapsed buildings, can be seen adjacent to some of the ponds.

Location: Northeastern California, approximately 11 miles east of Cedarville.

Primitive/developed: Primitive, except for the damming up of the creek and the remains of the resort.

Best time of year: Year-round. Roads may be muddy and slippery in wet weather.

Restrictions: None.

Access: Most passenger cars can make the trip.

Water temperature: 144 degrees F at source, decreasing as it flows down the small creek. All the pools are very hot. The largest and most appealing is approximately 120 degrees F (too hot for bathing).

Nearby attractions: Eagleville Hot Spring, Glenn's Hot Spring, Applegate Hot Springs.

Services: None; nearest gasoline, food, and supplies can be found in Cedarville, approximately 11 miles away. Cedarville is a small town, however; don't count on getting lodging there. Alturas, a larger town, is approximately 23 miles west on California Highway 299.

Camping: There does not appear to be any restrictions against camping at this spot. Please respect the privacy of others, pack out all trash, and keep in mind that there are several houses and ranches in the nearby valley.

Map: USGS topographic, Cedarville, CA, quadrangle, 1:100,000 scale.

Finding the spring: From Cedarville, travel north on Surprise Valley Road for approximately 5 miles to County Road 18 (49 Lane). Turn right (east) on this paved road, and drive approximately 4.5 miles (it will turn into a graded dirt road, but is well maintained). The road will make a major bend to the right. The springs are off to your right, past a small corral. A small road leads to the ruins of a swimming pool and several buildings adjacent to the hot springs.

Leonard's Hot Spring; Glenn's Hot Spring; Applegate Hot Springs; Eagleville Hot Spring

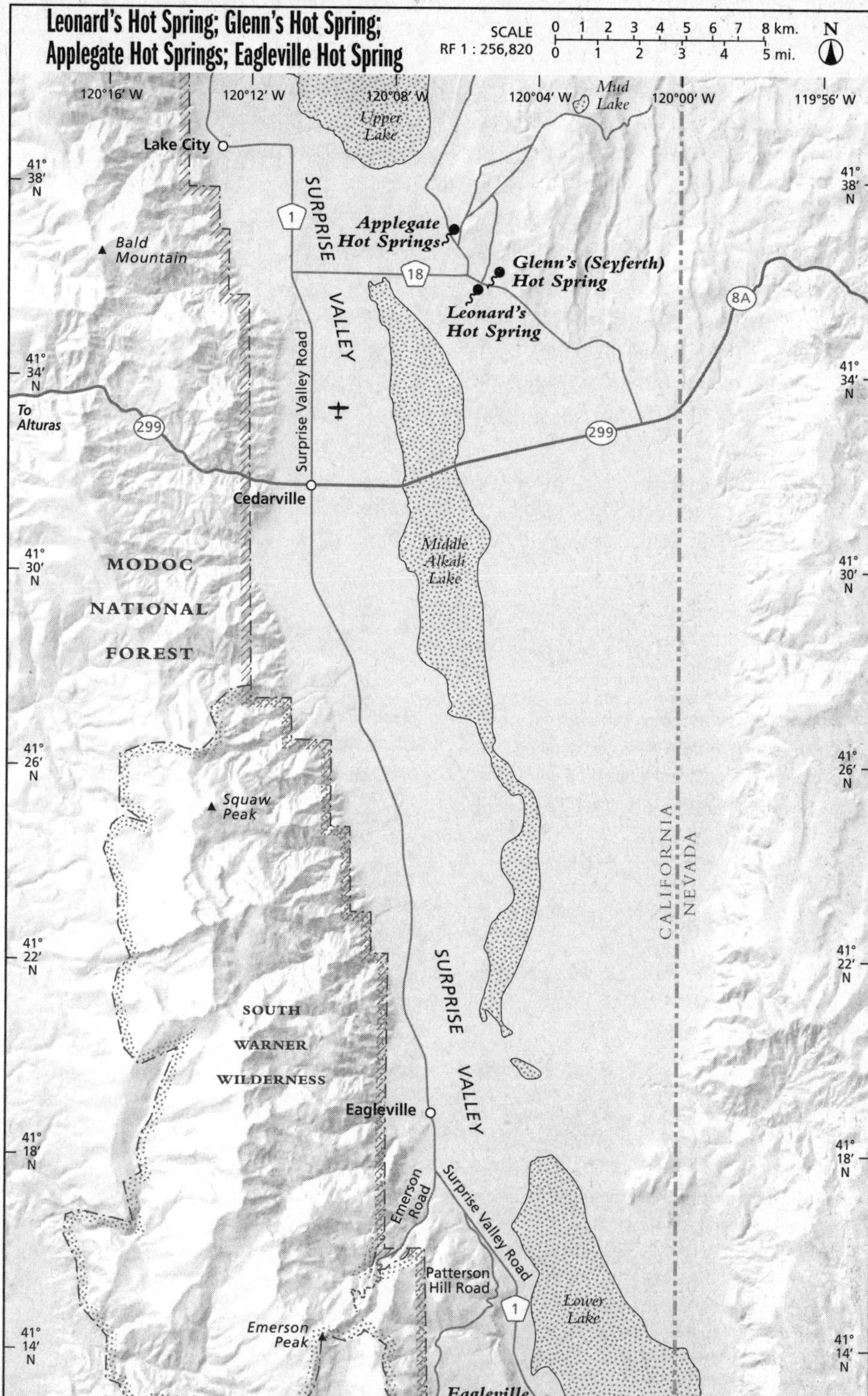

The Hot Spring

Once you get to the secondary dirt road off CR 18 (49 Lane), drive less than half a mile to the largest bathable pond. Follow the creek that is created by the hot spring water to find other ponds that have been constructed. Most of these are either too muddy or are unappealing. You will see the remains of the old hot spring resort. There are some other smaller ponds to bathe in on this side of the road. Most of these other ponds, however, are rather shallow and have been silted up. The largest pond, near the hot spring source, is your best bet for a bath and is approximately 120 degrees F. The pond itself is about 3 by 5 feet and 3 feet deep. Be careful before getting in, as the water temperature has a tendency to change.

This is a nice spot in a scenic valley in an underpopulated part of northern California. On a weekday you can generally expect to have this spot to yourself. It does get a few visitors on weekends, however. Do keep in mind that you are not totally out in the middle of nowhere, and only a few miles from a town. Glenn's Hot Spring, Applegate Hot Springs, and Eagleville Hot Spring are all relatively close by, and all three can be easily visited the same day.

2 Glenn's (Seyferth) Hot Spring

See map on page 17.

General description: A second series of ponds created by the damming up of a creek of hot spring water in an isolated part of northeastern California, near Leonard's Hot Spring.

Location: Northeastern California, approximately 11 miles from Cedarville.

Primitive/developed: Primitive, except for the damming up of the creek.

Best time of year: Year-round. Roads may be muddy and slippery in wet weather.

Restrictions: None.

Access: Most passenger cars can make the trip. The secondary dirt road from County Road 18 (49 Lane) to the spring is a little rough, and some low-clearance passenger cars may have problems.

Water temperature: 185 degrees F at source, decreasing as it flows down the small creek. Average pond temperature is approximately 120 degrees F (too hot for bathing).

Nearby attractions: Eagleville Hot Spring, Leonard's Hot Spring, and Applegate Hot Springs.

Services: None; nearest gasoline, food, and supplies can be found in Cedarville, approximately 11 miles away. Cedarville is a small town, however; don't count on getting lodging there. Alturas, a slightly larger town, is approximately 23 miles west on California Highway 299.

Camping: There does not appear to be any restrictions against camping at this spot. Please respect the privacy of others, pack out all trash, and keep in mind that there are several houses and ranches in the nearby valley.

Map: USGS topographic, Cedarville, CA, quadrangle, 1:100,000 scale.

Finding the spring: From Cedarville, travel north on Surprise Valley Road for approximately 5 miles to CR 18. Turn right (east) on this road and drive for approximately 4.5 miles, turning left on a small dirt road, approximately 100 yards past Leonard's Hot Spring (immediately before a small creek goes under CR 18). Follow this secondary dirt road for approximately 0.25 mile to the various sources of hot spring water.

The Hot Spring

Similar to Leonard's Hot Spring, these springs are also rather primitive. Many of the springs are also much hotter than those at Leonard's, and as such you should be very careful before entering any of them. There are several ponds in the creek that parallels the small road leading to the source. By the time the water crosses under the county road, however, it is a small trickle and there are no more bathing opportunities. As with Leonard's, many of the springs are unappealing due to silting, but with some selecting and perhaps some digging, you may find a good bathing opportunity.

3 Applegate Hot Springs

See map on page 17.

General description: A series of small ponds created by the damming up of a creek of hot spring water in an isolated part of northeastern California, near Leonard's and Glenn's Hot Springs.

Location: Northeastern California, approximately 11 miles from Cedarville.

Primitive/developed: Primitive, except for the damming up of the creek.

Best time of year: Year-round. Roads may be muddy and slippery in wet weather.

Restrictions: None.

Access: Most passenger cars can make the trip. The secondary dirt road to the springs themselves is a little rough, and some low-clearance passenger cars may have problems.

Water temperature: 185 degrees F at source, decreasing as it flows down the small creek. Average pond temperature is approximately 120 degrees F (too hot for bathing).

Nearby attractions: Eagleville Hot Spring, Leonard's Hot Spring, Glenn's Hot Spring.

Services: None; nearest gasoline, food, and supplies can be found in Cedarville, approximately 11 miles away. Cedarville is a small town, however; don't count on getting lodging there. Alturas, a slightly larger town, is approximately 23 miles west on California Highway 299.

Camping: There does not appear to be any restrictions against camping at this spot. Please respect the privacy of others, pack out all trash, and keep in mind that there are several houses and ranches in the nearby valley.

Map: USGS topographic, Cedarville, CA, quadrangle, 1:100,000 scale.

Finding the springs: From Cedarville, travel north on Surprise Valley Road for approximately 5 miles to County Road 18. Turn right (east) on this road and drive for approximately 4.5 miles to the first major bend to the right just before Leonard's Hot Spring. As the road makes the first bend to the right, follow a smaller dirt road to the left (at the bend in the road). Follow this graded dirt road for approximately 1 mile to a small dirt road on the right (immediately after crossing a small creek). Follow this small unimproved road for a few hundred yards to the hot spring sources.

The Hot Springs

Applegate Hot Springs are located near Leonard's and Glenn's Hot Springs and are equally hot. They also do not currently provide any good bathing opportunities, but this could change if volunteers construct pools and hot water is diverted into them. They are, however, interesting nonetheless, and worth a visit while in this area. The hot springs were located along the so-called Applegate Trail of the California Trail, and were often used as a campground by emigrants. They were frequently described in many emigrant diaries. A small sign was erected near the springs to commemorate the passage of the many emigrants through this area.

4 Eagleville Hot Spring

See map on page 17.

General description: A fantastic hot spring in a scenic valley immediately off a seldom-used highway. Hot water emerging from the side of the hill is channelized into a small pond and a large redwood hot tub.

Location: Northeastern California, approximately 23 miles from Cedarville.

Primitive/developed: Primitive, except for the piping of the water into the small pond and redwood hot tub.

Best time of year: Year-round.

Restrictions: None.

Access: Any vehicle can access the hot spring, as it is immediately off a paved highway.

Water temperature: 130 degrees F at source, approximately 110 degrees F in the pond, and 105 degrees F in the hot tub.

Nearby attractions: Leonard's Hot Spring, Glenn's Hot Spring, Applegate Hot Springs.

Services: None; nearest gasoline, food, and supplies can be found in Cedarville, approximately 23 miles away. Cedarville is a small town, however; don't count on getting lodging there. Alturas, a slightly larger town, is approximately 45 miles west on California Highway 299. Eagleville has few to no services.

Camping: This is not a place to camp, as the only parking is on the highway itself. There is plenty of public land in the surrounding countryside where undeveloped camping is available, however. Just be sure not to trespass.

Map: USGS topographic, Cedarville, CA, quadrangle, 1:100,000 scale.

Finding the spring: From the town of Cedarville, travel south on Surprise Valley Road 15 miles to the town of Eagleville. From Eagleville, travel another 7.5 miles south to a large turnout on the left side of the road. This turnout is immediately south of the 5.5 mile marker. Park here and walk the short but steep trail to the spring.

The Hot Spring

One of the better soaking opportunities in the area, Eagleville Hot Spring is in a beautiful location, is easy to get to, and has ideal water temperature. You will see the spring once you get out of your car at the turnout. The steep path to the spring is less than 50 yards. Be careful, however, as it is rather slippery. The hot spring water emerges from the side of the hill and is deposited into a small pond via tubing. This pond is approximately 10 feet across and 2 feet deep, with crystal clear water. The water is also transported into a large redwood tub with a slightly cooler water temperature than the pond. The tub is small but rather deep, with enough room for two.

The view from Eagleville Hot Spring is beautiful, and like so many described in this book, looks out on a vast valley flanked by large mountain ranges. You can usually expect to have this spring to yourself, though it does seem to be well

Eagleville Hot Spring

known by those few who drive the road that bypasses it. If there is someone at the spring, you usually don't have to wait long to get it to yourself. Weekend nights you may find local partyers hanging out at the spring until late. Recently a sign has been put up at the hot springs indicating that they are on private property and are open at the discretion of the landowner. Please respect this private property, and obey all signs.

Other books provide directions to another hot spring a short distance to the south of Eagleville Hot Spring (called Wild Mint Hot Springs by some). These springs, however, are on private property and are not open for public use at this time. NO TRESPASSING signs are in place and should be obeyed.

SOUTHERN CASCADE MOUNTAINS REGION

Immediately to the west of the Surprise Valley lie the Warner Mountains and other ranges comprising the Cascade Mountains. Within these mountains lie some of the best backcountry in the state and some of the best hot springs. The Cascades, which extend into Oregon and Washington, border the Sierra Nevada to the south in this region, roughly at Lassen Volcanic National Park. Because the Cascades are an active chain of volcanoes, there is an abundance of hot spring activity within and adjacent to them. It is believed that the Sierra Nevada range actually extends below the Cascades (which are younger), emerging again in northwestern California in the Trinity and Siskiyou regions.

A large part of the area is controlled by the Forest Service and is therefore unpopulated. Several national monuments and national parks are also interspersed throughout the region, offering abundant sightseeing and recreation. Roads in this region are few, but most areas can be accessed with ease. Because the elevations in these mountains can be quite high (well over 8,000 feet in places), winter travel is not recommended. Snow is common, and many of the roads described are subject to closure due to snow accumulation. Hiking, hunting, fishing, camping, and general sightseeing opportunities are plentiful. Prior to any trip you make, a map of the region within which you are traveling should be obtained. USGS topographic maps are an excellent place to start, though a Forest Service map is also recommended if you plan on entering a national forest. Also be sure to contact the local government agency (usually the Forest Service) in charge of the land in which you propose to travel.

5 West Valley Warm Springs

General description: A small warm spring feeding two small pools in a picturesque, quiet valley in northeastern California.

Location: Northeastern California, approximately 25 miles from Alturas.

Primitive/developed: Primitive, except for the creation of two small rock pools.

Best time of year: Year-round.

Restrictions: None.

Access: The warm springs are located along a fairly well-maintained secondary dirt road. The road will become wet and muddy during rain.

Water temperature: 90 degrees F at source, lukewarm in the small ponds.

Nearby attractions: West Valley Reservoir, Blue Lake.

Services: None; nearest gasoline, food, and supplies can be found in Alturas, approximately 25 miles away. The small community of Likely has a general store and a bar.

Camping: There is quite a bit of level space where people have camped adjacent to the spring. Be sure to obey any signs that may appear in the future.

Map: USGS topographic, Alturas, CA, quadrangle, 1:100,000 scale.

Finding the springs: From the town of Alturas, travel south on U.S. Highway 395 for approximately 20 miles to the small town of Likely. Turn left (east) onto paved Jess Valley Road (County Road 64). Follow this road for approximately 2.5 miles to West Valley Road (County Road 66), where you turn right (south). Follow this graded dirt road for approximately 2.5 miles to a Y in the road. The main road goes left to the West Valley Reservoir; bear right here onto a lesser road. Follow this road for approximately 3.5 miles to a smaller road on your left. Turn here and drive 100 yards or so to the warm springs.

The Hot Springs

This is a small collection of warm springs feeding a small meadow used for grazing cattle. One of the warm spring sources has been used to form two rock pools. These pools are small and lukewarm, however, and not the best bathing opportunity. But the meadow is beautiful and provides a lovely setting for a picnic or short adventure. West Valley Reservoir is also nearby, as are numerous campgrounds in the Warner Mountains to the east (including the picturesque Blue Lake).

Lava Beds National Monument: Approximately 50 miles northwest of Canby is Lava Beds National Monument. The monument is a huge lava field, formed hundreds of years ago when nearby volcanoes spewed molten rock into the area. As the lava cooled, large caverns, deep chasms, and tunnels were formed. Because of this mazelike landscape, the lava beds were the site of the Modoc Indians' last-ditch battle against U.S. forces between 1872 and 1873. Following confrontations between the Modocs and local settlers, the U.S. Army fought a series of small engagements with the Indians. During a peace treaty council, a group of Modocs

West Valley Warm Springs

West Valley Warm Springs

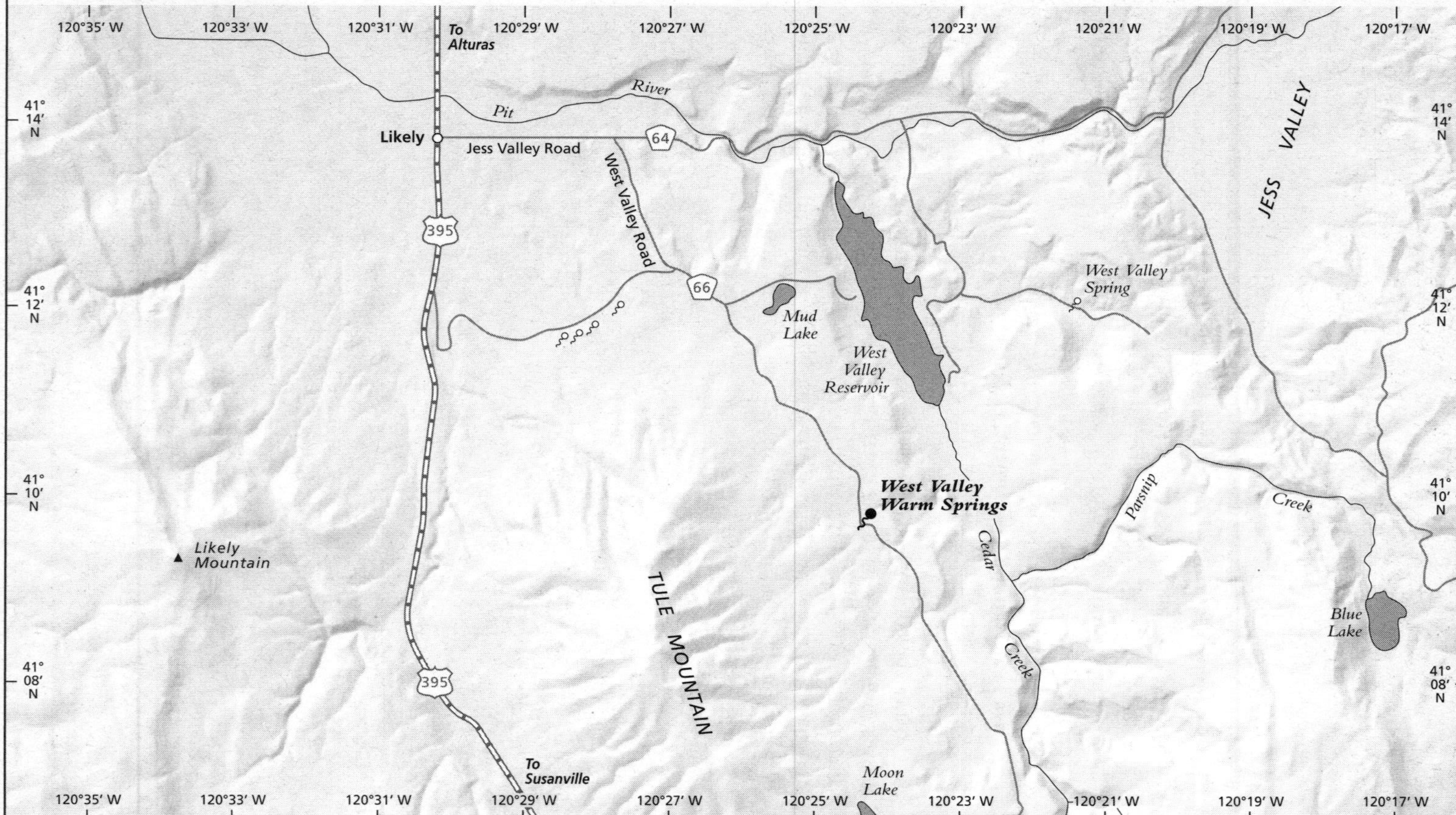

planned and carried out a surprise attack on the white officials, killing a number of them. Following the treacherous attack, the army pursued the Modocs in earnest, forcing them into this volcanic maze-land. The Modocs were able to hold out in the area for months, but they were eventually driven out, forced to surrender, and executed or shipped to Oklahoma for imprisonment.

The monument offers undeveloped camping, hiking trails, a visitor center, and interpretive displays. There are no services available. To reach the lava beds, travel north out of Canby on California Highway 139 to Toinessta Road, and follow the signs west to the park. Travel another 17 miles to the monument headquarters. For further information, contact the Lava Beds National Monument at (916) 667–2282.

6 Big Bend Hot Springs

General description: A series of hot springs on the banks of the Pit River, currently harnessed by a rustic resort. There are several soaking opportunities ranging from concrete tubs to rock-lined pools in the river.

Location: Northern California, approximately 52 miles east of Redding.

Primitive/developed: Primitive, though some of the pools are man-made with concrete.

Best time of year: Year-round.

Restrictions: This is a private resort, and pools are open to guests only.

Access: Any vehicle can access the resort, as it is at the end of a paved road.

Water temperature: Varies; some of the sources are 180 degrees F, but tub temperatures can be regulated with cold water.

Nearby attractions: Lake Shasta, Lassen Volcanic National Park.

Services: The resort provides camping, water, and primitive toilets. Groceries can be found in the town of Big Bend, 0.5 mile away. Nearest gasoline is in Burney, approximately 16 miles away.

Camping: There is camping at the resort, and there are also many campgrounds in the nearby Trinity and Shasta National Forests.

Map: California Highway Map.

Finding the springs: From the town of Redding, travel east on California Highway 299 for 35 miles to Big Bend Road, following the signs for the town of Big Bend, where you will turn left (north). Travel on this smaller paved road for approximately 15 miles to Hot Springs Road, where you turn left. Continue to the end of this road for 0.5 mile to the hot spring resort. The turnoff to Hot Springs Road is immediately before you cross the Pitt River. If you wish to get supplies, there is a small store near the river.

The Hot Springs

Big Bend Hot Springs is a rustic resort providing campsites near the edge of the Pit River. Several hot springs in different locations feed this pleasant resort in a beautiful location. There are three man-made pools on the resort grounds where the temperature is controlled by adding or subtracting river water. There are also several hot springs at the rivers edge, which can be channelized with rocks to form small pools. Here again river water can be added or subtracted to create the ideal temperature. Although this is not a secluded hot spring experience, you

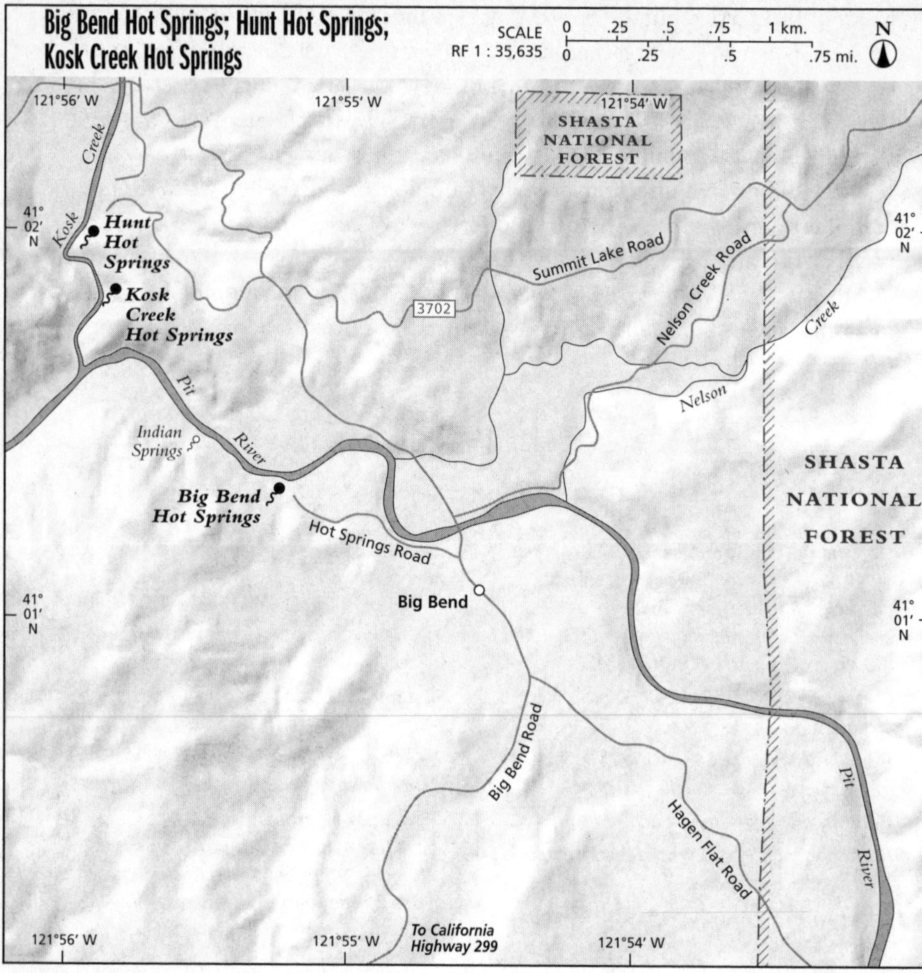

can generally have one of the pools to yourself and feel a sense of solitude.

Located at approximately 2,000 feet elevation, the resort is low enough to avoid snow and is therefore open year-round. The main baths are located in the middle of the resort, adjacent to the Pit River. Several other collections of hot springs are found in the area as well. A small trail provides access to a group of high-temperature hot springs known as Indian Springs. These have not been improved in any way, though occasionally small rock pools are built in the river to catch the hot water. Pools are open to guests of the resort or for day use at $10 per person. For more information, contact the resort at (530) 337–6606 or (530) 337–6602. Their mailing address is P.O. Box 116, Big Bend, CA 96011; e-mail rod jbbhs @299e.net.

7 Hunt Hot Springs

See map on page 26.

General description: A series of small hot springs, with one large soaking pool, near the Big Bend Resort. Also located near the Pit River, these pools are substantially less developed than those at Big Bend, as they are 1 mile down a rough dirt road.

Location: Northern California, approximately 55 miles east of Redding.

Primitive/developed: Primitive, though some of the pools are man-made with concrete.

Best time of year: Year-round, but don't try this road when it is wet.

Restrictions: None.

Access: High-clearance vehicle is recommended. You may need four-wheel drive when the road is wet.

Water temperature: The hot spring source is 136 degrees F. The pool temperature ranges, though it is generally 102 degrees F.

Nearby attractions: Big Bend Hot Springs, Kosk Creek Hot Springs, Lake Shasta, Lassen Volcanic National Park.

Services: None; groceries and food can be found in the town of Big Bend, approximately 0.5 mile away. Nearest gasoline is in Burney, about 16 miles away.

Camping: There does not appear to be any restrictions against camping at this site, though there are no developed campsites in the immediate area. There are plenty of campsites in the Trinity and Lassen National Forests nearby.

Map: USGS topographic, McArthur, CA, quadrangle, 1:100,000 scale.

Finding the springs: From the town of Redding, travel east on California Highway 299 for 35 miles to Big Bend Road, following the signs for the town of Big Bend, where you will turn left (north). Travel on this smaller paved road for approximately 15 miles to Big Bend. Continue on the same road through town, crossing

Hunt Hot Springs

the Pit River. After crossing the river, continue 1 mile. Pass Forest Service Road 3702 on your right, and take the next small dirt road on your left (approximately 100 yards from FR 3702). Bear right at the first fork in the road (approximately 0.2 mile). Continue on this road for approximately 1 mile to its end at the creek. Do not try this road with a low-clearance vehicle, and if it's wet, you will need four-wheel drive.

You will pass a small cemetery on your left shortly before reaching the river. The road has been washed out at times in the past, particularly at the culvert near the cemetery. If this is the case when you visit, you can walk the rest of the way to the hot springs. Once you reach the creek, the hot springs will be slightly downstream, on the left. The largest pool is a short walk, at the edge of the creek.

The Hot Springs

Hunt Hot Springs are located along Kosk Creek, near its confluence with the Pit River. Several hot springs emerge from the side of the hill, some of which feed a large concrete tub at the water's edge. Although the hot springs are located at the end of a relatively rough road in an isolated part of the state, they are well known. Your best bet for solitude is during the week. Nevertheless, the location is nice, and it's worth a visit. The large concrete pool is generally 102 degrees F, though it does vary. Several other smaller concrete tubs are nearby. As always, be sure to pack out all trash and respect private property wherever you encounter it.

8 Kosk Creek Hot Springs

See map on page 26.

General description: Another series of small hot springs, immediately downstream of Hunt Hot Springs. A large concrete and rock pool is immediately adjacent to the creek.

Location: Northern California, approximately 55 miles east of Redding.

Primitive/developed: Primitive, though some of the pools are man-made with concrete.

Best time of year: Year-round, but don't try this road when it is wet.

Restrictions: None.

Access: High-clearance vehicle is recommended. You may need four-wheel drive when the road is wet. The hot springs require a short hike up a steep hill from Hunt Hot Springs.

Water temperature: The hot spring source is approximately 104 degrees F. The pool temperature ranges, though it is generally 100 degrees F.

Nearby attractions: Big Bend Hot Springs, Hunt Hot Springs, Lake Shasta, Lassen Volcanic National Park.

Services: None; groceries and food can be found in the town of Big Bend, approximately 0.5 mile away. Nearest gasoline is in Burney, about 16 miles away.

Camping: There are no camping opportunities at the hot springs themselves. There are plenty of campsites in the Trinity and Lassen National Forests nearby.

Map: USGS topographic, McArthur, CA, quadrangle, 1:100,000 scale.

Finding the springs: From the town of Redding, travel east on California Highway 299 for 35 miles to Big Bend Road, following the signs for the town of Big Bend, where you will turn left (north). Travel on this smaller paved road for approximately 15 miles to Big Bend. Continue on the same road through town, crossing the Pit River. After crossing the river, continue

Kosk Creek Hot Springs

1 mile. Pass Forest Service Road 3702 on your right, and take the next small dirt road on your left (approximately 100 yards from FR 3702). Bear right at the first fork in the road (approximately 0.2 mile). Continue on this road for approximately 1 mile to its end at the creek. Do not try this road with a low-clearance vehicle, and if it's wet, you will need four-wheel drive. You will pass a small cemetery on your left shortly before reaching the river. The road has been washed out at times in the past, particularly at the culvert near the cemetery. If this is the case when you visit, you can walk the rest of the way to the hot springs. From Hunt Hot Springs, look for a small trail that leads up a steep hill (behind the hot springs). Follow this small trail for approximately 0.25 mile down to the river's edge and the hot springs.

The Hot Springs

Kosk Creek Hot Springs are located immediately downstream of Hunt Hot Springs, near the confluence of Kosk Creek and the Pit River. A well-made concrete and rock pool captures the hot spring water immediately above the river, providing a wonderful bath. The setting is beautiful and worth the short hike from Hunt Hot Springs. The road to Hunt Hot Springs is rough and should only be attempted by vehicles with high clearance. Four-wheel drive will be required in wet weather. The hike is easy, except for the first part, which takes you up a steep hill.

9 Drakesbad Guest Ranch

General description: A wonderful historic resort in the high country of Lassen Volcanic National Park. Several hot springs supply a warm swimming pool at the resort. The resort provides small cabins, as well as meals, horseback riding, hiking, and other activities. Numerous other natural hot springs can be visited in the surrounding countryside.

Location: Northern California, approximately 17 miles north of Chester, surrounded by Lassen Volcanic National Park.

Primitive/developed: Developed, though kept rather rustic.

Best time of year: June 4 to October 11.

Restrictions: This is a private establishment. Reservations are required for overnight stays. You must also pay an entrance fee to enter Lassen Volcanic National Park in order to reach the guest ranch.

Access: Drakesbad is located at the end of a paved and graded dirt road, accessible by most vehicles.

Water temperature: The source temperature for the hot springs is 151 degrees F. The swimming pool is generally maintained at 95 degrees F.

Nearby attractions: Lassen Volcanic National Park, Boiling Springs Lake, Terminal Geyser.

Services: The ranch provides cabins and meals. Nearest gasoline, food, and supplies can be found in Chester, approximately 17 miles away.

Camping: There is no camping at the ranch. The Warner Valley Campground is located a short distance away, on the road to Drakesbad.

Map: USGS topographic, Lake Almanor, CA, quadrangle, 1:100,000 scale.

Finding the springs: From the town of Chester, travel northwest on Feather River Drive from California Highway 36 (at the fire station). On Feather River Drive, follow the signs for Drakesbad for 16 miles to the ranch. The road's name eventually changes to Warner Valley Road. The last few miles of the road are graded dirt.

The Hot Springs

Drakesbad Guest Ranch is a historic facility, surrounded by Lassen Volcanic National Park. The ranch has been serving guests for over a hundred years. Natural hot springs emerge from the side of a hill across Hot Springs Creek from the ranch and are piped into a large swimming pool. Although the water comes out of the ground at over 150 degrees F, the pool is kept at approximately 95 degrees F. The ranch provides numerous cabins as well as meals. Horseback riding and massage services are also available. The ranch is located in an incredibly beautiful valley, surrounded by national park. Hiking and exploring opportunities are endless. The ranch is kept at a slightly rustic level, with each room containing a wash basin and toilet. A bathhouse is provided for bathing. Contact Drakesbad Guest Ranch for current rates, information, and reservations. During the off-season call (530) 529–1512, extension 120. During the summer season call AT&T long-distance and ask for area code 530 to Drakesbad Toll Station No. 2. Their Web site is www.drakesbad.com.

Short history of Drakesbad: Edward R. Drake (1830–1904) was the first European to settle in the valley that would later bear his name. Some sources indicate that he arrived as early as 1875. He lived in the Warner Valley before moving

Drakesbad Guest Ranch; Boiling Springs Lake and Terminal Geyser Hot Spring

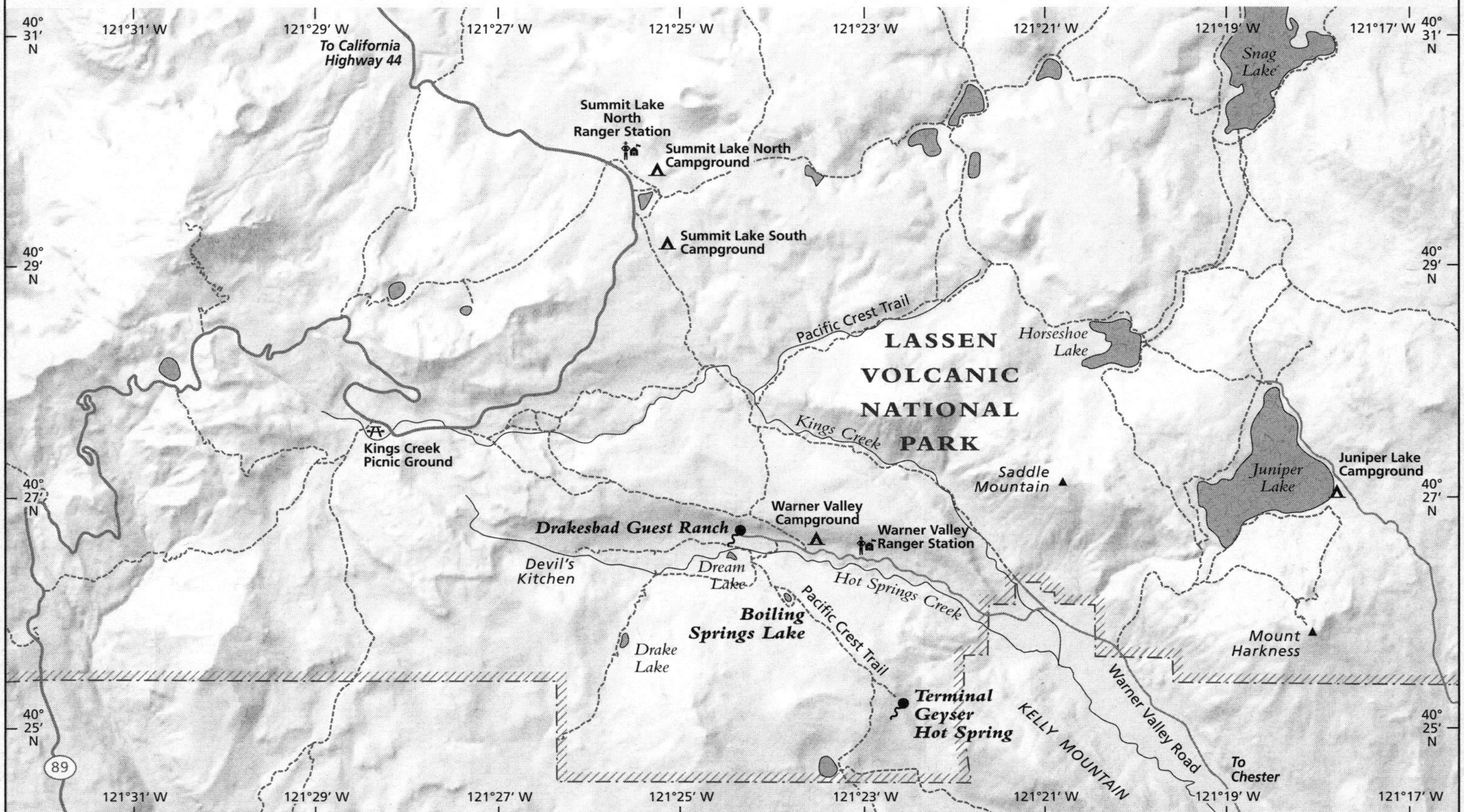

The pool at Drakesbad Guest Ranch

to what is now Drakesbad. Here he built a small log cabin, barn, and bathhouse. In 1890 he built a larger log cabin at the location of the current lodge. Drake acquired patents to several tracts of land over the next several years, until he owned over 400 acres at the turn of the century. This land is now all within Lassen Volcanic National Park. Campers stayed on his property, with his permission, and enjoyed the hot spring waters. Drake apparently moved down to the Lake Almanor area during winters.

In 1900 the Sifford family from Susanville visited Drake's home in the high country and camped in the valley. Alexander Sifford drank the hot spring water in hopes that it would cure his ailing stomach. The two men appear to have struck up a friendship, and soon Drake (who was over seventy years old) agreed to sell the property to Sifford for $6,000. The family soon moved to the valley, naming it Drakesbad (Drake's Baths) in 1908 to honor their pioneer friend. The family lived in the valley for the next sixty years. They worked hard to improve the property and were hospitable to the increasing number of campers who came to visit. In 1912 the family formed the Drakes Spring Company and obtained several investors. With this money they built a dining room with a kitchen, a barn, a cement pool, tent cabins, and bridges over the creek. In 1916 Lassen Volcanic National Park was created, resulting in more visitors. In 1938 the Siffords constructed a new lodge, replacing the one constructed by Drake in 1890. The same lodge serves visitors today.

In recent years the lodge has been undergoing repairs and rehabilitation by a team of historic preservation experts with the National Park Service. Extreme care is used to ensure that the historic character and materials of the building are maintained. For more information, see Tandy Bozeman's Web site on the history of Drakesbad at www.drakesbad.com.

10 Boiling Springs Lake and Terminal Geyser Hot Spring

See map on page 31.

General description: Two of several fantastic geothermal features in Lassen Volcanic National Park, near Drakesbad Guest Ranch. Short hikes (1 mile and 2.7 miles) are required to reach the springs. Though bathing is not permitted, the features provide a glimpse at the workings of an active volcano and are worth a visit.

Location: Northern California, approximately 17 miles north of Chester, surrounded by Lassen Volcanic National Park.

Primitive/developed: Primitive.

Best time of year: Summer, early fall, and late spring. Snow falls in the winter, making the trail impassable.

Restrictions: The springs are located in Lassen Volcanic National Park. No bathing is permitted. Previously, visitors made small pools with rocks in which to bathe. The Park Service forbids this activity today.

Access: Most passenger vehicles can reach the trailhead, as it is located at the end of a paved and graded dirt road. A 1-mile and 2.7-mile (respectively) hike are required to get to Boiling Springs Lake and Terminal Geyser.

Water temperature: The hot springs feeding Boiling Springs Lake are 190 degrees F, and the Terminal Geyser is 205 degrees F!

Nearby attractions: Drakesbad Guest Ranch, Lassen Volcanic National Park.

Services: None; nearest gasoline, food, and supplies can be found in Chester, approximately 17 miles away. The Drakesbad Guest Ranch at the trailhead rents cabins and provides meals, but reservations must be made ahead of time.

Camping: The nearest campground is Warner Valley, a short distance away from the trailhead. Check with Lassen Volcanic National Park for current camping rules and restrictions.

Maps: Lassen Volcanic National Park Official Map and Guide; USGS topographic, Lake Almanor, CA, quadrangle, 1:100,000 scale.

Finding the springs: From the town of Chester, travel northwest on Feather River Drive from California Highway 36 (at the fire station). On Feather River Drive, follow the signs for Drakesbad for 16 miles to the ranch. The last few miles of the road are graded dirt. At the Drakesbad Guest Ranch, you will see the trailhead for the Pacific Crest Trail (near the horse corrals and the lodge). Follow the trail west and south across Hot Springs Creek, and follow the signs to Boiling Springs Lake and Terminal Geyser. Boiling Springs Lake is approximately 1 mile, and Terminal Geyser is another 2 miles. Another trailhead is located immediately before you reach Drakesbad Guest Ranch, at a small parking lot. The bridge over Hot Springs Creek was out of commission as of summer 2004, but may be reopened by the time you read this. Either trailhead can be used.

The Hot Springs

Though people previously formed rock pools in which to catch the hot water from Terminal Geyser for bathing, this is no longer allowed by the park. Boiling Springs Lake provides no bathing opportunities and, in fact, is quite dangerous. Several

Boiling Springs Lake

people have been scalded here. If you are interested in seeing the raw energy of the earth at the flanks of an active volcano, these two springs are a must-visit. They are located a short hike from the Drakesbad Guest Ranch. There are several other hot springs in the park, but all of them are also far too hot to bathe in and can be quite hazardous. The springs see a few visitors during peak hiking and backpacking season in the late summer.

Lassen Volcanic National Park: When visiting Drakesbad, Boiling Springs Lake, and the Terminal Geyser Hot Spring, you will be surrounded by Lassen Volcanic National Park. The park consists of over 100,000 acres of largely volcanic landscape. The most dominant feature of the park is Mount Lassen, standing 10,457 feet high and considered an active volcano. Several other smaller volcanoes dot the region, most of which are also considered active. The region is named for Peter Lassen, the California pioneer, explorer, and settler made most famous by his ranch in the area as well as his blazing a new route from the Applegate Trail. The Lassen area was last active in eruptions in 1915, and evidence of its sleeping power can be seen in the countless fumaroles, boiling springs, boiling lakes, mud pots, hot springs, and lava flows. Before the eruption of Mount St. Helens in 1980, Lassen was the most recent volcanic eruption in the contiguous forty-eight states. In addition to the many volcanic points of interest in the park, there are countless trails connecting the traveler to many backcountry lakes. The park is open year-round, but because of high winter snowfall, most roads are closed from late October to June. Winter activities (cross-country skiing, snowshoeing, etc.) can be enjoyed from the Lassen Chalet, which is located near the southern entrance station on California Highway 89. Before venturing into the backcountry, contact the park for the latest information on wilderness permits, access, and other issues at (530) 595–4444. The park Web site is www.nps.gov/lavo.

NORTHERN SIERRA NEVADA REGION

Lying to the south of the Cascades is the Sierra Nevada. Geologically quite different from the Cascades, the Sierras are similar in the fact that they provide limitless high-country recreation. The northern Sierra Nevada is also largely controlled by the Forest Service, limiting settlement in the region. Although the region is dotted with small towns and crisscrossed by a variety of paved and dirt roads, it is generally isolated, and all travel precautions should be taken. High-country travel is best done during spring, summer, and fall, as winter weather brings hazardous conditions. Sierraville Hot Springs lies a relatively short distance from Reno, and can be an easy day trip from the little city.

11 Woody's Hot Springs

General description: A small cement tub located adjacent to an old lodge and resort (now closed) at the edge of the Feather River and a state highway.

Location: Northeastern California, 15 miles northwest of Quincy.

Primitive/developed: Primitive. Although originally part of a resort, the hot springs are now left as is with minimal upkeep.

Best time of year: Year-round.

Restrictions: The tub is located on private property, but it is open for public use during daylight hours for a small donation ($1.00 per person).

Access: The hot springs are located immediately off a highway.

Water temperature: 99 degrees F at the source. The tub is generally 95 to 98 degrees F.

Nearby attractions: Feather River, Lake Almanor.

Services: There are no longer any services available at the site. Nearest services are available in Quincy, approximately 15 miles away.

Camping: Camping is not permitted. There are numerous Forest Service campgrounds located nearby, however.

Map: California Highway Map.

Finding the springs: From Quincy, travel north on California Highway 89 for 11 miles to the intersection with California Highway 70. Turn left here, and travel 4 miles west. The old resort will be on your left near milepost 29. Pull off the highway here, and park in a small dirt parking lot. A sign will indicate the way to the hot spring tub, which is a short walk.

The Hot Springs

Woody's Feather River Hot Springs was for many years a popular resort with cabins and hot tubs supplied with natural hot spring water. Recently, however, the resort closed, but the main hot tub was left open for public use. The tub is fed by hot springs coming out of the ground at approximately 99 degrees F. The temperature in the tub itself is approximately 95 degrees F, making for a nice, but not too hot, bath. The hot springs are still located on private property, but the public is

Bathers at Woody's Hot Springs

allowed to use them during daylight hours. A $1.00 entry fee/donation is required. The hot tub is well known, and it sees a large number of visitors. Many prefer to use the tub in the nude. The tub is located immediately adjacent to the Feather River and is a very nice place for a soak. Please keep this place clean, and therefore open for all to use.

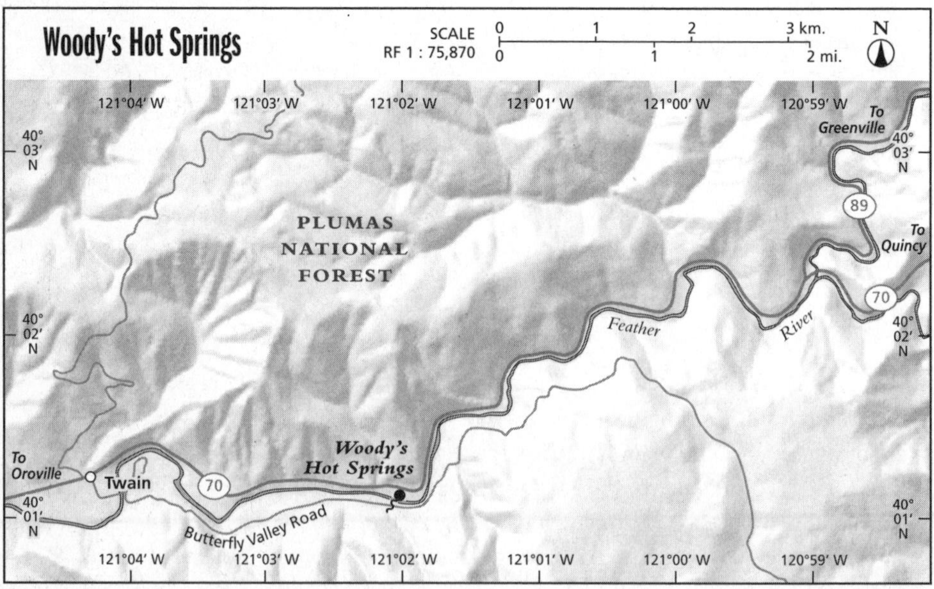

12 Sierraville Hot Springs

General description: An unusual hot spring resort in a beautiful valley in northeastern California. The resort is a membership facility, but the tubs are generally open for guests staying at the lodge and for day use. There is a wide variety of tubs to choose from, from private rooms to a communal pool. This is a clothing-optional facility in and around the tub areas.

Location: Northeastern California, 57 miles west of Reno.

Primitive/developed: Developed, though retaining a rustic feel.

Best time of year: Year-round.

Restrictions: This is a private membership facility, but you can join on the first visit, and the tubs can generally be rented for day use.

Access: Any vehicle can make the short drive on the dirt road off the highway.

Water temperature: Varies depending upon the tub chosen.

Nearby attractions: Plumas National Forest, historic mining town of Downieville.

Services: Lodge rooms are available at Sierraville Hot Springs, along with a small restaurant. Gasoline and groceries can be found in Sierraville, a few miles away. Other hotel accommodations can be found in Reno, 57 miles away, or in Truckee, 25 miles away.

Camping: Campsites can be rented from Sierraville Hot Springs. There are also many developed and undeveloped Forest Service campgrounds in the area.

Map: California Highway Map.

Finding the springs: From Truckee, take California Highway 89 north out of town for 25 miles to the town of Sierraville. At the intersection of California Highways 89 and 49, take CA 49 to Lemon Canyon Road. Turn right on Campbell Hot Springs Road, adjacent to the airport. Follow this road to Sierraville Hot Springs.

The Hot Springs

Supplied by several natural hot springs, the Sierraville Hot Springs have harnessed them in unique ways. The resort has undergone several changes in the past few years, with many of the tubs being renovated and improved. Located in a beautiful setting, with a view of the surrounding valley, almost all of the tubs at the resort offer a part of this view. There are several different tubs to choose from. Individual rooms with a tub inside can be rented by the hour, offering a private soak. There is a redwood tub on a wooden deck, large enough to accommodate up to six people comfortably. A communal area with a larger pool and several other contiguous tubs offer a choice for those who are less private. Keep in mind that this is a clothing-optional resort, and if you are uncomfortable with this, choose one of the private rooms.

MENDOCINO NATIONAL FOREST AND NORTHWESTERN CALIFORNIA

The Mendocino National Forest lies within the Coast Range mountains, extending along the majority of California's coast, roughly to Ventura County. The Coast Ranges are largely north–south-trending mountains with rugged terrain. The range is significantly lower than either the Cascades or Sierra Nevada, providing quite different flora and fauna from the other two ranges. Dominated by lower scrub vegetation and occasional forests, the Coast Ranges are also somewhat drier than their larger neighbors. In places, however, the mountains are high enough to support forest biotas. As always, contact the local land management agency before venturing out into the backcountry. The Mendocino National Forest at Upper Lake can be reached at (707) 275–2361.

13 White Sulphur Springs Inn and Spa

General description: A beautiful and peaceful historic resort in the Napa Valley, complete with several spa services, pools, and overnight accommodations.

Location: Northwestern California, immediately outside the town of St. Helena.

Primitive/developed: Developed, except for the land surrounding the ranch.

Best time of year: Year-round.

Restrictions: This is a private resort, and pools are only open to guests and for day use for a charge ($30). Contact the resort ahead of time for reservations at (707) 963–8588 or (800) 593–8873.

Access: Located at the end of a paved road, any vehicle can make the trip.

Water temperature: The hot spring source varies, though the water generally comes out of the ground at 97 degrees F. There are several pools to choose from, with the Jacuzzi being 104 degrees F. Another smaller pool closest to the source is approximately 94 degrees F.

Nearby attractions: Napa Valley wine country, Calistoga.

Services: The resort offers a variety of accommodations as well as a full range of spa services. All other services can be found in St. Helena, about 2 miles away.

Camping: Not permitted at the resort, but can be found at several locations within a few hours' drive.

Map: California Highway Map.

Finding the springs: From Napa, travel north on California Highway 29 to the small town of St. Helena (approximately 18 miles). Once in St. Helena, look for Spring Street (with a small sign to White Sulphur Springs Inn and Spa). The street is in the middle of town (do not turn on Sulphur Springs Avenue south of town). Turn left on Spring Street, and drive approximately 2.2 miles to the small resort.

White Sulphur Springs Inn and Spa

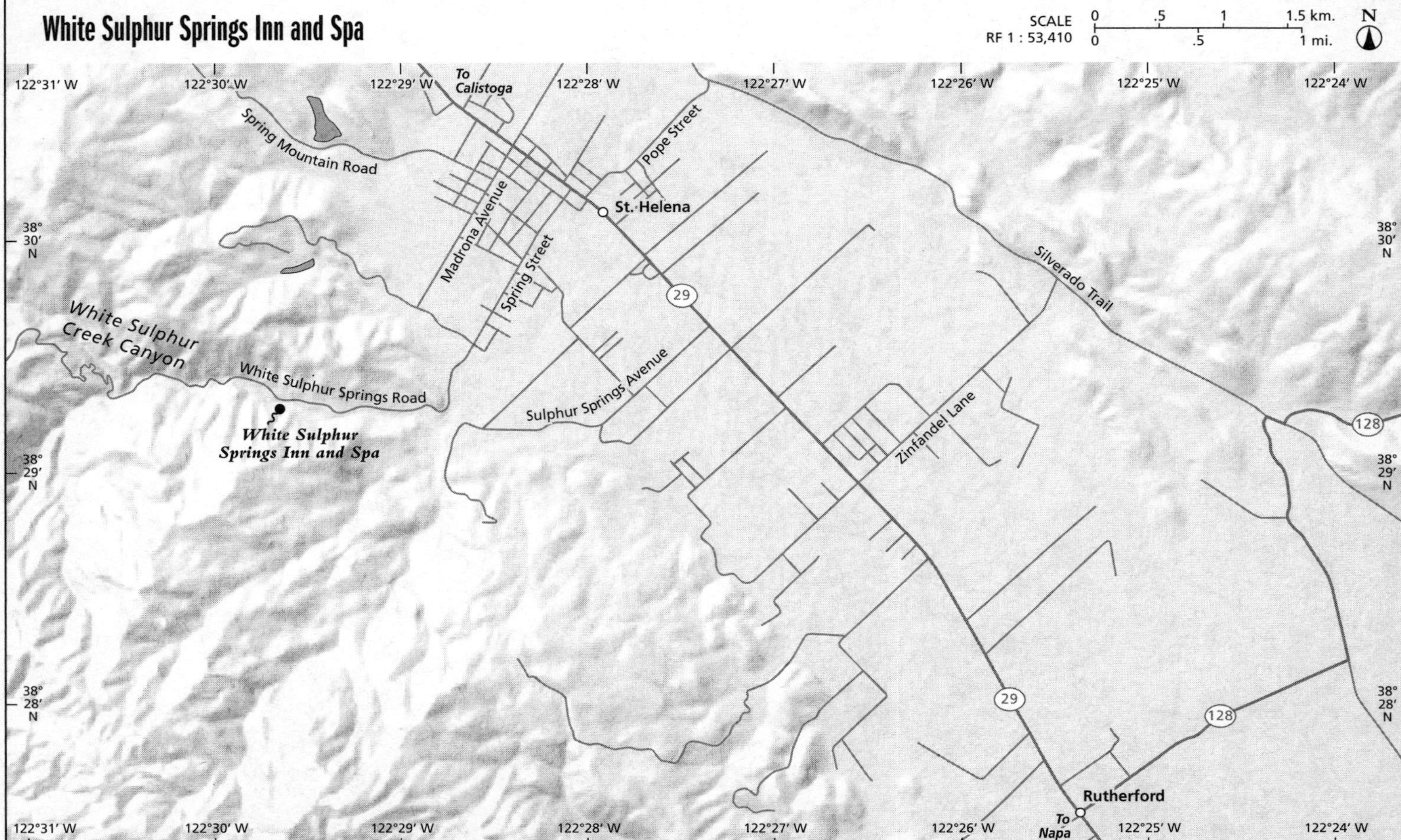

White Sulphur Springs Inn and Spa

The Hot Springs

White Sulphur Springs Inn and Spa is a great way to enjoy a historic hot spring mineral spa, away from the hustle and bustle of nearby Napa Valley. The strong smell of sulphur is found near the source of the namesake spring, which flows down a hill and over a few small waterfalls. A small warm tub is located near this source, adjacent to the spa building. A hotter (104 degrees F) hot tub/jacuzzi as well as a warm swimming pool are in place on the other side of the road. All of these pools are open to guests. Accommodations consist of creekside cottages, a fifteen-room inn, and the two-story, fourteen-room Carriage House. A full range of spa services is also available, including outdoor massages. The resort maintains a peaceful environment, which guests seem to love. Rooms are frequently booked months in advance, particularly for weekends. Be sure to call ahead for reservations.

Established in 1852, White Sulphur Springs has gone through several owners, but it still retains its historic feel. Several of the buildings were refurbished by the current owners, who purchased the property in 2001. Prior to that time, the resort had been closed to the public for almost twenty years and had deteriorated in the process. There are many vestiges of the historic White Sulphur Springs resort on the grounds of this forty-five-acre property. The remains of a large concrete dam can be found slightly upstream of the resort, near a beautiful redwood grove. The dam provided a swimming pool for resort guests for years. Foundations and old buildings can be found in various places, lending to the historic feel of this property. Hiking trails are open to visitors to explore the beautiful scenery provided by the White Sulphur Creek Canyon.

14 Vichy Springs Resort and Inn

General description: A peaceful, historically significant resort complete with a variety of warm pools, massage services, full breakfast, and acres of property to explore, including a creek and a waterfall.

Location: Northwestern California, immediately outside the town of Ukiah.

Primitive/developed: Developed, except for the waterfall and the land surrounding the ranch.

Best time of year: Year-round.

Restrictions: This is a private resort, and pools are only open to guests and for day use for a small charge. Contact the resort ahead of time for reservations.

Access: Any vehicle.

Water temperature: 90 degrees F at the source; varies depending upon pool chosen. Water is heated to approximately 105 degrees F for use in some pools.

Nearby attractions: Clear Lake, Pacific coast, Sonoma and Napa Valley wine country.

Services: The resort offers cottages and lodge rooms, along with a full breakfast. All other services can be found in Ukiah, 3 miles away.

Camping: Not permitted at the resort, but can be found at several locations within a few hours' drive.

Map: California Highway Map.

Finding the springs: From U.S. Highway 101, exit onto Vichy Springs Road in the town of Ukiah. Travel east out of town on Vichy Springs Road for slightly less than 3 miles, following the National Historic Landmark signs pointing you to the resort.

The Hot Springs

The Vichy Springs Resort and Inn is a historic landmark, set in the front of a beautiful, sprawling 700-acre ranch. The current owners of the property have expended a great deal of time and energy renovating the resort, while maintaining its historic character. Almost all of the buildings at the resort are original, and all retain their historic integrity nicely. Boasting the state's only natural effervescent spring, the hot water is fed from the spring into a series of small bathtub-shaped pools for single or double use. The spring's source, the pride of the resort, produces approximately one hundred gallons of water per minute. One of the most unusual aspects of the spring is the fact that it is naturally carbonated, the only one of its kind in the country. The pools can be enjoyed outside or inside a small structure sheltering the tubs from the weather, with two tubs to a room. The water is also fed into a large warm swimming pool and into a modern Jacuzzi-style tub where the temperature is raised to approximately 105 degrees F.

Many people swear by the curative benefits of the natural hot spring water at Vichy. As the water is high in calcium carbonate and boron, it does tend to soften your skin considerably. Along with the various baths, massages can also be obtained. A waterfall is accessible via a short hike, open to all guests and day-users of the resort. The waterfall is an equally invigorating experience on a warm day. Phone ahead for more information and reservations: (707) 462–9515.

A historic resort: Originally constructed in 1854, Vichy Springs is the oldest continuously operating mineral water resort in California. Named after natural mineral springs in France, whose chemistries are strikingly similar, the Vichy resort is a historical treasure. The first developer of the property was William Day, who built several cabins, a bathhouse, baths, and a dining room by 1861. In 1867 the resort passed into the hands of William Doolan, who operated it for the next thirty years, building the first large swimming pool on the property and several new buildings. During Doolan's ownership, the springs became a popular destination for the rich and famous. Such celebrities as Ulysses S. Grant, William Harrison, Mark Twain, Jack London, and Grace Hudson, among others, visited the springs for varying lengths of time. Following another change of ownership, the resort was bought by A. F. Redemeyer in 1901. Redemeyer leased the operation of the resort to others, including Bob Jones in 1914. Jones remodeled portions of the resort and undertook additional construction measures, including an auto garage, a lounge, a lobby, and a double bowling alley (much of which still remains today).

Following the Great Depression of the 1930s, the resort fell into disuse and decline until the current owners bought it in 1977. Gilbert and Marjorie Ashoff acquired the property originally to bottle the water, but soon got to work on remodeling the resort. As the resort buildings and grounds were in disrepair, a great deal of effort was expended to update the buildings without losing their historical feel. Following a variety of bureaucratic roadblocks, lawsuits, and other

Hot Pool with a replica of Monet's Bridge crossing Vichy Creek

obstructions, the Ashoffs succeeded in renovating the resort. The baths and buildings that await you at Vichy are basically unchanged from the original resort of the 1860s. Vichy Springs is definitely worth a visit.

CENTRAL CALIFORNIA

Central California as defined here is another area of contrasts. In the east the region is dominated by the Sierra Nevada. The mountains slope gradually upwards from the west to their peak elevations before dropping off rapidly to the east. U.S. Highway 395 serves as a lifeline to the eastern side of the mountains, providing access into the backcountry and connecting California with Nevada. The highest point in the state, Mount Whitney at 14,494 feet, is a short distance from the small town of Lone Pine, sitting on the Owens Valley floor. Within the High Sierra attractions abound, the most popular being Yosemite National Park, accessed from the east on California Highway 120. There is plenty of open space for outdoor recreation. During winter months most of the roads leading into the mountains are closed due to snowfall. The best time to enjoy these mountains is in summer and portions of fall and spring.

Lying to the west of the mountains is the Great Valley, the agricultural heartland of California—and of the country. Beyond the Great Valley the elevation rises again in the Coast Ranges before meeting the Pacific Ocean. Much of this country is rugged and unpopulated. The main thoroughfares through central California are north–south trending, following the contours of the state. Interstate 5 connects California with Oregon and points north and is the fastest way to traverse the state. U.S. Highway 101 lies to the west, connecting many of the larger towns, and is a more scenic way to travel the state.

Owens Valley Warm Spring

CARSON RIVER AREA

Although originating in the high country of the Sierra Nevada, the majority of the Carson River extends into Nevada, eventually terminating in the Lahontan Reservoir. The two hot springs described for this region are quite different, one harnessed for use in a swimming pool in a state campground, the other a collection of largely unaltered springs at the end of a difficult dirt road on the East Carson River. Named for famed mountain man, explorer, and trailblazer Christopher "Kit" Carson, the river was first recognized as a travel corridor through Nevada and an entryway into the high country by Carson. The Carson River Route became one of the most popular paths into California among the emigrants of the 1840s–1860s. Today the area offers hunting, fishing, hiking, and camping (among other outdoor activities) from the high country around Grover Hot Springs, to lower elevations and Carson River Hot Springs, near the state line. Because of the high elevations at Grover, wintertime driving is not advised, particularly during storms.

15 Carson River Hot Springs

General description: Two sets of natural hot springs on the East Carson River, far from civilization and requiring either a raft trip or a grueling drive to reach.

Location: Eastern California, approximately 20 miles southwest of Gardnerville, Nevada.

Primitive/developed: Primitive.

Best time of year: Spring, summer, and fall. Road may be impassable during periods of snow and rain.

Restrictions: Although located on national forest property, the road to these springs passes through privately held land. Access is generally granted, however.

Access: You will need a high-clearance vehicle at the least, and four-wheel drive is highly recommended. Do not try this road with any vehicle in wet weather.

Water temperature: The water emerges from the source at approximately 105 degrees F, and cools depending upon the amount of river water admitted into the pools.

Nearby attractions: Carson River.

Services: There are no services at this location. Nearest food, gasoline, and lodging can be found in Gardnerville, approximately 20 miles away.

Camping: Camping is permitted at this location, but there are no developed sites. Contact the Toiyabe National Forest ahead of time for up-to-date rules and restrictions: (760) 932–7070 or (775) 331–6444.

Map: Toiyabe National Forest Map.

Finding the springs: From Carson City, travel south on U.S. Highway 395 for 11 miles to the town of Gardnerville. Continue south on US 395 for approximately 12 miles to Leviathan Mine Road on your right (west). Turn right here, then continue for approximately 1.7 miles to Forest Service Road 189 and turn right. Travel on this increasingly smaller and less maintained road for approximately 3.8 miles to a fork in the road. Continue straight at this fork. Pass through a cattle gate (close it behind you), and drive another 4 miles to the East Carson River. Park here, cross the river, and walk the last 50 yards to the springs on the other side. The second set of hot springs is approximately 0.5 mile upstream from the first set. I recommend hiking to this set as crossing the river can be difficult, and the road becomes more difficult on the other side. If you wish to arrive at these springs by raft instead of by car, contact one of the many river-rafting guide companies operating in the area. Do not try the trip by yourself.

The Hot Springs

Both sets of hot springs are on the bank of the East Carson River, and both provide excellent bathing opportunities. Both pools have been dug out of the soil by volunteers and are kept up by continuous digging and placement of rocks, as the pools get washed out. Although difficult to get to by car, the hot springs are relatively popular and well known. During rafting season (May to August), most trips stop and visit the springs. The road you take to reach the springs passes through private property, but so far the landowner has allowed access. Be sure to respect posted signs. Come prepared on this trip, as the road is quite difficult. I recommend you bring plenty of food and water, a spare tire with sufficient air in it, a car jack, and plenty of tools. Also, let someone know where you are going and when you expect to be back.

16 Grover Hot Springs

General description: A state-run hot springs with a communal warm pool, adjacent to a campground in the High Sierra.

Location: Eastern California, outside the small town of Markleeville and approximately 38 miles southwest of Carson City.

Primitive/Developed: Developed.

Best Time of the year: Year-round, except in heavy snowfall during winter. Campground is closed from October through May.

Restrictions: This is a state park, and all rules and regulations must be obeyed. The pool is limited to fifty people at any given time. Park hours vary depending on the time of year; phone ahead for hours and for rules and regulations.

Access: Any vehicle can access the park, as it is on a paved highway. Roads may be closed in winter, particularly during storms.

Water temperature: Approximately 148 degrees F at its source, the hot spring water is cooled to approximately 100 degrees F in the pool.

Nearby attractions: Hot Springs Trail, Burnside Lake.

Services: Some services can be found in the nearby town of Markleeville. For complete services, however, Minden and Garnerville are approximately 20 miles away.

Camping: There is a campground at the park. Make reservations ahead of time, as it fills up quickly. Reservations can be made through MISTIX at (800) 444–PARK.

Map: California Highway Map.

Finding the springs: From the town of Minden, travel southwest on U.S. Highway 88 for approximately 15 miles to Woodfords, where you turn left on California Highway 9. Approximately 5 miles later you will reach Markleeville. Follow the signs to Grover Hot Springs State Park for 3 miles to the entrance station.

The Hot Springs

Grover Hot Springs is located within a 519-acre state park in Hot Spring Valley. The park contains two concrete pools that are fed by the runoff from six natural hot springs. The large, communal warm pool is quite pleasant despite the usual crowds encountered. As the occupancy limit of the pool is fifty, you may have to wait until someone leaves before being able to get in. The natural source of the pool is uphill a few yards, and it's an interesting sight. The water is treated and flushed constantly, and a constant temperature is maintained. The park is open year-round, offering all types of vacationers access to a hot soak throughout the year. The park lies at 6,000 feet elevation, so summers are generally mild (80s). Winters can be very cold, however, and the road will occasionally be closed due to snowstorms. The springs are especially enjoyable in the winter, when steam can be seen wafting from the large pool, creating a surrealistic look. The water also feels that much better when the air temperature is in the 40s and 50s. The park offers camping sites and several interesting hikes. A particularly enjoyable hike is the Hot Springs Creek Trail, leading you to a waterfall and eventually to Burnside Lake. Trail maps can be obtained at the park. For further information, contact the park at (916) 694–2248.

THE EASTERN SIERRA—THE HOT SPRING JACKPOT

Lying along the base of the Sierra Nevada, U.S. Highway 395 south of Carson City provides access into some of the best hot spring country in the nation. From north of Bridgeport to south of Lone Pine, hot springs of all types abound. Most of these springs are completely natural, with only enough alterations made to provide bathing opportunities, while a few have been partially or totally harnessed. The springs described in this region are all excellent bathing hot springs, and you could spend weeks sampling them all. Because US 395 sees a substantial amount of traffic, many of these springs are well known. Seclusion can be had, however, particularly during the tourist off-season and also during the week. On weekends, and particularly holidays, the springs see heavy visitation. Several towns dot the landscape, providing ample services along the way.

From US 395 there is easy access to a variety of attractions, from the low deserts in the east to alpine mountains in the west. The numerous creeks and rivers draining the Sierra Nevada offer countless fishing opportunities. Mono Lake is a bird-watchers paradise, and cross-country and downhill skiers will love the Mammoth Lakes region. Camping and hiking can be enjoyed year-round. The region is also rich in history and prehistory, and only a little extra time is needed to enjoy these aspects of the area.

17 Fales Hot Spring

General description: A closed and abandoned resort with several unfinished pools and structures. Currently off-limits to bathing, there have been rumors of the resort opening again someday. The hot water from the old resort flows under the highway into a pool that makes for a nice bath.

Location: Eastern California, immediately off U.S. Highway 395, approximately 13 miles north of Bridgeport.

Primitive/developed: Developed, though the resort is now closed and in disrepair.

Best time of year: Spring, summer, and fall. US 395 may be difficult to impassable during winter storms.

Restrictions: The resort itself is on public land, but several NO TRESPASSING signs have been posted. There is also private property behind the resort, which should be respected.

Access: Any vehicle, as the hot springs are immediately off US 395. The road can be treacherous during winter storms.

Water temperature: 180 degrees F at the source, cooling rapidly as it flows down the creek.

Nearby attractions: Mono Lake, Yosemite National Park.

Services: There are no services at the old resort but in Bridgeport, approximately 13 miles away.

Camping: There is no camping allowed at Fales. This is not a good place to camp anyway, as it is immediately off the highway. There are several Forest Service campgrounds in the

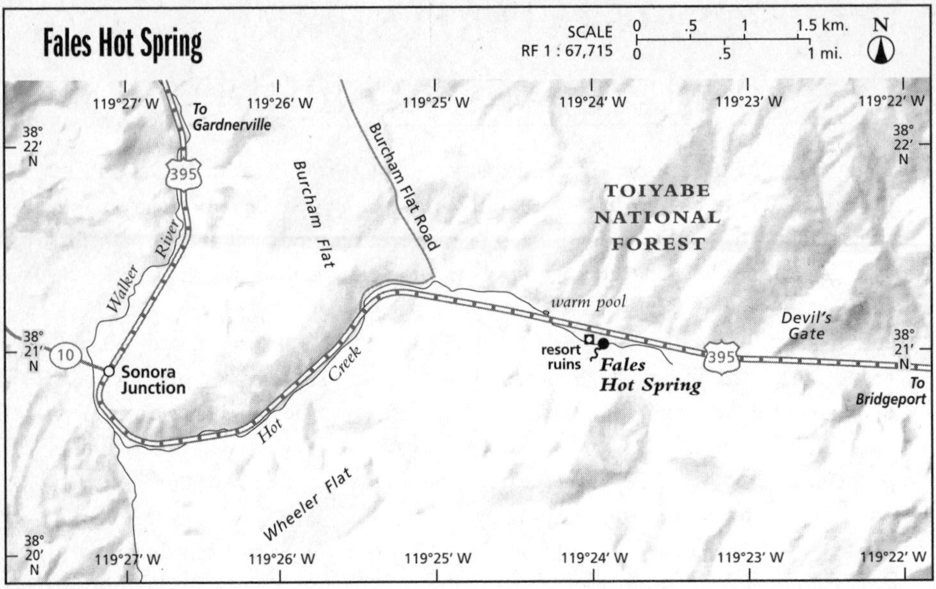

vicinity, however, including two a few miles north on US 395.

Map: California Highway Map.

Finding the spring: From the town of Bridgeport, travel northwest out of town on US 395 for 13 miles to the ruins of the resort on your left. The pond where bathing is possible is located west of the resort, on the north side of the road, 0.3 mile away. It is not visible from the road, so slow down and look for a small pullout on the north side of the highway.

The Hot Spring

Fales Hot Spring was at one time a substantial resort, as is apparent from the large pools, buildings, and individual rooms, now all in disuse. The water at the source is extremely hot! Do not go near this water, as it could be fatal. Follow the hot spring water as it flows into a small stream by several individual rooms. The individual bathhouses were constructed with local stone and cement, immediately over the stream in which the hot water flows. Baths in each room, the water in which could be altered, provided the best soaking opportunities but now are dry. Eventually the hot creek water forms a pool, but keep going. Several NO TRESPASSING signs have been posted here. The water does, however, flow under the highway into a good-size pond that makes for a good bathing spot. The water here is approximately 90 degrees F. It is not visible from the road, so keep your eyes open.

Originally the hot springs were used as a way station on a toll road in the 1870s. In 1878 the first direct route between San Francisco and Bodie was completed with the Sonora-Mono Wagon Road. The road was designed to be a passenger and freight route from the productive mines at Bodie to markets in San Francisco. It followed the Stanislaus River, then an old Indian trail over the pass to

Fales Hot Spring

Leavitt Meadows, then to Fales and Bridgeport, and finally to Bodie. It is unknown what type of facilities were constructed at Fales during this time period, but it is clear that the resort aspect of the spring was developed later. The hot water at Fales was eventually harnessed for use in a resort, with several small bathhouses constructed, along with a lodge. As this enterprise largely failed, the resort fell into disuse. Another more recent attempt was made to reopen the hot spring resort, but it never fully materialized. Foundations for a large swimming pool were laid out, and a few improvements were made to some of the buildings, none of which were ever finished. Time will tell what becomes of this fascinating historic location and high-temperature hot springs.

18 Travertine Hot Springs

General description: A series of natural hot springs, bolstered to provide several bathing opportunities. A popular hot spring in the eastern Sierra area, Travertine Hot Springs, as the name suggests, are most notable because of the multicolored travertine formations associated with the pools.

Location: Eastern California, 2 miles south of Bridgeport.

Primitive/developed: Primitive, though several pools have been dug to provide better soaking opportunities, and one has been cemented in.

Best time of year: Year-round. The road to the springs may be impassable in wet weather.

Restrictions: None.

Access: Although a high-clearance vehicle is recommended, most standard vehicles can

The lower pool at Travertine Hot Springs

make the short dirt road drive to the springs, but during wet weather you will need four-wheel drive.

Water temperature: The main source for the hot spring is 180 degrees F. There are several pools with temperatures ranging from 90 to 110 degrees F.

Nearby attractions: Twin Lakes, Bodie, Buckeye Hot Springs.

Services: There are no services at Travertine Hot Springs but 2 miles away in Bridgeport.

Camping: Camping is allowed at the springs, but there are no developed sites. As this is a popular hot spring, respect the privacy of others. Also, do not monopolize the springs by camping immediately next to any of the pools. There are several Forest Service campgrounds in the area also. Check in at the local ranger station for details.

Map: USGS topographic, Bridgeport, CA, quadrangle, 1:100,000 scale.

Finding the springs: From Bridgeport, travel south out of town on U.S. Highway 395 for approximately 0.5 mile and turn left on Jack Sawyer Road, a few hundred yards north of the ranger station. Drive on this paved road for approximately 0.3 mile to where the road begins to bend to the right, and turn left on a dirt road here. Travel on this dirt road for approximately 1.2 miles, staying right at the first Y in the road. Although the road has been washed out in places in the past, it is in pretty good condition today, and most vehicles should have little trouble. As you approach the top of the hill, you will see the multicolored travertine where the hot springs are. Continue until you reach the top cement pool. From here, follow the ridge of travertine down to the other pools. Do not try to drive next to the lower pools, as there is no road to them and the ground is very muddy in places.

The Hot Springs

Travertine Hot Springs not only offers several soaking opportunities, it also presents interesting geology and a beautiful setting. The upper hot spring (the first you come to) has a small concrete pool adjacent to it. This bathtub-shaped pool presents the best soaking opportunity, as it is approximately 105 degrees F. This is also the most popular spring, however, and there will generally be people in it. The lower pools are formed from water dripping off the ridge of travertine into small crude pools constructed by hot spring goers. There are several of these pools ranging in temperature from 90 to 105 degrees F, and all are only a foot or two deep. The water is a little murky here, but who cares? The view from the lower pools is fantastic. As always, respect other people's privacy, and do not leave any trash behind. So far this spring has stayed clean, free from trash, and open. Let's keep it that way.

Twin Lakes offers lake and stream fishing, camping, and hiking. The resort provides a complete marina, boat rentals, general store, and RV park. On the road to Twin Lakes, Doc and Al's Resort provides cabins and camping, along with excellent creek fishing. To reach Twin Lakes, travel west out of town on Twin Lakes Road for approximately 15 miles.

Bodie: To the southeast of Bridgeport, in the dry sage country, lies the ghost town of Bodie. Run by the California State Parks Department and a cadre of dedicated volunteers, Bodie is maintained in a state of "arrested decay" to give the visitor a glimpse of what the old town looked and felt like in the 1880s.

Gold was discovered as early as 1859 by Warterman Bodey, but mining did not occur on a large scale for several years. By 1864 there were only twenty buildings in the town, and in the early 1870s there had not been much more growth. In 1872, however, another vein was found, and the town was "discovered." With the creation of the Standard Consolidated Mining Company in 1877, miners flocked to the town. From 1876 to 1884 the town witnessed boom growth, typical of so many other western mining towns of the era. In 1879 the town's population was over 10,000, and the name was changed to Bodie to ensure its proper pronunciation. Over $30 million in gold and a million ounces of silver were extracted from the mines.

During its heyday Bodie was known as one of the roughest towns in the country. Although the gunslinging that occurred at Bodie has undoubtedly been overplayed, the leading cause of death was from bullets, and the death rate per capita was extremely high. A future resident, upon learning that she was to live in the infamous town, remarked in her diary: "Goodbye God, I'm going to Bodie." Despite Bodie's decline in the late 1880s, several people hung around, and Bodie became the first mining town to have electricity in 1893. Several fires have ravaged the town through the years, but an amazing number of buildings remain today. The outlines of streets can also be seen clearly, especially when looking at the town from a higher elevation, giving the visitor an idea of just how big this town was in its heyday.

To reach Bodie, travel south out of Bridgeport on US 395 for approximately 7 miles to signs for Bodie State Historic Park. Turn east on California Highway 270 and travel for approximately 12 miles to the park. The last few miles of the road is dirt, but most passenger cars will have no problem. The park is open year-round from 9:00 A.M. to 7:00 P.M. in the summer, 9:00 A.M. to 4:00 P.M. the rest of the year. CA 270 is generally closed to motor vehicles during the winter months due to snowfall. The park can be reached by snowmobile, skis, or snowshoes during the winter. Contact the Mono County Sheriff's Office in Bridgeport (760–932–7549) for road and weather conditions before making the trip. For further information, contact Bodie State Historic Park at (619) 647–6445.

19 Buckeye Hot Spring

General description: Two hot spring sources feeding two soaking pools adjacent to a clear stream on the eastern slope of the Sierra Nevada. One of the pools is on the hillside and the other is creekside, both offering excellent bathing opportunities.

Location: Eastern California, 10 miles northwest of Bridgeport.

Primitive/developed: Primitive, except for the damming up of the pools for bathing.

Best time of year: Spring, summer, and fall. There is substantial snow here in the winter, but you can ski to the spring relatively easily.

Restrictions: None.

Access: A high-clearance vehicle is recommended, but most sturdy passenger vehicles with decent clearance make it OK. During wet weather you will need four-wheel drive.

Water temperature: The sources are approximately 140 degrees F, and the water cools to approximately 100 degrees F in the pool on the hillside. Temperatures in the creekside pools vary depending upon amount of creek water admitted in.

Nearby attractions: Travertine Hot Springs, Mono Lake, Yosemite National Park.

Services: There are no services at the hot springs themselves, but some can be found 10 miles away in Bridgeport.

Camping: There is a Forest Service campground (Buckeye) less than a mile away from the spring.

Map: USGS topographic, Bridgeport, CA, quadrangle, 1:100,000 scale.

Finding the spring: In Bridgeport at the north end of town, turn left on Twin Lakes Road (right before the last gas station in town). Travel on Twin Lakes Road for approximately 7.1 miles to Doc and Al's Resort, where you turn right on a dirt road (Forest Service Road 017). Travel on this dirt road for approximately 2.7 miles, following signs to Buckeye. After crossing Buckeye Creek (about 2.5 miles), stay straight and look for a large flat area to park on your right. The springs are approximately 100 yards downstream from this parking area. Buckeye Campground is to the right after crossing the bridge.

An alternate route is to travel north out of Bridgeport for approximately 5 miles on U.S. Highway 395 to the ranger station, then turn onto a dirt road to the left (west). A Forest Service sign at the road will indicate Buckeye Campground. Travel on this one-lane dirt road for approximately 5 miles to a small parking lot overlooking Buckeye Creek. Walk down the steep trail to the spring at the edge of the creek. The other pool will be slightly upstream and uphill half the way. This route is more difficult and can be impassable in wet weather. As the road is one lane in places, take it slow and look out for other vehicles.

Creekside pools at Buckeye Hot Spring

The Hot Spring

The two main sources at Buckeye Hot Spring emerge from the side of the hill and cool rapidly at they flow downhill. In cold weather the hot spring will be easy to spot with all of the steam. In warmer weather look for color changes on the side of the hill where the algae is growing in the hot springs. One of the sources flows into a small (7 by 3 foot) pool that maintains a temperature of approximately 100 degrees F. The other source is larger and flows into the creek, where it has been dammed up with rocks, forming several pools. Each of these pools differs slightly in temperature, ranging from 95 to 110 degrees F. The temperature will vary greatly depending upon the amount of creek water flowing into the pools. The largest pool is under an overhang created by the hot spring water and offers a small cavelike setting. The water coming off the overhang also produces a small waterfall. This is a fantastic hot spring, adjacent to a clear stream stocked with rainbow and brown trout. The water is a little hot in places at Buckeye, so use caution. Also be careful coming down the hill to the creekside pools, as the ground is quite slippery. This is another popular hot spring in the area, and you can count on sharing it with others during weekends in the summer. If you choose to visit it during the snowy part of winter, you should have it to yourself.

20 Dechambeau Hot Springs

General description: A series of very high-temperature hot springs feeding ponds that provide a bird sanctuary near Mono Lake. The bathing opportunities are limited, but the springs are interesting, there is a lot of wildlife, and several other bathable springs are in the vicinity.

Location: Eastern California, approximately 15 miles northeast of Lee Vining.

Primitive/developed: Primitive, though a large well has been dug and several other changes have been made recently to promote the bird sanctuary.

Best time of year: Year-round. The road to the springs may be difficult in wet weather.

Restrictions: The springs are within a bird sanctuary run by the state, and all posted rules must be obeyed. There is also substantial private property in the area, which should be respected.

Access: Most passenger vehicles can access the springs. There are some slightly sandy spots in the road, but four-wheel drive is not needed.

Water temperature: 151 degrees F at the source, cooling off rapidly in the ponds.

Nearby attractions: Mono Lake, Yosemite National Park.

Services: There are no services at Dechambeau Hot Springs, but some can be found 7 miles away in Lee Vining.

Camping: There does not appear to be any restrictions against camping near the springs, but you can't drive up to the springs anyway. As much of the land in the immediate area is private, I do not recommend camping here. There are several developed and undeveloped campgrounds in the vicinity. Contact the Mono Lake Visitor Center (760–647–6331) and the Lee Vining Ranger Station (760–647–3000) for campsites in the area.

Map: USGS topographic, Bridgeport, CA-NV, quadrangle, 1:100,000 scale.

Finding the springs: From Lee Vining, travel north on U.S. Highway 395 for 8 miles to California Highway 167, where you turn right (east). Travel on CA 167 for approximately 5 miles to Cemetery Road, where you turn right. Follow this dirt road for approximately 1 mile, where you turn left on a lesser dirt road. Continue for another 0.5 mile until you see the sign for the bird sanctuary. Park at the sign and walk the few hundred yards to the several hot spring sources.

The Hot Springs

Although too hot to really be a bathable hot spring, Dechambeau offers ample scenery. The hot springs themselves have been dammed up in the past, but the pools have not really survived. Apparently the springs were discovered accidentally while drilling for oil. The well itself still remains and is fenced off to protect the public from its scalding water. The hot spring water feeds several ponds that are used by waterfowl. The ponds themselves are too cold for bathing, and portions of the hot springs are too hot. Be careful at Dechambeau, and obey all the posted rules. The area is managed under cooperation by the California Department of Transportation, USDA Forest Service, Mono Lake Committee to Restore Seasonal Wetlands and Moist Meadowlands, and Ducks Unlimited as a wetland restoration project. The nearby ranch is on private property, as is much of the surrounding land.

The pond at Dechambeau Hot Springs

21 Navy Beach Hot Spring

General description: A deep pond formed by a single hot spring on the shores of Mono Lake on state property. It was once open to bathing, but the state forbids it now, claiming that bacteria levels have risen to an unnatural level.

Location: Eastern California, 10 miles from Lee Vining.

Primitive/developed: Primitive.

Best time of year: Year-round. The road to the spring may be impassable in wet weather.

Restrictions: This is a state park, and bathing is not allowed currently. Check in with the Mono Lake Visitor Center, immediately south of Lee Vining, for current regulations.

Access: Any vehicle. Although the dirt road does have some sandy spots, as long as you stay on the road, you should have no problem.

Water temperature: Approximately 100 degrees F in the pond.

Nearby attractions: Mono Lake, Yosemite National Park.

Services: None; nearest gasoline, food, and lodging can be found in Lee Vining, approximately 10 miles away.

Camping: Camping is not allowed at Navy Beach. There are several campgrounds nearby, however. Contact the Mono Lake Visitor Center (760–647–6331) or the Lee Vining Ranger Station (760–647–3000).

Map: California Highway Map.

Finding the spring: From Lee Vining, travel south on U.S. Highway 395 for approximately 5 miles to California Highway 120; turn left (east). Travel on CA 120 for approximately 4 miles to a state park sign for the Tufa Reserve. Turn left on this dirt road, following the signs to Navy Beach for approximately 0.5 mile to the parking area. From the west side of the parking area, walk 0.25 mile on a trail to the spring.

The Hot Spring

Bathing is no longer permitted at the Navy Beach Hot Spring, which is located a few hundred yards from the shore of Mono Lake. But there is plenty to see in this area to make up for the lack of bathing. Fabulous scenery, interesting geology, and tons of birdlife will greet you at Navy Beach.

Mono Lake: Surrounded by a 116,000-acre National Scenic Area, Mono Lake is a beautiful and multifaceted natural area. The youngest mountain range in California, the Mono Craters to the south of the lake, and actually one of its islands, erupted as recently as 600 years ago. The Mono Craters can be seen off to the east when traveling south on US 395, their volcanic character obvious. Several of the volcanoes in the Mono Lake region are obsidian domes. Obsidian is a particularly glassy type of lava that is black in color; it was a favorite tool material among Native Americans. Picnic areas abound in the obsidian domes area, south of the lake and west and east of US 395. The volcanic activity in the area is also evidenced by the many hot springs in the vicinity, including the two described above. Other hot springs exist throughout the lake area, the most dramatic of which lies on Pahoha Island in the middle of the lake. This extremely high-temperature hot spring was at one time used as a resort, but has long since been abandoned, its buildings and baths in ruin.

Mono Lake itself is over 700,000 years old, and with no natural outlet the water in the lake is too salty to support fish populations. Brine shrimp do live in the water, however, providing abundant food for the many birds in the area. Several types of birds and waterfowl come to Mono Lake every year to nest and to feed on brine shrimp and flies. The many islands provide secure havens from predators for these migratory birds. One of the most remarkable features of the lake are its tufa towers, formed when lake levels were higher and calcium carbonate was precipitated at springs, eventually forming these sometimes large outcrops. There are ample back roads to explore in this region, but close to the lake most of these roads are too sandy. Winter weather can be treacherous in the Mono Lake region and the surrounding area. The best time to visit is summer, early fall, and late spring. An excellent visitor center was recently constructed north of Lee Vining and is a must first stop. For further information, contact the visitor center at (619) 647–3000.

Mono Mills: Immediately off CA 120, past the turnoff for Navy Beach, 20 miles from US 395, lies the remains of a large lumber mill used between 1876 and 1916. Trees from the surrounding mountains were cut and brought to this mill, where it was processed for use in the mining town of Bodie. Wood was such a necessity in building Bodie, and for use in the mines, that a narrow-gauge railway was constructed from the town all the way to this mill (see Mono Basin Warm Springs). Some of the remains of the mill itself, and the camp where the workers lived, can still be seen today.

22 Mono Basin Warm Springs

General description: A series of warm springs on the isolated east shore of Mono Lake, requiring a long ride on a sandy road and four-wheel drive. Bathing opportunities are currently limited, but could be improved with a little work.

Location: Eastern California, approximately 25 miles from Lee Vining.

Primitive/developed: Primitive.

Best time of year: Spring, summer, and fall. The road may be very difficult in wet weather.

Restrictions: The springs are located immediately adjacent to Mono Lake Tufa State Reserve. Please drive only on the road.

Access: A four-wheel-drive vehicle is required due to several areas of deep sand.

Water temperature: The water comes out of the ground at approximately 88 degrees F. In the only makeshift pond currently existing, the water is about 85 degrees F.

Nearby attractions: Mammoth Lakes, Long Valley hot springs area.

Services: None; the nearest services can be found approximately 25 miles away in Lee Vining.

Camping: There are no campgrounds in the area, but several Forest Service campgrounds and private resorts are located near Lee Vining. Undeveloped camping is possible.

Map: USGS topographic, Excelsior Mountains, CA-NV, quadrangle, 1:100,000 scale.

Finding the springs: From Lee Vining, travel north on U.S. Highway 395 for 7 miles to California Highway 167, where you turn east. From Bridgeport, travel south on US 395 for 18 miles to CA 167. Drive east on CA 167 for approximately 12 miles (passing the road to Dechambeau Hot Springs). Look for a small road on your right (south) with a small historical marker for the Bodie and Benton Railroad. Turn here. Follow this small dirt road for approximately 6.2 miles. You will pass through several sandy areas, so shift into four-wheel drive. Look for a road on your right, leading to a cattle gate. Follow this road, passing through the cattle gate, and travel about 0.5 mile to the springs flowing toward the lake. The springs are not easy to spot, but are visible from the dark green vegetation growing around them.

The Hot Springs

The Mono Basin Warm Springs consist of a collection of small seeps of warm water (about 88 degrees F) flowing out near the eastern shore of Mono Lake. They are located in a beautiful, peaceful setting, with great views of the lake and surrounding mountains. There is one small makeshift pool offering very limited bathing. This collection of warm springs is located immediately adjacent to the historic Bodie and Benton Railroad, which ran from Mono Mills to Bodie. The railroad was constructed in 1883 in order to carry wood from Mono Mills to the thriving mining community of Bodie, 32 miles to the north. The narrow gauge railroad operated until 1918, when mining activity declined and the railroad was no longer needed. The tracks were removed, while many of the timber ties were abandoned in place. Many of these ties can still be seen along the railroad grade paralleling the road to the warm springs.

Mono Basin Warm Springs

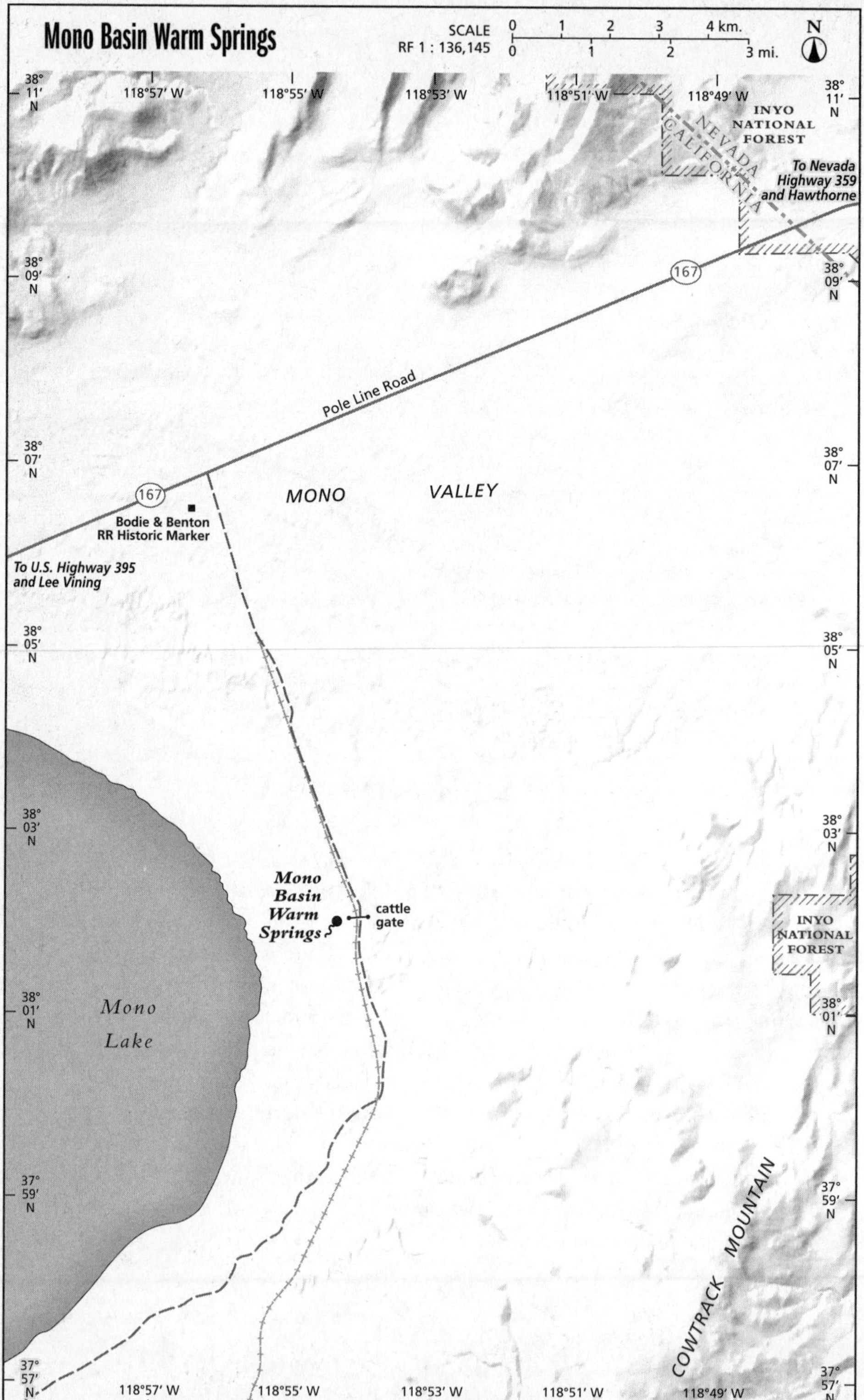

LONG VALLEY PRIMITIVE HOT SPRINGS

There are probably more hot springs in this one valley than in any other area described in this book. Many of these natural springs have been channelized, dammed up, or diverted into soaking pools. Although not well known a few years ago, this area has recently become quite popular. You should, however, still be able to find a nice pond or tub for a great soak, always in a majestic setting. Roads to the springs vary. The main access road east of U.S. Highway 395 is paved (Benton Crossing Road), and another is a graded dirt road (Forest Service Road 2S07). The other roads leading from these two roads are unimproved dirt surfaces, sandy in places. During wet weather these roads become very treacherous and should not be attempted. Much of the land in this area is owned by the Los Angeles Department of Water and Power (LADWP), which generally allows daytime use. Some of the springs are located on public land, where there are usually no restrictions against camping. LADWP land will be marked with large white signs. Obey these signs so public access won't be denied in the future.

Long Valley is a large volcanic complex and actually represents the remains of a massive caldera (collapsed volcano) that erupted roughly 760,000 years ago. The valley is the remains of this volcano after it erupted. The ash (known as the Bishop Tuff) can be found great distances away, indicating the severity of the eruption. The latest eruption occurred 600 years ago. The area is still active, and according to geologists, a resurgent dome in roughly the center of the valley has been uplifted over 1 meter since 1980 alone. In the recent past renewed earthquake activity caused concern that another eruption was in the making. As a result, the U.S. Geological Survey has been studying the area closely. It appears that magma is moving beneath the surface, causing geological unrest in the form of earthquakes and gas emissions.

23 Hot Creek Geothermal Area

General description: A series of hot springs feeding into a cold-water creek in a Forest Service park. The hot springs vary widely in temperature, but it is possible to find a few warm spots in the creek where the mixture of water is perfect. The park is a popular bathing spot. Use caution and bathe only in the main beach area, and obey all signs.

Location: Eastern California, 9 miles southeast of Mammoth Lakes.

Primitive/developed: The hot springs in the creek have not been developed, but dressing rooms, toilets, and a parking lot have been constructed above the creek.

Best time of year: Spring, summer, and fall. The road to the springs may be closed in winter.

Hot Creek

Restrictions: Hot Creek is only open during daylight hours.

Access: Any standard passenger vehicle should have no problem on the graded dirt road leading to the creek.

Water temperature: Varies depending upon source; some of the springs are extremely hot (199 degrees F), while other sources are slightly cooler. The few bathable spots also vary in temperature depending upon the exact place in the creek.

Nearby attractions: Mammoth Lakes, Long Valley hot springs area.

Services: There are no services at Hot Creek, but 9 miles away in Mammoth Lakes.

Camping: Camping is not allowed at Hot Creek, as it is only open during daylight hours. There are several Forest Service campgrounds in the area, and there is plenty of public land nearby where camping is permitted.

Map: USGS topographic, Benton Range, CA-NV, quadrangle, 1:100,000 scale.

Finding the springs: From the junction of U.S. Highway 395 and California Highway 203 outside of Mammoth Lakes, travel south on US 395 for approximately 3 miles. Turn left (east) on Hot Creek Road; this will turn into Owens River Road. Take this paved road for 0.8 mile to the sign for Hot Creek Geothermal Area and turn right. Travel another 3 miles on this paved and graded dirt road to the parking area for Hot Creek. The hot springs are downhill in the creek, along a steep paved path.

The Hot Springs

A popular place for those visiting the Mammoth Lakes area, Hot Creek can be quite busy on weekends, particularly in the summer. Although the road may be closed during the winter, you can reach the springs by cross-country skiing, if you

Hot Creek Geothermal Area; The Hot Tub; Shepherd Hot Spring; Crab Cooker; Crowley (Wild Willy's) Hot Spring; Hilltop Hot Spring (Pulky's Pool); Alkali Lake Hot Spring

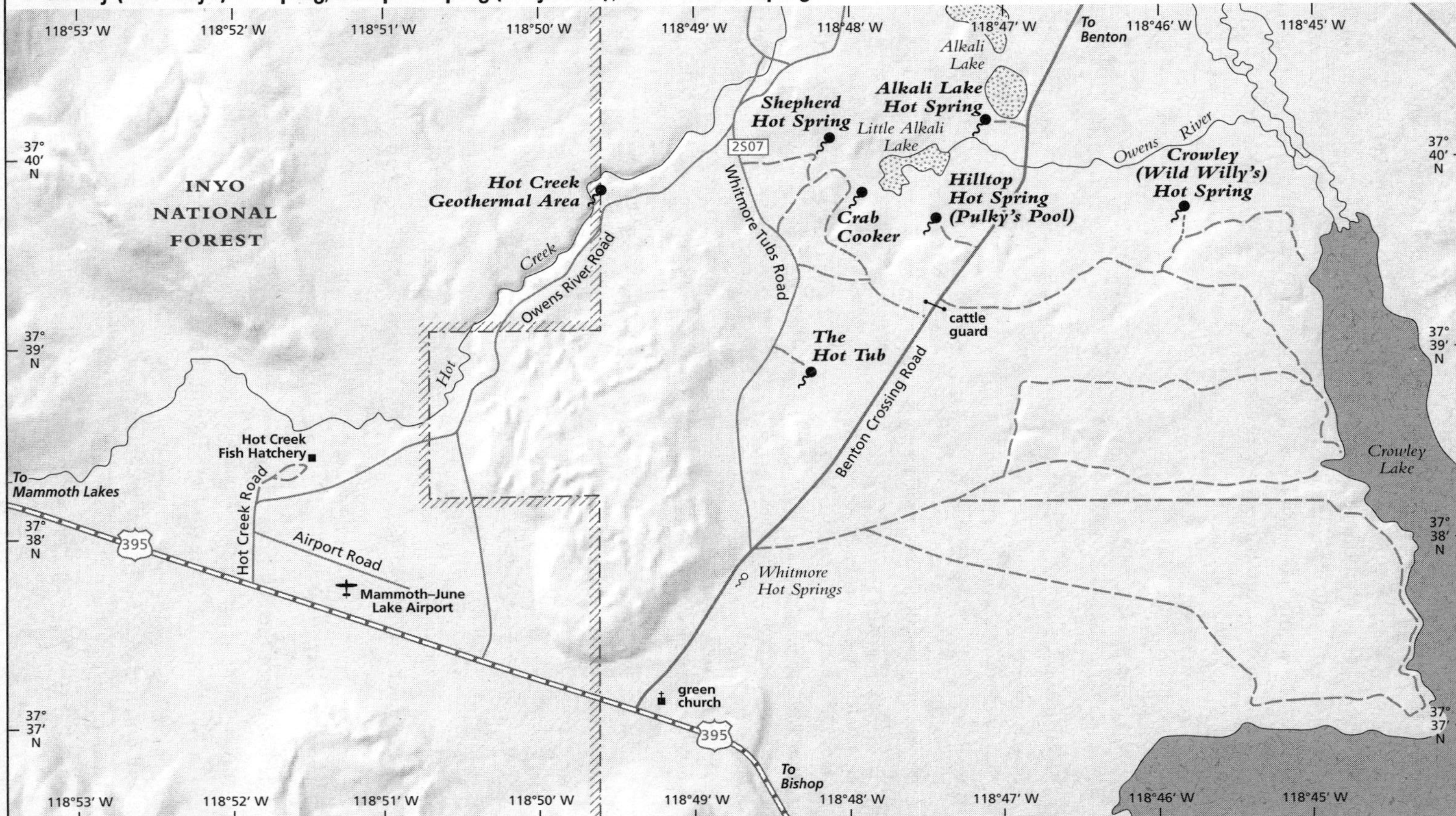

are so inclined. Most of the springs feeding the cold creek are extremely hot, as you can see by the vast amount of steam produced. In the main bathing area there are several springs bubbling up from the creek bottom that are also quite hot but, mixed with the cold water, make an exhilarating bath. Be extremely careful here, as most of the springs are boiling and will scald you. Bathe only in the main beach area, and take caution here also. Not the place for seclusion, Hot Creek is another interesting geologic area and is worth an hour or two for a bath.

24 The Hot Tub

See map on page 63.

General description: A large bathtub-size pool fed by a natural hot spring in the eastern Sierra. The tub is built out of rocks and cement, and water is piped into it from a spring a short distance away. One of the best bathing spots in the state.

Location: Eastern California, 11 miles southeast of Mammoth Lakes.

Primitive/developed: Primitive, except for the construction of the hot tub and the piping of the water into it.

Best time of year: Year-round. The road may have occasional snow in the winter and should be avoided during this time, as it can get a little muddy.

Restrictions: None.

Access: Any vehicle can make the short drive on the well-maintained, graded dirt road.

Water temperature: The temperature at the source is approximately 167 degrees F, but in the tub itself it's closer to 100 degrees F, varying slightly.

Nearby attractions: Mammoth Lakes, Hot Creek.

Services: There are no services at this location, but some can be found 11 miles away in Mammoth Lakes.

Camping: Camping is generally allowed at the spring, though there is frequently someone already there. There are several Forest Service campgrounds in the area and plenty of public land nearby where camping is permitted.

Map: USGS topographic, Benton Range, CA-NV, quadrangle, 1:100,000 scale.

Finding the spring: From the junction of U.S. Highway 395 and California Highway 203 outside of Mammoth Lakes, travel south on US 395 for approximately 9 miles. Turn left (east) on Benton Crossing Road at the large green church. Travel on this paved road for approximately 1.2 miles (passing Whitmore Hot Springs) to the first graded dirt road on your left. This is Forest Service Road 2S07 (Whitmore Tubs Road). Travel on this road for approximately 1.1 miles to where you come upon a small hill. Take the faint dirt road on your right here. You will soon see the source, and if you follow the road for less than 100 yards, you will reach the tub.

The Hot Spring

This is one of the best places for a soak in the state. The tub is perfectly sized for several people, is approximately 2 feet deep, and has a temperature in the low 100s. The tub also faces the Sierra Nevada, which provides an awesome backdrop. Several years ago resourceful volunteers diverted the water from the hot spring up the hill through a PVC pipe to this concrete and rock pool that they constructed. The tub has been improved over the years, with a patio-like area being constructed most recently. Although it is only a short distance off the main dirt road, the Hot

The Hot Tub

Tub is not visible from the road, providing a good deal of privacy. The tub, however, is also one of the most popular springs in the area, and you can generally expect to find others there before you. Your best chance for seclusion is during the week in the winter or fall. Please help to keep the area pristine by packing out all your trash and staying on the established roads.

25 Shepherd Hot Spring

See map on page 63.

General description: Another fantastic tub created by the diversion of hot spring water into a small concrete pool. This spring is similar to the others in the area, but requires driving on a rougher road than that to the Hot Tub.

Location: Eastern California, 12 miles southeast of Mammoth Lakes.

Primitive/developed: Primitive, except for the construction of the hot tub and the piping of the water into it.

Best time of year: Spring, summer, and fall. The road may be quite difficult during wet weather and may be impassable in the snow.

Restrictions: The tub itself is on land owned by the LADWP, and their rules must be obeyed (no camping).

Access: A high-clearance vehicle is recommended, though I've seen all kinds of passenger vehicles make it. If the road is wet, avoid it unless you have four-wheel drive.

Water temperature: The temperature at the source is approximately 120 degrees F, and cools to about 110 degrees F in the tub. The water can get quite hot if you sit in it for a while. You can cool it off some by diverting the water out of the tub and waiting for it to cool.

Nearby attractions: Mammoth Lakes, Hot Creek.

Services: There are no services at this location, but some can be found 12 miles away in Mammoth Lakes.

Camping: Camping is permitted on public land a few hundred yards to the west. Do not camp at Shepherd Hot Spring itself. There are also several Forest Service campgrounds in the area and a semideveloped campground at Benton Crossing, a few miles east on Owens River Road.

Map: USGS topographic, Benton Range, CA-NV, quadrangle, 1:100,000 scale.

Finding the spring: From the junction of U.S. Highway 395 and California Highway 203 outside of Mammoth Lakes, travel south on US 395 for approximately 9 miles. Turn left (east) on Benton Crossing Road at the large green church. Travel on this paved road for approximately 1 mile, past Whitmore Hot Springs, to the first graded dirt road on your left. This is Forest Service Road 2S07 (Whitmore Tubs Road). Travel on this road for approximately 2 miles (passing the road to the Hot Tub), and turn right on a smaller dirt road (a few yards before the lone tree). Travel on this lesser-maintained road for approximately 0.8 mile. The road will curve around a boggy area and fork. Stay to the left and drive the last few yards to the tub on your right.

The Hot Spring

This is another fantastic place to soak, though not quite as secluded as the Hot Tub. The water is also somewhat hotter, not allowing you to stay in as long. Apparently sheepherders built this tub quite a few years ago by diverting hot spring water through a plastic pipe into a cement and rock tub. The tub is approximately 6 by 5 feet and 2 feet deep. It can be emptied by removing a drain plug at the end of the tub and diverting the water. People generally keep it clean by replacing the water and scrubbing the sides with a brush. This spring has also been kept clean and free from trash—do your part to keep it that way. Though camping was allowed at one time, a few years ago the LADWP posted signs forbidding it. There is plenty of public land to the west where camping is allowed. You can always camp there and walk to the tub.

26 Crab Cooker

See map on page 63.

General description: Another bathtub-size pool fed by a natural hot spring in the eastern Sierra. This tub is also built out of rocks and cement, and water is piped into it from a spring a short distance away. A little less popular than the other tubs in the region, the Crab Cooker is another great place to soak.

Location: Eastern California, 12 miles southeast of Mammoth Lakes.

Primitive/developed: Primitive, except for the construction of the hot tub and the piping of the water into it.

Best time of year: Spring, summer, and fall. The road may be quite difficult during wet weather, and may be impassable in the snow.

Restrictions: The tub itself is on land owned by the LADWP, and their rules must be obeyed (no camping).

Access: A high-clearance vehicle is recommended, though I've seen all kinds of passen-

The Crab Cooker

ger vehicles make it. If the road is wet, avoid it unless you have four-wheel drive. The last few hundred yards to the spring can be difficult, and can be walked if you are unsure your car can make it.

Water temperature: The temperature is extremely hot at the source, which has been covered over. The water cools off substantially, however, and averages approximately 105 degrees F in the tub itself.

Nearby attractions: Mammoth Lakes, Hot Creek.

Services: There are no services at this location, but some can be found 12 miles away in Mammoth Lakes.

Camping: Camping is not allowed at the spring, but you can park a few hundred yards to the west and camp there. There are also several Forest Service campgrounds in the area.

Map: USGS topographic, Benton Range, CA-NV, quadrangle, 1:100,000 scale.

Finding the spring: From the junction of U.S. Highway 395 and California Highway 203 outside of Mammoth Lakes, travel south on US 395 for approximately 9 miles. Turn left (east) on Benton Crossing Road at the large green church. Travel on this paved road for approximately 1 mile, past Whitmore Hot Springs, to the first graded dirt road on your left. This is Forest Service Road 2S07 (Whitmore Tubs Road). Travel on this road for approximately 2 miles (passing the road to the Hot Tub), and turn right on a smaller dirt road (a few yards before the lone tree). Travel on this lesser-maintained road for approximately 0.8 mile. The road will curve around a boggy area and fork. To get to the Crab Cooker, turn right at this fork, and go down the hill a few hundred yards to a large grassy area. If you don't think your car can make the last part of the drive, walk the short distance to the spring. Stay on established roads, as there is a good chance you will get stuck in the boggy marsh if you don't.

The Hot Spring

The Crab Cooker is a nice place for a bath, and is similar to the Hot Tub and Shepherd Hot Spring. It is a little shallower than the others, but is big enough for several people and also provides beautiful scenery. Recently, a valve has been installed that allows you to fill the tub when you are ready to bathe in it. You can also empty the tub by releasing a drain at the other end. As with Shepherd, camping used to be permitted at the tub but is now prohibited. You can camp a few hundred yards west, however. In some ways this regulation is better, as you will generally not find a group of people camping at the spring and monopolizing it for their own use. Be sure to keep the area clean and free of trash.

Another tub was developed roughly halfway between Shepherd Hot Spring and the Crab Cooker, beneath a small ridge. As of this writing, however, the water entering the tub is cool, and no bathing opportunities exist. You can find it by stopping at a large, broad flat that serves as an unofficial parking area on your left as you drive from Shepherd Hot Spring going toward the Crab Cooker. This parking area is often lined with rocks. The tub is located beneath the small hill from this parking area, toward the Alkali Lakes to the east.

27 Crowley (Wild Willy's) Hot Spring

See map on page 63.

General description: A larger pond and smaller tub fed by a couple of hot spring sources in the scenic eastern Sierra. Although you must walk the last 100 yards to Crowley, it is still a popular spring and generally has people at it.

Location: Eastern California, 14 miles southeast of Mammoth Lakes.

Primitive/developed: Primitive, except for the construction of the pool and tub and the diversion of water into them.

Best time of year: Spring, summer, and fall. The road can be difficult to impassable in wet weather, particularly in the snow.

Restrictions: You are not allowed to drive out to the spring itself, and camping is not permitted.

Access: Most passenger vehicles can make the 1.2-mile drive on the dirt road to the spring. Do not try the road when it is wet, and especially in the snow.

Water temperature: The temperature at the source is approximately 115 degrees F. The pool is approximately 95 degrees F, the tub about 105 degrees F.

Nearby attractions: Mammoth Lakes, Hot Creek.

Services: There are no services at this location, but 14 miles away in Mammoth Lakes.

Camping: Camping is not allowed at the spring itself. There is plenty of public land nearby, however, where undeveloped camping can be had. There are also several Forest Service campgrounds in the area.

Map: USGS topographic, Benton Range, CA-NV, quadrangle, 1:100,000 scale.

Finding the spring: From the junction of U.S. Highway 395 and California Highway 203 outside of Mammoth Lakes, travel south on US 395 for approximately 9 miles. Turn left (east) on Benton Crossing Road at the large green church. Travel on this paved road for approximately 3.1 miles (passing Forest Ser-

Crowley Hot Spring

vice Road 2S07). As you cross a cattle guard, there is a small dirt road on your right; turn here. Follow this dirt road around the fence line and eventually downhill for approximately 1.2 miles to a parking area, past a large rock outcrop. Park here and walk a few hundred yards to the spring and the pools. Again, stay on the main road and you will not get stuck. When this soil gets wet, it is extremely mucky, and you will get mired.

The Hot Spring

Crowley has a nice, big pool complete with a wooden deck on the edge. Recently, the Bureau of Land Management has been attempting a revegetation project in the area and has installed a gravel walkway and boardwalk all the way from the parking lot to the hot springs. Please stay on this walk. The pool was built out of concrete quite a few years ago and is approximately 9 by 12 feet and 3 feet deep. The smaller tub is also enjoyable, with enough room for one, and possibly two. The tub, which is a few degrees F hotter than the pool, was also constructed quite a few years ago, out of wood. The area is kept clean, particularly now that cars are forbidden from driving right to the springs. As with most of the other springs, camping used to be permitted at the spring itself, but is no longer allowed. Again, there is plenty of public land nearby where camping is allowed. Just obey any signs you see and you should be fine.

28 Hilltop Hot Spring (Pulky's Pool)

See map on page 63.

General description: A newer, smaller concrete tub fed by a hot spring source a few yards away. Located on the top of a hill, this spring also has a fantastic view of the surrounding countryside and the Sierra Nevada.

Location: Eastern California, 13 miles southeast of Mammoth Lakes.

Primitive/developed: Primitive, except for the construction of the hot tub and the piping of the water into it.

Best time of year: Year-round. Because it is located a short distance off the paved road, you can walk to the tub if the dirt road is too muddy or covered in snow.

Restrictions: The land on which it is located is owned by the LADWP, and camping is not allowed. Obey all signs.

Access: The spring is only 0.25 mile off the paved road on a decent dirt road. When it is dry, most standard passenger vehicles can make the trip. When the ground is wet, however, you are much better off walking from the paved road. The soil here gets extremely mucky when it's wet, and you stand a good chance of getting hopelessly mired.

Water temperature: The temperature at the source is approximately 120 degrees F, but cools to about 100 degrees F in the tub. Tub temperature can be altered easily by diverting water out and letting it cool.

Nearby attractions: Mammoth Lakes, Hot Creek.

Services: There are no services at this location, but some can be found 11 miles away in Mammoth Lakes.

Camping: Camping is generally allowed at the spring, though there is frequently someone already there. There are several Forest Service campgrounds in the area and plenty of public land nearby where camping is permitted.

Map: USGS topographic, Benton Range, CA-NV, quadrangle, 1:100,000 scale.

Finding the spring: From the junction of U.S. Highway 395 and California Highway 203 outside of Mammoth Lakes, travel south on US 395 for approximately 9 miles. Turn left (east) on Benton Crossing Road at the large green church. Travel on this paved road for approximately 3.4 miles (0.2 mile past the road to Crowley Hot Spring) to a dirt road on your left. Turn here and drive approximately 0.25 mile to a parking area. Park and walk the short distance up the hill to the tub. If the ground is wet, do not drive on this dirt road, as it passes through a low spot where water collects, and the ground becomes quite slippery. Pull off the paved road and walk the short distance instead.

The Hot Spring

Hilltop Hot Spring is a relatively new tub in the area, and is sometimes known as Pulky's Pool. The tub is otherwise similar to the others in the area, consisting of a concrete tub fed by a hot spring.

29 Alkali Lake Hot Spring

See map on page 63.

General description: A small concrete-lined tub fed, through PVC pipe, by a hot spring source a few yards away. This hot spring currently presents limited bathing opportunities, but could be improved with a little work.

Location: Eastern California, 14 miles southeast of Mammoth Lakes.

Primitive/developed: Primitive, except for the construction of the hot tub and the piping of the water into it.

Best time of year: Year-round. Because it is located a short distance off the paved road, you can walk to the tub if the dirt road is too muddy or covered in snow.

Restrictions: The land on which the spring is located is presumably owned by the LADWP, and camping is generally not allowed. Obey all signs.

Access: The spring is located a short walk off of the main paved road, and a large parking area is located nearby.

Water temperature: The temperature at the source is approximately 120 degrees F. The water in the bathtub is about 118 degrees F, 115 degrees F in the concrete-lined tub. Tub temperature can be easily altered by diverting water out and letting it cool.

Nearby attractions: Mammoth Lakes, Hot Creek.

Services: There are no services at this location, but 13 miles away in Mammoth Lakes.

Camping: Camping is not permitted at the spring itself, but there are several Forest Service campgrounds in the area and plenty of public land nearby where camping is permitted.

Map: USGS topographic, Benton Range, CA-NV, quadrangle, 1:100,000 scale.

Finding the spring: From the junction of U.S. Highway 395 and California Highway 203 outside of Mammoth Lakes, travel south on US 395 for approximately 9 miles. Turn left (east) on Benton Crossing Road at the large green church. Travel on this paved road for approximately 4.2 miles (0.8 mile past the road to Hilltop Hot Spring) to a very hard-to-see dirt road on your left. This road will be after Benton Crossing Road makes a bend to the left, and shortly before it makes a bend to the right. Turn here and drive a short distance to a parking area next to a large alkali lake. Park here and walk west, across a small dry creek, for approximately 100 yards to the spring. You will see a galvanized metal culvert at the hot spring source and the bathtub nearby. You may also notice steam on colder days.

The Hot Spring

This hot spring consists of a single source that has been captured by a large galvanized metal culvert stuck in the ground. The hot water (approximately 120 degrees F) is diverted into a bathtub, far too hot to bathe in. The water is also diverted into a small, shallow concrete-lined tub that is also rather hot for bathing. Water could be diverted and allowed to cool, however. With improvement this tub could make for a great bath. It is, however, located within view of the road.

30 Little Hot Creek Hot Springs

General description: A hotter, larger spring and tub removed a few miles from the other hot springs in the area. A great place for a hot soak, Little Hot Creek is also located in a beautiful setting with fantastic views.

Location: Eastern California, 16 miles southeast of Mammoth Lakes.

Primitive/developed: Primitive, except for the construction of the hot tub and the piping of the water into it.

Best time of year: Spring, summer, and fall. The secondary roads can be difficult in wet weather and impassable in the snow.

Restrictions: None.

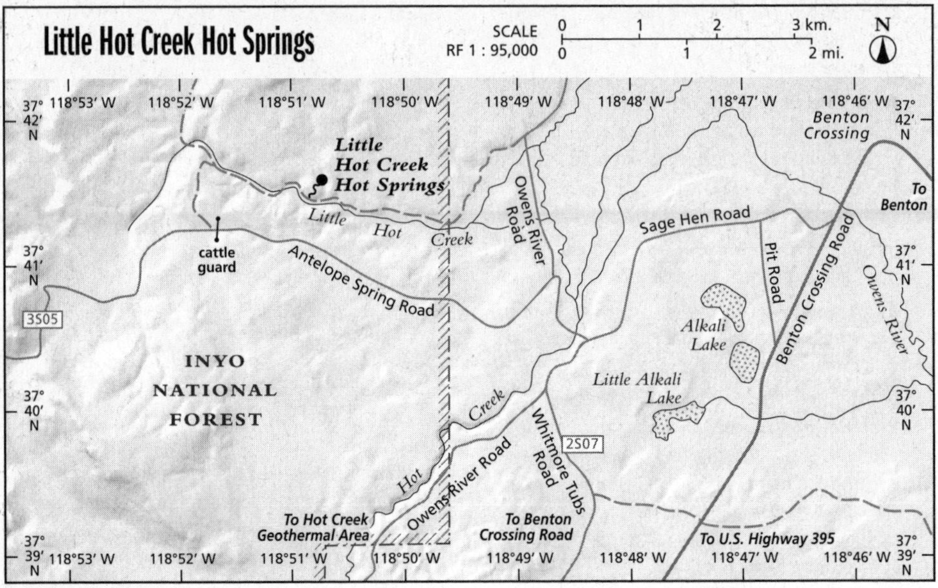

Access: Most standard passenger vehicles should be able to make the drive without too much trouble when the road is dry. Avoid it altogether when wet.

Water temperature: The temperature at the source is approximately 180 degrees F, but cools to about 115 degrees F by the time it reaches the tub itself. As this is still too hot, divert the water for a while to cool it off.

Nearby attractions: Mammoth Lakes, Hot Creek.

Services: There are no services at this location, but some can be found 11 miles away in Mammoth Lakes.

Camping: The hot spring is on Forest Service land, and there does not appear to be any restrictions against camping. Do not camp immediately adjacent to the spring itself, however. There are several developed Forest Service campgrounds in the area and plenty of public land nearby where camping is also permitted.

Map: USGS topographic, Benton Range, CA-NV, quadrangle, 1:100,000 scale.

Finding the springs: From the junction of U.S. Highway 395 and California Highway 203 outside of Mammoth Lakes, travel south on US 395 for approximately 9 miles. Turn left (east) on Benton Crossing Road at the large green church. Travel on this paved road for approximately 1 mile, past Whitmore Hot Springs, to the first graded dirt road on your left. This is Forest Service Road 2S07 (Whitmore Tubs Road). Travel on this road for approximately 3.3 miles, passing the roads to the Hot Tub, Shepherd Hot Spring, and the Crab Cooker. Turn left on a dirt road that may not be labeled. Continue across the creek and turn left at the next intersection, Antelope Spring Road (0.7 mile). This road is not as well maintained as Owens River Road, but should be fine as long as it's dry. Drive on Antelope Spring Road for approximately 2.5 miles, crossing a cattle guard. Immediately past the cattle guard, turn right and travel another 0.8 mile to the springs. You will need to walk a few yards through a cattle-proof gate to the tub itself.

Another option is to stay on Owens River Road (instead of turning on Antelope Spring Road) for 1 mile, where you turn left on a small dirt road. Travel on this poor road for 1.6 miles to the hot spring.

The Hot Springs

The extremely hot water is diverted from one in a cluster of hot springs through several yards of pipe into a concrete pool, where the water remains hot. A series of fences have been built around the spring to reduce cattle damage. The tub is approximately 8 by 9 feet and 2 feet deep. Be careful here as the water is hot. Before getting in, feel the water temperature and divert the pipe from the tub to let the water cool down. This tub is the least-known of the springs in the area, but that does not guarantee seclusion. The road to the tub is longer than the others, but is passable to most vehicles when it is dry. Unlike the other springs, this tub is located on Forest Service land, and there does not appear to be any restrictions against camping here. As with the other springs, however, do not camp immediately adjacent to the tub, and please pick up after yourself.

31 Benton Hot Springs

General description: A pleasant hot spring resort, campground, and hotel in eastern California, complete with several outdoor hot tubs. Benton Hot Springs is a historic town, with numerous historic buildings and a bed-and-breakfast.

Location: Eastern California, 47 miles north of Bishop and 50 miles southeast of Lee Vining.

Primitive/developed: Developed, though rustic.

Best time of year: Year-round. Summer can be hot.

Restrictions: This is a private establishment with usage fees.

Access: Located on a paved highway. California Highway 120 is often closed during winter,

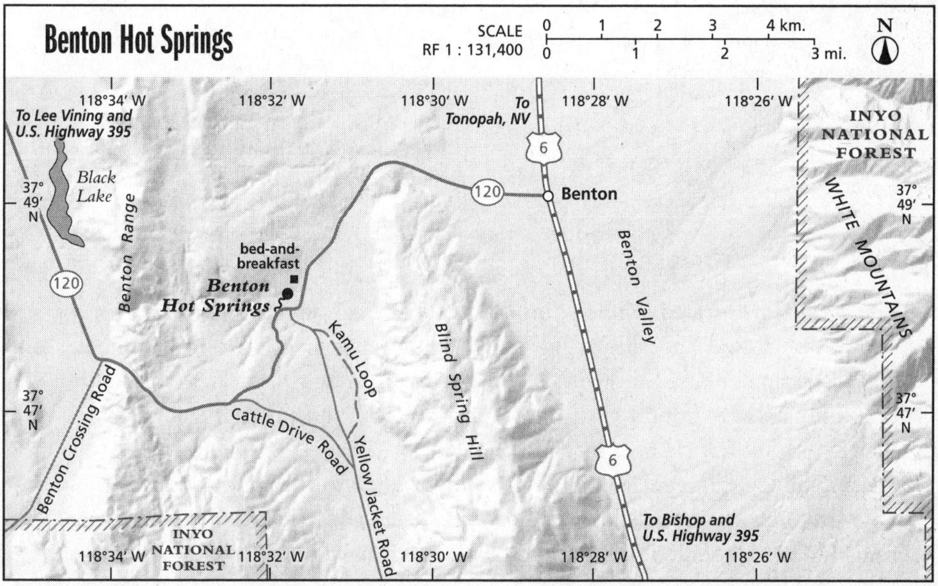

The tub at Benton Hot Springs

so drive from Bishop to Benton Hot Springs during these months.

Water temperature: The hot spring source is 134 degrees F. Water temperature in the tubs ranges between 100 and 104 degrees F. The temperature can be controlled by adding cold water.

Nearby attractions: White Mountains.

Services: The small town of Benton Hot Springs has a bed-and-breakfast. Other services (gas and food) can be found in Benton, 3 miles away. More complete services are found in Bishop, 47 miles away.

Camping: Campsites are available at the resort, complete with a private outdoor hot tub.

Map: California Highway Map.

Finding the springs: Benton Hot Springs is located on CA 120. From Bishop, travel north on U.S. Highway 6 for 35 miles to the town of Benton. Turn left (west) onto CA 120 and follow it for 3 miles to Benton Hot Springs. The resort will be on your right, after the bed-and-breakfast. From Lee Vining, travel south on U.S. Highway 395 for 5 miles to CA 120. Turn left and follow CA 120 for 45 miles to Benton Hot Springs. The resort will be on your left.

The Hot Springs

The springs are located in one of the oldest surviving towns in Mono County, Benton, which was once a thriving silver-mining center with up to 5,000 inhabitants. The small house (known as the Old House) where you check in to use the tubs and the campground sells antiques and gifts. The house itself dates back to the 1870s, with few changes made since that time. There are numerous other historic buildings scattered around the grounds and the town. Currently there are six hot tubs to choose from, all fed by a natural spring with a source temperature of roughly 134 degrees F. The redwood tubs are all located outside, with small privacy fences. Prices are $6.00 per person, or $15.00 per tub per hour. Down the road is the Inn at Benton Hot Springs, a bed-and-breakfast. The resort is open year-round, but keep in mind that CA 120 frequently closes during winter. The resort can be accessed from Bishop during these months. For more information, contact the Old House at Benton Hot Springs, Route 4, Box 58, Benton, CA 93512, or call (760) 933–2507.

OWENS VALLEY REGION

South of the Long Valley region lies the lower Owens Valley, with the communities of Bishop, Big Pine, Independence, and Lone Pine. This area is generally warmer than regions to the north and is less watered. The Owens River flows through the valley, where it is picked up by a Los Angeles' Department of Water and Power (LADWP) canal. The river at one time flowed into Owens Lake, and eventually disappeared into the desert to the south, but the lake is now dry. Ample creeks draining the high Sierra from the west flow under U.S. Highway 395 and into the Owens River. Most of these creeks are stocked with various types of game fish and make excellent fishing spots. Campgrounds and picnic areas also abound along US 395 between Bishop and Lone Pine. All services can be obtained in any of the four towns, though Bishop is by far the largest.

32 Keough Hot Ditch

General description: A group of pools of varying temperature formed in a creek of hot spring water. Located off U.S. Highway 395, the hot spring water forming these pools is from a source that supplies a bath house uphill.

Location: Eastern California, 8 miles south of Bishop.

Primitive/developed: Primitive, except for the damming up of some of the pools.

Best time of year: Year-round.

Restrictions: This is LADWP land, and is only open to the public during the daytime.

Access: Any passenger vehicle can make the short drive along the dirt road off the highway. To access some of the pools, there are a couple of spots that will require some clearance.

Water temperature: The sources are quite hot, approximately 130 degrees F at the top of the hill. The water cools as it flows downhill, and each pool is therefore cooler as you go down the hill. Temperatures range from 110 degrees F on the hillside to 90 degrees F on the other side of the road.

Nearby attractions: Owens Valley Warm Spring, Lake Sabrina, Owens River, numerous fishing creeks.

Services: There are no services at this location, but 8 miles away in Bishop.

Camping: Camping is not allowed. There are several Forest Service and private campgrounds in the area, however.

Map: USGS topographic, Bishop, CA, quadrangle, 1:100,000 scale.

Finding the springs: From the town of Bishop, travel south on US 395 for approximately 7 miles to Keogh Hot Springs Road (there will be a yellow highway sign), where you turn right. Drive on this paved road for approximately 0.6 mile to an old paved road near power lines, where you again turn right. Drive on this road (old US 395) for approximately 0.25 mile to where you will see the springs on your left, up a smaller road. There are also three groups of springs on your right. Take your pick of the many pools here.

Keough Hot Ditch

The Hot Springs

The Keough Hot Springs Resort, which recently reopened, is up the road from Keogh Hot Ditch. This historic resort is also worth a visit and is open for day use. It contains a large swimming pool with snack bar and picnic areas. Keogh Hot Ditch is formed from several sources uphill that flow in a small creek, dammed up in places for bathing opportunities. The pools are fairly large in size and decrease in temperature as you go downhill. The water is generally clear and inviting in all of the pools. The second collection of pools is across the old paved road and slightly downhill. These pools are a little cooler (high 90s) and are also fairly large in size. Although this is a rather popular place, with so many pools to choose from, you should be able to find one to yourself. If all the pools are full when you arrive, wait awhile and one may come open. So far, trash has not been too much of a problem at Keogh, but there is a fair amount of broken glass, so be careful.

33 Owens Valley Warm Spring

General description: A warm spring feeding a small pond at the base of the mountains near the Owens River.

Location: Eastern California, approximately halfway between Bishop and Big Pine.

Primitive/developed: Primitive, except for the placement of several culverts to channel the water downhill from the pond.

Best time of year: Spring, summer, and fall. The road to the spring may be impassable in wet weather.

Restrictions: None.

Access: The road to the spring is passable by most vehicles with decent ground clearance. Many passenger cars will have trouble, however. Avoid it altogether when the ground is wet.

Water temperature: The temperature at the source is approximately 85 degrees F. The water cools off rapidly in the pool, but remains lukewarm.

Nearby attractions: Keogh Hot Springs and Ditch.

Services: There are no services at this location but 9 miles away in Big Pine.

Camping: There is very little room for camping at the spring, and it may not be permissible. Instead, camp in one of the many campgrounds near Big Pine.

Map: USGS topographic, Bishop, CA, quadrangle, 1:100,000 scale.

Finding the spring: From the town of Big Pine, travel east on California Highway 168 for 1.9 miles (crossing the Owens River) to Leighton Road on your left. Turn on this paved road heading north for approximately 3.3 miles toward the Owens Valley Radio Observatory. Immediately before reaching the gate, turn right on a dirt road and travel approximately 1 mile to the east. This road will intersect another dirt road, where you turn left. Follow this road north for approximately 2.8 miles to the spring on the right side, at the base of the mountains. It is possible to reach the spring from Bishop, but the route from Big Pine is more direct and clearer.

The Hot Spring

This small warm spring feeds a pond that provides a picturesque oasis in an otherwise dry valley. The spring water was, at one time, extended further along a concrete ditch that irrigated a much larger field. Today, however, this ditch is dry. The water in the pond is amazingly clear and contains numerous fish. The ownership of this spring is unclear, so be sure to obey all signs. Currently there are no restrictions against visiting it. Bathing is possible, but don't expect a hot bath here.

The road to the radio observatory follows the abandoned grade of the Carson and Colorado Railroad, beginning at the remains of Zurich Station. This was the hub of activity (particularly Big Pine) for this area prior to the dissolution of the railroad. A small historic marker is located near the intersection. Be sure to check it out.

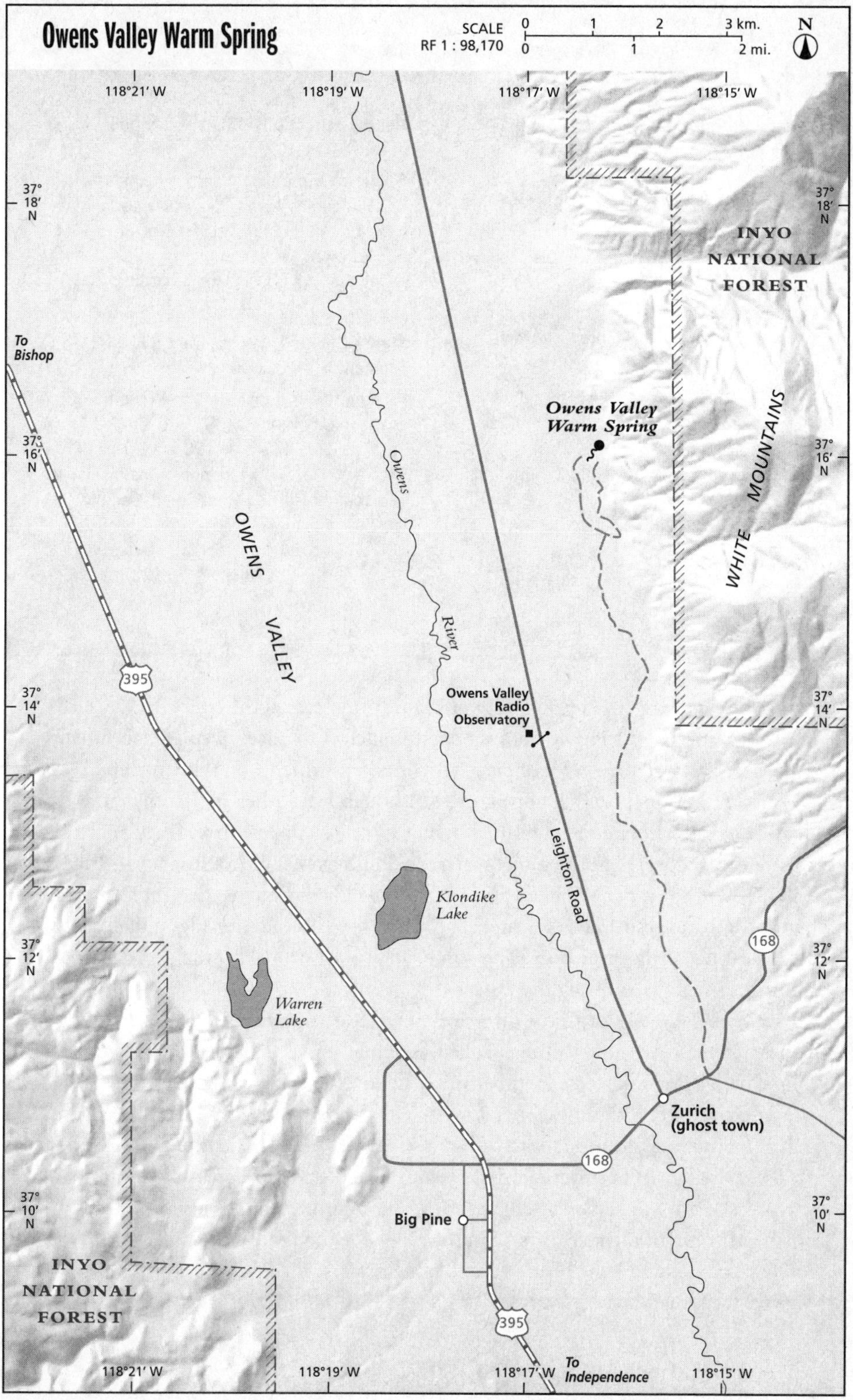
Owens Valley Warm Spring
SCALE
RF 1 : 98,170
0 1 2 3 km.
0 1 2 mi.
N
118°21′ W
118°19′ W
118°17′ W
118°15′ W
37° 18′ N
37° 16′ N
37° 14′ N
37° 12′ N
37° 10′ N
INYO NATIONAL FOREST
To Bishop
Owens Valley Warm Spring
WHITE MOUNTAINS
OWENS VALLEY
Owens River
Owens Valley Radio Observatory
395
Leighton Road
Klondike Lake
Warren Lake
168
Zurich (ghost town)
Big Pine
INYO NATIONAL FOREST
To Independence

34 Dirty Sock Hot Spring

General description: A large pool formed from a hot well near the edge of the dry Owens Lake. The warm-water pool can be bathed in, but the large amounts of algae give it a murky appearance.

Location: Eastern California, 26 miles south of Lone Pine.

Primitive/developed: Although this is a man-made pool, there are few other improvements at this isolated location.

Best time of year: Fall, winter, and spring. Summer can be too hot.

Restrictions: None.

Access: Any vehicle can make the trip, as the hot spring is located at the end of a paved road.

Water temperature: Approximately 90 degrees F in the center of the pool, cooler in other places.

Nearby attractions: Death Valley, ghost towns of Darwin and Keeler.

Services: There are no services at this location, but can be found 26 miles away in Lone Pine. There are a few small hotels in Olancha, 5 miles away.

Camping: There does not appear to be any restrictions against camping at Dirty Sock.

Map: USGS topographic, Darwin Hills, CA, quadrangle, 1:100,000 scale.

Finding the spring: From Lone Pine travel south on U.S. Highway 395 and turn left (east) onto California Highway 190 toward Death Valley. Travel on CA 190 for approximately 5 miles to an unmarked, degraded paved road on the left. Follow this road for approximately 0.25 mile to the pond at the end of the road.

The Hot Spring

Dirty Sock is a large (30 by 30 feet) pool of warm water on the edge of a dry lake in the dry Owens Valley. The pool is approximately 4 to 5 feet deep and about 90 degrees F. The water has a lot of algae growing in it, which won't hurt you but gives it a rather unappealing appearance. Although it is rather well-known, the spring does not receive many visitors due to its murky appearance. Dirty Sock was apparently discovered accidentally when the Southern Pacific Railroad was drilling wells and hit hot water. An enterprising individual later bought the property and built a pool and resort at the spring. The resort failed rather quickly, and all that remains today is the large pool. The name Dirty Sock probably emerged from the sulfurous smell given off by the waters.

Owens Valley: Prior to the diversion of water out of the Owens River by Los Angeles in the early 1900s, Owens Lake was actually a lake. Named in the 1850s by John Charles Fremont for a member of his third expedition to the West, the lake was measured to be 15 miles long, 9 miles wide, and 50 feet deep in 1891. As hard as it is to imagine, steamboats actually traversed this lake at one time. During the 1860s, at the height of production of the mines at Cerro Gordo (in the mountains to the east), ore was hauled over the mountains and down to Swansea, on the northeast shore of the lake. From Swansea it was loaded onto the steamship *Bessie Brady,* steamed across the lake, and unloaded at Cartago, on the southwest shore. This 85-foot steamboat saved freighters over 50 miles and four days' travel around

Dirty Sock Hot Spring

the lake. Fuel, wood, and charcoal was in turn carried from Swansea, on the steamship *Molly Stevens,* for use in the smelters on the north shore of the lake. From Cartago the ore was freighted to Los Angeles and from there shipped to San Francisco for refining. The massive amount of ore from the Cerro Gordo mines ($15 million worth) is believed to have been the impetus for the initial growth of Los Angeles in the 1870s.

Following a decline in mining at Cerro Gordo, a rejuvenation occurred in the late 1870s. In conjunction with this rejuvenation, the Carson and Colorado Railroad was constructed in 1883 from Carson City to its terminus at the new town of Keeler, on the east shore of Owens Lake. The mines thereafter declined rapidly, however, and the railroad saw little use. Today the line is long since abandoned, but the depot can still be seen in the semi–ghost town of Keeler.

White settlers began living in the Owens Valley in the 1860s, largely to take advantage of the Cerro Gordo trade. Hay was grown for feeding the many teams plying the region. A variety of other crops were grown, supplying the large numbers of miners throughout the 1860s and 1870s. Sheep and cattle ranching also prospered in the region. Other mining areas such as Darwin, Candelaria, Ballarat, and Panamint City were supplied by these Owens Valley farms and ranches in subsequent decades.

In 1904 the growing city of Los Angeles sought out additional sources of water, finding it in the Owens River. By 1907 an aqueduct was completed (portions of which can still be seen today), linking the water with Los Angeles, over 250 miles away. As the city grew, more water was needed, and more water was drawn out of the valley. The local ranchers and farmers fought the city for their water, with numerous skirmishes occurring, through the 1920s. Los Angeles was the eventual victor, however, buying up enough property to acquire control of the water. The once-fertile farms and ranches soon thereafter dried up, leaving only a handful of settlers able to make a living off the land.

THE SALINE VALLEY

One of the most isolated, unpopulated, and foreboding regions in California, a trip to the Saline Valley is an expedition. Located to the northwest of Death Valley National Monument, Saline is in many ways far more treacherous. The only roads leading into and out of the valley are poor, unimproved dirt surfaces, winding long distances from the nearest paved highway. Portions of these roads are sandy, steep, and lined with large rocks. Any vehicle attempting to enter the region should have high clearance (four-wheel drive is recommended) and be in good working order. For those willing to take the long trek into the valley, there are several hot springs waiting as a reward.

All precautions should be taken before attempting the trip. Contact the Bureau of Land Management in Ridgecrest (760–384–5483) and Death Valley National Monument (760–786–3200) for up-to-date regulations, road conditions, and restrictions. Notify someone of your planned trip and when you plan on returning. Bring more food and water than you could possibly use, along with tools, camping equipment, and other supplies listed at the beginning of this book.

35 Saline Valley Hot Springs

General description: An extremely isolated series of hot springs in a low, dry desert—a beautiful environment. Despite their isolation, however, the springs are heavily visited, and groups of people stay at the location for extended periods of time. Several concrete tubs have been constructed at the three sets of hot springs in Saline Valley.

Location: Eastern California, 105 miles northeast of Lone Pine.

Primitive/developed: Although these hot springs are natural, there have been substantial improvements made, including the construction of concrete tubs, a shower, a toilet, and a camp setup. The upper hot springs are primitive, with no improvements made to them.

Best time of year: Fall, winter, and spring. Summer can be extremely hot.

Restrictions: The springs are on National Park Service land (as a part of Death Valley National Park), and park regulations must be obeyed. These include a thirty-day camping limit, as well as removal of all trash brought in.

Access: This is a very difficult road and requires a sturdy vehicle in sound condition. High clearance is necessary, and you may need four-wheel drive if the road has been washed out at all. Do not try this drive if the roads are wet or rain is approaching. Count on at least three hours to get to Saline Valley from U.S. Highway 395.

Water temperature: The temperatures vary depending upon the hot springs chosen. Most of the concrete tubs are around 100 degrees F.

Nearby attractions: Death Valley, ghost towns of Darwin and Cerro Gordo.

Services: There are no services at this isolated location, but they can be found 105 miles away in Lone Pine.

Camping: Camping is permitted for up to thirty days, and volunteers have made quite a comfortable camp, which includes dish basins, makeshift showers, plenty of shade, and couches.

The improved tub at the lower springs of Saline Valley Hot Springs

Maps: Death Valley National Monument map; USGS topographic, Darwin Hills, CA, quadrangle, 1:100,000 scale.

Finding the springs: From Lone Pine, travel south out of town on US 395 to California Highway 136 toward Death Valley. Take CA 136 for 18 miles to where it intersects with California Highway 190 and stay left, following CA 190 toward Death Valley for approximately 17 miles to a sign for Saline Valley. Turn left here, and travel on Saline Valley Road, staying right at the first fork, and then right again at the next fork, which leads you down a steep canyon. Be careful to stay on the main road. After approximately 44 miles you will see another dirt road marked with either a sign or a painted rock. Travel on this road for approximately 10 miles, staying left at another fork, and eventually reaching a palm tree where the first set of hot springs (Lower Warm Springs) is located. The second set, Palm Springs, is approximately 1 mile up the same road. The undeveloped springs are another 5 miles of treacherous road beyond Palm Springs.

The Hot Springs

Located in a newly acquired portion of Death Valley National Park, there are three hot springs here in Saline Valley. **Lower Warm Springs** is the first cluster of springs you will come to, and with a source of about 110 degrees F, the water cools to roughly 90 degrees F in the tub. **Palm Springs,** adjacent to Lower Warm Springs (farther up the road about 1 mile), is the hottest of the group, with a source temperature of approximately 120 degrees F, cooling to about 106 degrees F in the tub. **Upper Warm Springs,** located another 5 miles from Palm Springs, require a difficult drive to get to. They have been left in a natural state, with no concrete tubs constructed, and have a source temperature of roughly 90 degrees F.

An extensive camp and several concrete soaking pools have been constructed at the lower group of hot springs, which consists of Lower Warm Springs and Palm Springs. Upper Warm Springs comprises several natural pools. The two lower springs are visited frequently during the nonsummer months, with most of the people staying for days, weeks, and even months at a time. The springs are very well maintained by these volunteers, and you get a real sense of cooperation and decency among those who so painstakingly take care of the area. The camp has almost every convenience of a developed campground, but still maintains a sense of isolation. If you want seclusion, your best bet is to come during the week and make the extra 5-mile trip to the upper springs.

The National Park Service has designated the hot springs as clothing optional. Be forewarned that many of the visitors to Saline Valley Hot Springs prefer to go clothesless. Also, be sure to plan ahead before making this trip. Pack plenty of extra water and food (more than you think you will need), a complete tool kit, shovel, spare tire, and car jack. Check your car over thoroughly, and let someone know where you are going and when you are coming back. This is an enjoyable hot spring to visit, but the trip can be very dangerous if you are not prepared.

CALIFORNIA CENTRAL COAST

The central coast of California is what many people envision when they think of the state: spectacular coastline, rugged mountains, redwoods, and small quaint towns. Within the region are distinct geographic areas, each with its own topography, flora, biota, and settlement patterns. Though the region is rich in geothermic resources, only a few of the hot springs are open to the public. Below are some of the best.

Mono Hot Springs

36 Franklin Lakes Hot Well

General description: A concrete swimming pool and lake fed by a geothermal well, located a short distance outside the town of Paso Robles. A private aquaculture farm, Franklin Lakes is open to the public and makes for a nice bath.

Location: Coastal central California, a few miles outside the town of Paso Robles.

Primitive/developed: Developed, though simple and rustic.

Best time of year: Year-round.

Restrictions: The pool and lake are private property, but are open to the public for a $5.00-per-person day-use fee.

Access: Immediately off a paved road.

Water temperature: Approximately 104 degrees F at the source, while most of the swimming pool is about 98 degrees F.

Nearby attractions: Paso Robles Hot Springs & Spa.

Services: There are no services at this location, but some can be found approximately 4 miles away in Paso Robles. Portable toilets and changing rooms are provided at the swimming pool.

Camping: None currently, but there are several campgrounds in the nearby national forests and state parks.

Map: San Luis Obispo County Highway Map.

Finding the spring: From U.S. Highway 101 northbound in Paso Robles, exit at Spring Street and turn right at Niblick Road. Travel 1.7 miles on Niblick Road to Creston Road and turn right. Travel on Creston Road for 2.3 miles to the sign for Franklin Lakes on your right. Turn on the small dirt road to the lake and swimming pool. From US 101 southbound, exit at Sixteenth Street and turn left on Riverside Drive. Travel 0.7 mile to Thirteenth Street, and turn left. 13th Street becomes Creston Road, which you follow for approximately 4.5 miles to Franklin Lakes on your right.

The Hot Spring

Geothermal water was accidentally discovered here in the 1950s, while drilling for oil. Shortly thereafter a concrete swimming pool was constructed to take advantage of the hot water, which comes out of the ground at about 104 degrees F. Because so many people came to bathe in the water over the ensuing years (trespassing in the process), the owners decided to open it to the public and charge a small fee. The swimming pool's water is about 98 degrees F, and it's a fun place for a hot bath or swim. The water overflows into a small lake, which is stocked with a variety of game fish, including bass and catfish. Because this is a private enterprise, no fishing license is required if you pay the day-use fee. Currently the rate is $5.00 per person per day. The facility is open generally from sunrise to sunset, year-round. A couple of portable toilets along with two small changing rooms are provided, as are a few picnic tables under a ramada. It's a nice, low-key place to spend a lazy afternoon.

Franklin Lakes Hot Well

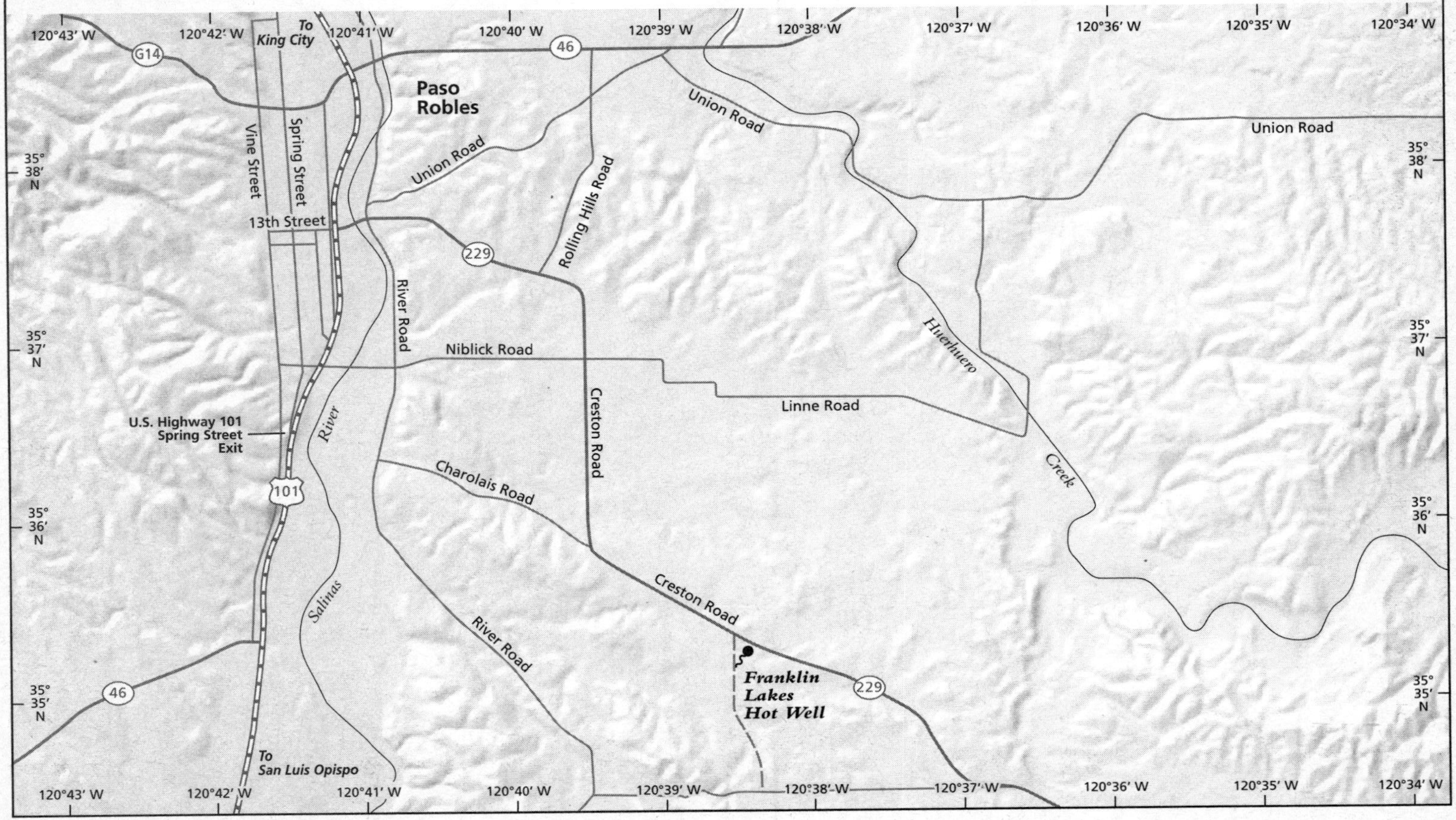

37 Paso Robles Hot Springs & Spa

General description: A new hot springs spa located immediately outside the town of Paso Robles.

Location: Coastal central California, a few miles from Paso Robles, at 3725 Buena Vista Drive.

Primitive/developed: Developed.

Best time of year: Year-round.

Restrictions: The hot springs spa is a private operation and charges various usage fees.

Access: Immediately outside the town of Paso Robles, on a paved road.

Water temperature: Varies at the source, though water in the tubs is generally maintained between 100 and 104 degrees F.

Nearby attractions: Franklin Lakes Hot Well, numerous wineries and golf courses.

Services: All services can be found in Paso Robles, 1.5 miles away.

Camping: Not permitted.

Map: San Luis Obispo County Highway Map.

Finding the springs: From the town of Paso Robles (or along U.S. Highway 101), travel east on California Highway 46. After crossing the Salinas River, make the first left turn on Buena Vista Drive. Travel 0.6 mile to a sign for Paso Robles Hot Springs & Spa on your left. Turn here, and drive for another 0.8 mile to the hot springs spa.

The Hot Springs

Paso Robles Hot Springs & Spa is one of the newer establishments in the area (opened in 2001) and provides several private hot mineral tubs as well as a variety of spa treatments. The private indoor and outdoor hot tubs can be rented by the

Paso Robles Hot Springs & Spa

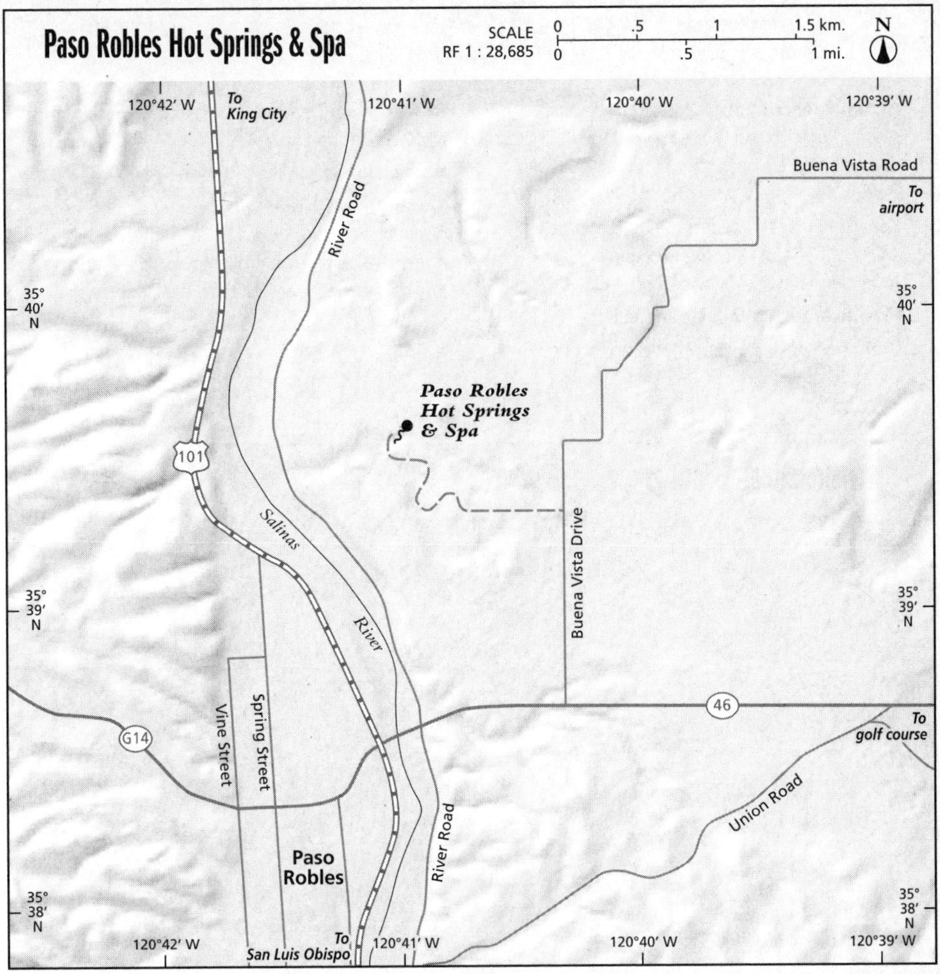

hour, currently for $10.00 per person per hour ($6.00 per half hour). Water in the tubs is generally kept between 100 and 104 degrees F, though hot or cold water can be let into the tubs to alter the temperature. All tubs are equipped with jets. The indoor tubs have half-walls that are open to the outdoors, ensuring plenty of air circulation. Various spa treatments, including massages, facials, waxing, and manicures, are also available. The Paso Robles Hot Springs & Spa is located in a beautiful parklike setting, adjacent to a small lake and extensive green grass. It is such a beautiful location that many weddings have been held here. The hot springs and spa are open every day, year-round. Call ahead for reservations, rates, hours, and additional information: (805) 238–4600.

38 Sycamore Mineral Springs

General description: A full-service hot springs spa and hotel based on a large natural mineral hot well, located near the community of Avila Beach.

Location: Coastal central California, 8 miles south of San Luis Obispo and a few miles from Avila Beach, at 1215 Avila Beach Drive.

Primitive/developed: Developed.

Best time of year: Year-round.

Restrictions: The spa is a private operation and charges various rates.

Access: Immediately off a paved road.

Water temperature: Water comes out of the ground at 110 degrees F. The water temperature varies in the hot tubs, though is generally maintained between 100 and 104 degrees F.

Nearby attractions: Avila Beach.

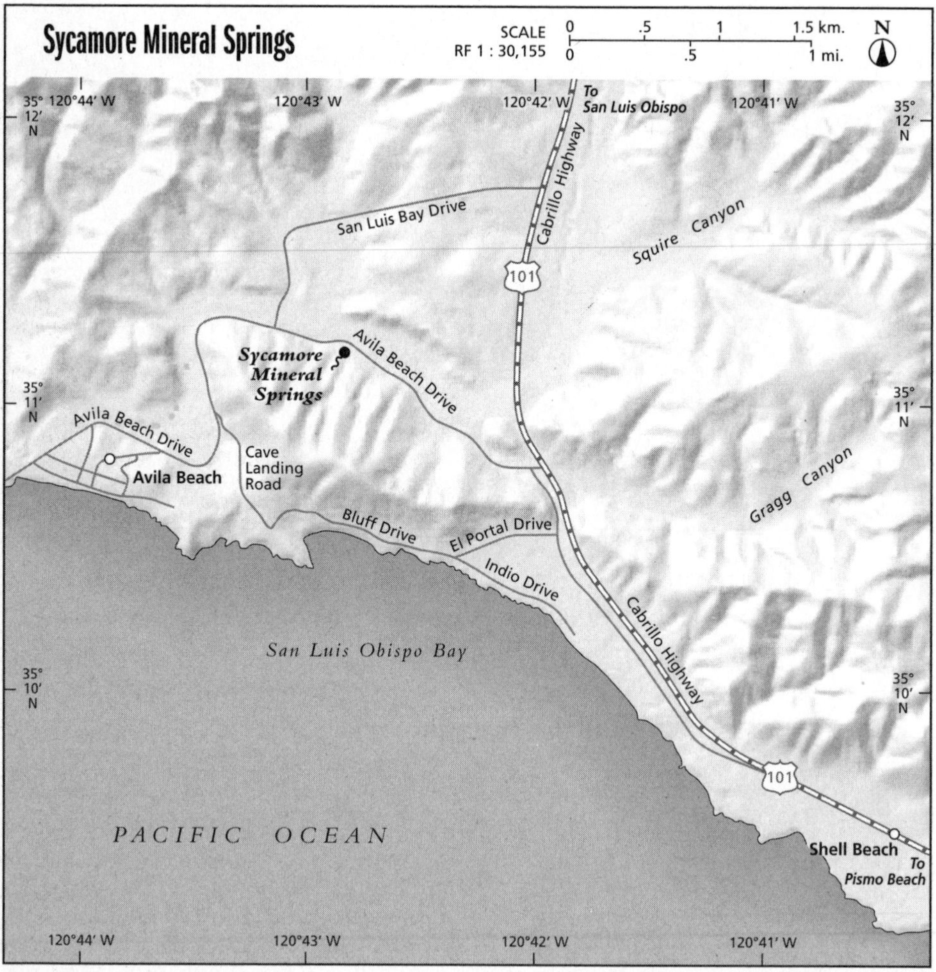

Services: The spa contains a full hotel with a variety of accommodations, as well as a restaurant. Other services are available in San Luis Obispo, approximately 8 miles away.

Camping: Not permitted.

Map: San Luis Obispo County Highway Map.

Finding the springs: From San Luis Obispo, travel south on U.S. Highway 101 to the San Luis Bay Drive exit (with signs for Avila Beach). Exit here and travel west to Avila Beach Drive, where you turn left. The resort will be a short distance on your right. Coming from the south, exit US 101 at Avila Beach Drive and travel west for approximately 1 mile to the resort on your left.

The Hot Springs

Sycamore Mineral Springs has been a resort for over a hundred years, and it shows no signs of slowing down today. It is very popular, and with good reason. The resort contains numerous private hillside wooden hot tubs available for hourly rental. Currently the rate is $12.50 per person per hour. They are open twenty-four hours a day. A large warm-water swimming pool and oversize hot tub are also available. In addition, full spa services can be obtained. A luxurious hotel on the premises provides each room with a private hot tub. The grounds are beautiful, as are many of the buildings. This is a great escape when in this part of the state. Call (805) 595–7320 for reservations and for further information, or visit www.sycamoresprings.com.

POINT SUR AND LOS PADRES NATIONAL FOREST

Big Sur is a small community located in the lushly vegetated Pacific coastal strip, immediately below a range of mountains. The mountains themselves are largely managed by the Los Padres National Forest. Although portions of the mountains are also well watered and lush in vegetation, a large percentage of the country is dry scrub vegetation with few trees. The mountains are rugged, with steep sides and canyons, cut by several year-round creeks. In addition to the three hot springs described in this section, others in the region include those at the Esalen Institute, near the town of Big Sur, which can be utilized by guests of the institute by calling (408) 667–3047. Another set of hot springs lies to the north, in the rugged mountains near the small community of Carmel Valley. Tassajara Springs is primarily a Buddhist meditation center, but the public may use it by calling ahead at (415) 431–3771.

39 Sykes Hot Spring

General description: A cluster of natural hot spring pools at a popular backpacking campground in the forested coast range of California. Only accessible by foot on a 10-mile trail, this spring is popular nonetheless and frequently visited.

Location: Western California, 10 miles east of the small town of Big Sur and 36 miles southeast of Monterey.

Primitive/developed: Primitive.

Best time of year: Year-round.

Restrictions: The spring is in the Los Padres National Forest, and you must obtain a wilderness permit ahead of time.

Access: Only by foot, and because of the distance, you will need to backpack to get to it.

Water temperature: Approximately 100 degrees F in the largest pond, slightly cooler in the smaller.

Nearby attractions: Pacific coast, Monterey.

Services: There are no services at this location, but all can be found 36 miles away in Monterey. There are some services in the small town of Big Sur, near the trailhead.

Camping: Backpack camping is permitted, but you must obtain a wilderness permit prior to your trip.

Maps: Los Padres National Forest Map; USGS topographic, Point Sur, CA, quadrangle, 1:100,000 scale.

Finding the spring: From Carmel (at the intersection with Rio Road), travel south on California Highway 1 for 26 miles. Continue past Pfeiffer Big Sur State Park for approximately 0.25 mile to a parking area and visitor center operated jointly by Caltrans, the Forest Service, and California State Parks. Pull in here, check in at the visitor center, pay a $4.00 registration, and get information on the trail you will be taking, the Pine Ridge Trail. The trailhead is located a short distance down the parking lot. The 10-mile hike is difficult for the first few miles as you climb in elevation through scrub vegetation with no shade. The trail eventually becomes more flat in the forest and is quite nice. You will eventually reach a substantial creek, which you will follow to the left for the last mile to the springs, on the banks.

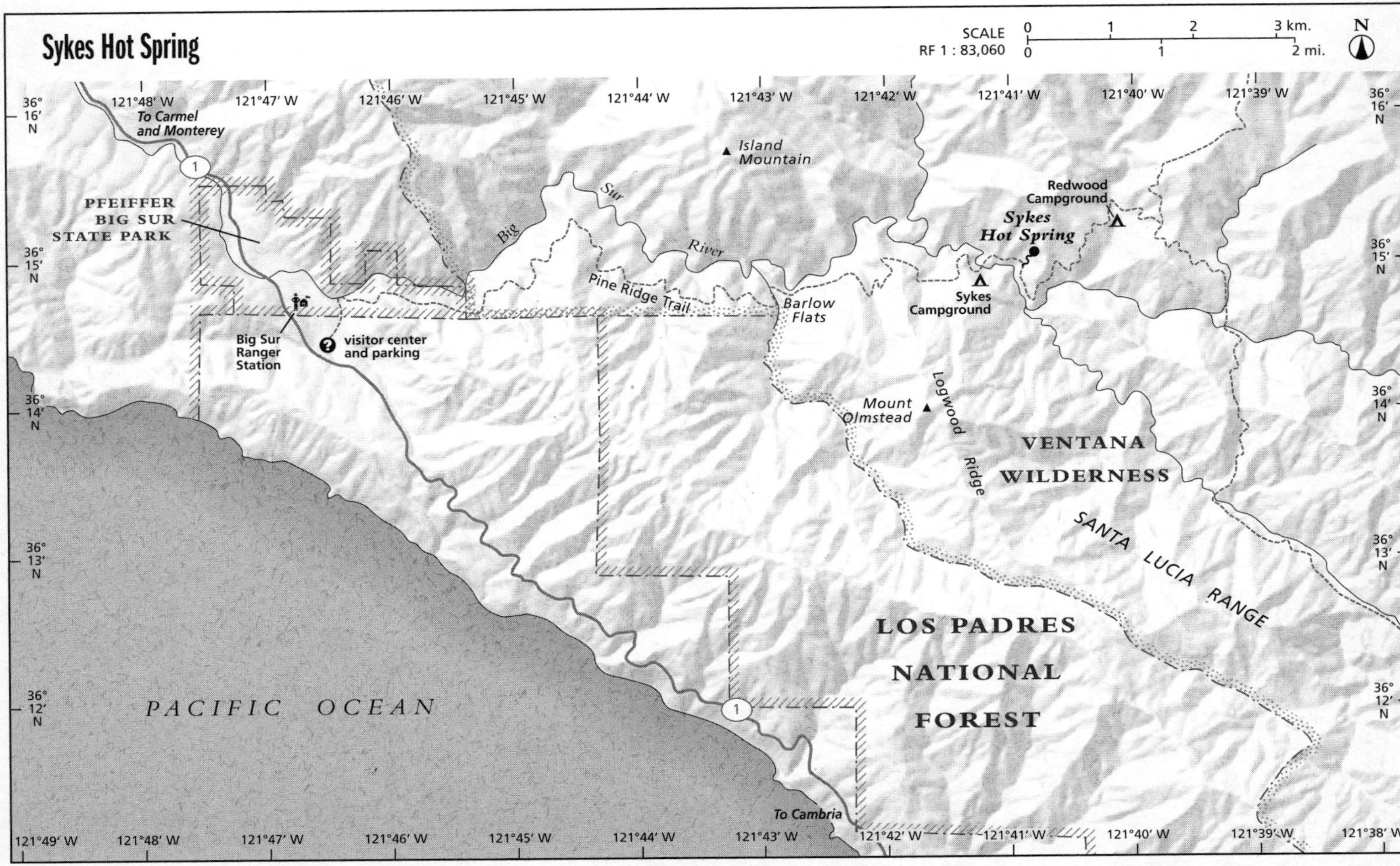
Sykes Hot Spring
SCALE
RF 1 : 83,060
0 1 2 3 km.
0 1 2 mi.
N
To Carmel and Monterey
1
PFEIFFER BIG SUR STATE PARK
Big Sur Ranger Station
visitor center and parking
Big
Sur
River
Island Mountain
Pine Ridge Trail
Barlow Flats
Sykes Campground
Sykes Hot Spring
Redwood Campground
Mount Olmstead
Logwood Ridge
VENTANA WILDERNESS
SANTA LUCIA RANGE
LOS PADRES NATIONAL FOREST
PACIFIC OCEAN
To Cambria
36° 16′ N
36° 15′ N
36° 14′ N
36° 13′ N
36° 12′ N
121°49′ W
121°48′ W
121°47′ W
121°46′ W
121°45′ W
121°44′ W
121°43′ W
121°42′ W
121°41′ W
121°40′ W
121°39′ W
121°38′ W

The Hot Spring

Sykes is a delightful natural hot spring adjacent to a rushing creek. The largest pool is sheltered on one side by a big boulder and by deadfall on the other. The water maintains a temperature of 100 degrees F, just the thing after a 10-mile hike. The long hike does not guarantee you of seclusion or of having the spring to yourself, as locals refer to Sykes as "Big Sur's worst-kept secret." There will generally be other people camping at the spring, particularly on weekends during the summer. If you prefer seclusion, try going midweek, and if people are there, wait till they vacate the spring to enjoy it. You will need to pack all your overnight necessities to this location, as it is much too far to do the round-trip in a day. Be sure to obey all backcountry rules and etiquette by packing out all your trash, not dumping waste of any kind in the creek, and generally making zero impact.

40 Mono Hot Springs

General description: A collection of hot springs in the high Sierra that previously served a thriving hot spring resort, but now remains only partially developed. Hot spring water is piped to a small bathhouse, while on the other side of the river there are several hot springs in a more natural state.

Location: Central California, in the high Sierra Nevada, approximately 17 miles from the small town of Lakeshore at Huntington Lake and about 95 miles from Fresno.

Primitive/developed: Primitive, except for the small bathhouse and outdoor pool.

Best time of year: Late spring, summer, and early fall. Roads will be closed during winter and much of spring and fall. The small resort is open from May 15 to November 1.

Restrictions: Some of the hot springs are located on national forest land, and the bathhouse is privately owned and operated.

Access: Located a long way from the nearest town on a very narrow and winding paved road. Any vehicle can make the trip (except in snow), though larger vehicles (RVs) are not recommended.

Water temperature: The sources vary, but most are 109 degrees F. The pool temperatures also vary, though most are between 100 and 104 degrees F. Water temperatures in the bathhouse vary between 100 and 105 degrees F.

Nearby attractions: Huntington Lake, Lake Thomas Edison, Florence Lake.

Services: All services can be found in the town of Shaver Lake, approximately 32 miles away. Lakeshore (at Huntington Lake) has food, camping, and lodging.

Camping: A Forest Service campground is located immediately adjacent to the hot springs.

Maps: USGS topographic, Mount Givens, CA, quadrangle, 1: 24,000 scale; Sierra National Forest Map.

Finding the springs: From Fresno, travel east on California Highway 168 for 60 miles to the town of Shaver Lake. Continue on CA 168 for 16 miles to Huntington Lake. Just before reaching the town of Lakeshore, look for signs for Mono Hot Springs and Lake Thomas Edison to the right. Turn right here (Forest Service Road 80, or Kaiser Pass Road) and travel 15 miles to the High Sierra Ranger Station. Continue 1 mile, and bear left to Mono Hot Springs. Travel another mile on this road, crossing a wooden bridge. Continue to a steel bridge (over the San Joaquin River), and turn left immediately after crossing the bridge, following the signs to Mono Hot Springs.

Mono Hot Springs

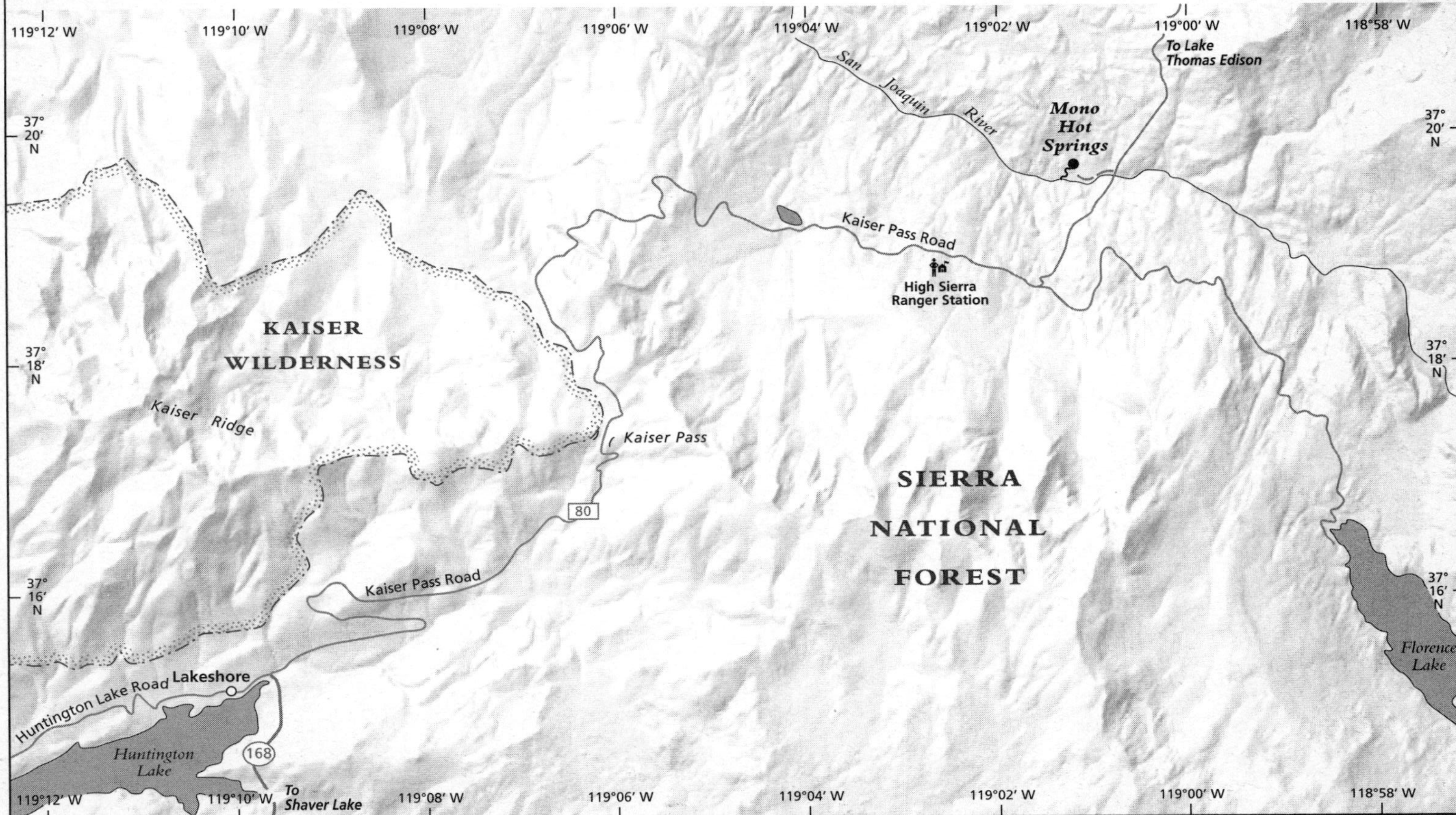

Mono Hot Springs

The Hot Springs

Mono consists of a collection of hot springs emanating from the side of a hill in the high Sierra Nevada. Some of the hot spring water is piped across a creek (the south fork of the San Joaquin River) to serve a small bathhouse and outdoor hot tub. Several private tubs are available in the bathhouse, and they range in temperature from 100 to 105 degrees F. An outdoor Jacuzzi tub is also available. Other facilities next to the bathhouse include a small store, cabins, and a restaurant. A Forest Service campground is located adjacent to the creek. From the bathhouse a small trail leads you across the creek to the hot springs themselves. Take care when crossing the creek! At the hot springs the remains of a large resort can be seen in a few places. Several concrete tubs still exist, along with natural pools, making for some great bathing opportunities. The various tubs and pools across the creek also vary in temperature, so you will have to do some experimenting and exploring to find one that suits your taste. Be careful, as the hillside can be quite slick and slippery due to the water flowing from the hot springs. The resort is open from May 15 to November 1. Call ahead for more information or reservations: (559) 325–1710.

SOUTHERN CALIFORNIA

Boasting California's largest concentration of people, southern California still offers the traveler many opportunities for seclusion. The majority of land encompassing southern California consists of the Mojave Desert, in the eastern portion of the region. The largest concentration of people lies to the west, along the coast from the Transverse Ranges in Santa Barbara in the north to San Diego and the international border with Mexico in the south. Although not a geothermally active region, there are a few hot springs to be enjoyed in this area, located in a variety of settings. In the desert region remote hot springs in the mountains and a funky hot spring resort near Death Valley await your visit. Closer to the city, there are hot springs immediately off major highways, as well as those requiring a few hours' drive off the main roads to reach. Most visits to the springs listed in this region can be combined with trips to other points of interest quite easily. Hot springs in other regions described in this book are also easily accessible to places described here.

Cahuilla Warm Springs

LAKE ISABELLA AND THE KERN RIVER

Located in the southern Sierra Nevada, a few hours from the farming community of Bakersfield, Lake Isabella lies in a geothermally active region. Lake Isabella was created from the damming up of the Kern River in the 1950s to provide flood control, irrigation, and recreational opportunities. The lake has allowed the San Joaquin Valley to develop as one of the most agriculturally productive regions in the country. Lake Isabella lies in a small valley bordered on all sides by high mountains, with ample outdoor recreation activities available. The lake is lined with countless boat ramps, picnic spots, campgrounds, and marinas, and it is a popular place for fishing, boating, and waterskiing during the summer.

The main thoroughfare through the area is California Highway 178, running from Bakersfield in the west to California Highway 14 and U.S. Highway 395 in the east. CA 178 east of Lake Isabella crosses the Sierra Nevada at Walker Pass, discovered by and named after mountain man Joseph Reddeford Walker in 1834. Other paved roads lead the traveler from the lake to high country in the Sequoia National Forest to the north. The community of Lake Isabella is the largest in the area, offering all services. Kernville, at the north end of the lake, and Weldon, on the east, also provide traveler services, including gas, food, and lodging. The hot springs described for this region are relatively easy to reach, with all three lying immediately off paved roads. Seclusion should not be expected but may be encountered at all of the springs. As with so many other hot springs described in this book, several in this region were at one time resorts. All that remains today are concrete tubs and traces of the old buildings.

While only three hot springs are profiled here, there are several other natural hot springs in the region, most of which are privately owned and inaccessible to the public. But two that are worth visiting can be accessed by raft or kayak. Despite numerous attempts, Delonegha Hot Springs has not been successfully developed as a resort. Several hot springs are on private property and closed to public use, but one set is located on public land and is accessible via the Kern River. Do not try to reach them on foot: No parking is available and walking along the highway is dangerous. The best way to visit these hot springs is from the river. Contact the Forest Service or one of the many raft guide companies in the area for further information.

China Gardens is a small collection of hot springs emerging from the side of a hill immediately adjacent to the north bank of the Kern River. Several foundations of large buildings are in place adjacent to the springs. Visit these hot springs by raft or kayak; they're located immediately downstream of the China Gardens Day Use Area.

41 Miracle Hot Spring

General description: Several cement soaking pools fed by natural hot spring water along the Kern River. At the location of an old resort, Miracle Hot Spring is now operated by a nonprofit group, which has designated it clothing-optional. There are several different hand-built pools. Immediately adjacent to a Forest Service campground, the spring is rather popular and heavily visited.

Location: Central California, 6 miles west of the town of Lake Isabella.

Primitive/developed: Primitive, except for the cement tubs.

Best time of year: Year-round. Summer can be a little hot.

Restrictions: None.

Access: Any vehicle can make the trip, as the hot springs are located close to a paved road.

Water temperature: Approximately 120 degrees F at the hottest pool, varying depending upon the spring chosen. Most average about 100 degrees F.

Nearby attractions: Lake Isabella, Kern River Canyon.

Services: There are no services at this location, but some can be found 6 miles away in Lake Isabella.

Camping: Camping is available at Hobo Campground (Forest Service).

Map: USGS topographic, Lake Isabella, CA, quadrangle, 1:100,000 scale.

Finding the spring: From Bakersfield, travel east on California Highway 178 toward Lake Isabella. The highway will enter the Kern River Canyon as it leaves the valley. Exit CA 178 at Borel Road, 4 miles west of Lake Isabella, then turn right on Kern River Canyon Road (Old Canyon Road). Travel west for approximately 1.5 miles to the Hobo Campground. Turn right into the campground, then bear right to the small trailer. There is a small parking area here. From the parking area, follow a short trail for approximately 100 yards to several hot spring pools at the river's edge. From Lake Isabella, travel west on CA 178 for 4 miles to the Borel Road exit, and follow the directions above.

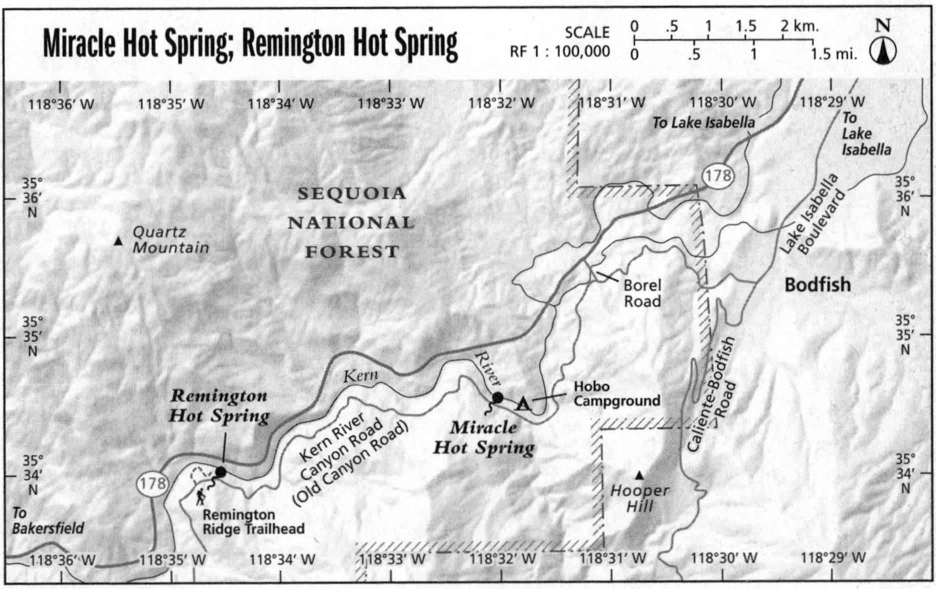

The Hot Spring

Once a hot spring resort, Miracle is another abandoned location, still offering a great soak. Today it is operated by a nonprofit group called the Friends of the Hot Springs. The group operates a trailer at the parking lot, where you pay a $5.00-per-person entrance fee, and has established the hot springs as clothing-optional. Hot spring water emerges from the side of the hill and is trapped in several pools of varying size and temperature. The hottest pool is too small to bathe in and is approximately 120 degrees F. The largest of the pools, constructed with concrete and rock, is approximately 105 degrees F. Located immediately adjacent to the Kern River, the pools do not generally get inundated by the river. This is a beautiful setting and a great place for a bath. Because it is so close to a campground, however, the springs are well-known, and your chances for privacy here are virtually nil. The Friends of the Hot Springs can be reached at (760) 379–4407.

Miracle Hot Spring has a fascinating history, having originally been known as Compressor Hot Springs or Clear Creek Hot Springs. Apparently, a miner built a turbine that ran a compressor used by workers in the nearby mining district of

Bathers at Miracle Hot Spring

Havilah. Later, during the construction of the Borel Power Plant, a makeshift camp was established near the hot springs, and so its name was changed to Hobo Hot Springs. In 1927 a hotel was built to take advantage of the hot springs. This hotel was successful for the next several decades, enough so that a post office was established at the site. By 1947 the hot springs became known as Miracle, for their miraculous healing powers. In 1975 the hotel burned, and public services were discontinued. Only traces of the foundation of the hotel can be seen today. The Forest Service took control of the property for the next few decades, until recently when the Friends of the Hot Springs began operating it. It is located on Forest Service property, however.

42 Remington Hot Spring

See map on page 101.

General description: Two cement soaking pools fed by natural hot spring water along the Kern River. Near Lake Isabella and a few miles from a campground, this hot spring has many visitors but is worth a stop for a soak.

Location: Central California, 6 miles west of the town of Lake Isabella.

Primitive/developed: Primitive, except for the cement tubs.

Best time of year: Year-round. Summer can be a little hot.

Restrictions: None.

Access: Any vehicle can make the trip, as the hot springs are located close to a paved road. A steep 300-yard hike is required to get to the tubs.

Water temperature: Approximately 113 degrees F at the source, 102 degrees F in the tub. The water can be drained relatively easily, thus allowing for control of the temperature.

Nearby attractions: Lake Isabella, Kern River Canyon.

Services: There are no services at this location, but some can be found 6 miles away in Lake Isabella.

Camping: Camping is not permitted at the parking area above the spring, and there is no room to camp at the spring itself. There is a Forest Service campground (Hobo) 1.5 miles to the east, however.

Map: USGS topographic, Miracle Hot Springs, CA, quadrangle, 1: 24,000 scale.

Finding the spring: From Bakersfield, travel east on California Highway 178 toward Lake Isabella. The highway will enter the Kern River Canyon as it leaves the valley. Exit CA 178 at Borel Road, 4 miles west of Lake Isabella, then turn right on Kern River Canyon Road (Old Canyon Road). Travel west for approximately 1.5 miles to Hobo Campground and Miracle Hot Springs. Continue east on Kern River Canyon Road. At 1.5 miles past the campground, pull off the road into a broad parking area at the edge of the canyon. This pullout is the second one you will pass, both with telephone poles in the middle of them. The parking area is also directly across the road from a trailhead for the Remington Ridge Trail. Park here and find a well-defined trail at the east side of the parking area down the steep hillside. Walk for approximately 0.25 mile to the river's edge, where there are two adjacent concrete and rock pools. From the riverside pools, there is another smaller pool uphill less than 50 yards.

A raft passes bathers at Remington Hot Spring

The Hot Spring

Remington Hot Spring is yet again another abandoned resort. Remains of the resort can be seen in several places, and the hot springs themselves have since been diverted into pools. Remington, like the other hot springs in the area, is in a beautiful setting, on the banks of the rushing Kern River. There are several pools along the river's edge, beautifully made of concrete with mosaic inlays. The larger pools are approximately 6 by 2 feet and 2 to 3 feet deep. The temperatures in the pools range on average from 95 to 105 degrees F. The pools are high enough above the river to prevent their inundation, though in rare floods this may not be the case. The higher pool is smaller and well enough away from the river to prevent its flooding. Remington is another well-known hot spring, and privacy is rare. Occasionally you may be the only one there, mainly on weekdays in the off-season (winter). Because the hot spring is off the beaten track, many people choose to bathe in the nude. While this is not how every visitor chooses to bathe, it is rather common. Be sure to pack out all trash when visiting Remington, and be careful when climbing down the steep trail to the spring. There is also an abundance of poison oak in the area, so don't venture off into the bushes, and take care not to come into contact with any plants you suspect might be poison oak. For information on the area, contact Sequoia National Forest at (760) 379–5646.

43 Pyramid Hot Spring

General description: A small, obscure hot spring in the Kern River Canyon, near Lake Isabella, and only accessible for the driest two months of the year.

Location: Central California, approximately 20 miles east of the town of Lake Isabella.

Primitive/developed: Primitive.

Best time of year: Late summer and early fall. Summer can be a little hot, and the pool may be submerged during extraordinarily high spring runoff.

Restrictions: None.

Access: Any vehicle can make the trip, as the hot spring is located close to a paved road. A short walk is required, along with crossing the creek to access the spring from where you park your car.

Water temperature: Approximately 105 degrees F throughout the natural pool.

Nearby attractions: Lake Isabella, Kern River Canyon.

Services: There are no services at this location but approximately 20 miles to the east in the town of Lake Isabella or in Bakersfield, about 15 miles to the west.

Camping: Camping is not permitted at the turnout in the road, nor would you want to camp here. There is a Forest Service campground (Live Oak) 1 mile to the east, however.

Map: Sequoia National Forest Map.

Finding the spring: Travel east on California Highway 178 from Bakersfield toward Lake Isabella. The road will eventually reach the Kern River Canyon as it rises out of the valley. From the beginning of the canyon, travel 4.2 miles to an unmarked turnout on your left (north). The turnout has an iron pole in the middle of it, approximately 5 feet tall, and a pyramid-shaped rock on the east end. Park here. Look across the Kern River from the turnout, slightly downstream. There will be a large cube-shaped rock, under which the hot spring is located. To reach the spring, follow a faint trail upstream from the turnout. The trail leads to the river, where there are several large boulders on which you can cross the water. From the other side, travel downstream approximately 100 yards to the cube-shaped rock.

The Hot Spring

The hot spring emerges from the ground immediately under the cube-shaped rock. Depending upon the level of the river, the spring may not be discernible. The best time to visit Pyramid Hot Spring is in the late summer and early fall, when river levels are lower. During spring runoff the hot spring will be completely submerged, and the river may be impossible to cross. If water levels are just right, however, this spring is a welcome surprise along the Kern River. Temperatures average approximately 100 degrees F, depending upon how much river water is mixed with the spring water. Although the spring is difficult to find, it is within view of the highway and therefore does not offer the highest degree of privacy. Because it is so close to the highway, however, the spring can be reached rather quickly, and so makes an enjoyable diversion when passing through or when visiting other springs in the region (including Remington and Miracle). Keep in mind, however, that you can only access the spring during the driest months of the year, when river levels are safe enough to cross.

Be careful when crossing the river, and do not attempt a crossing when water levels are high. Hundreds of people have lost their lives in the fast current of the Kern River in the past decades. Do not try to swim across, but instead stick to the boulders upstream, using care when stepping across. Contact Sequoia National Forest, Greenhorn Ranger District, at (760) 379–5646 for more information.

44 California Hot Springs

General description: A historic resort, reopened in 1985, providing a large outdoor swimming pool and two hot tubs.

Location: Central California, at the edge of Sequoia National Forest, near Sequoia National Monument. Approximately 75 miles northeast of Bakersfield, and 70 miles east of Visalia.

Primitive/developed: Developed.

Best time of year: Open year-round. Roads are generally kept open during the winter, as the resort is located at 3,100 feet.

Restrictions: Private resort with usage fees.

Access: Any vehicle can make the trip, as the hot springs are located on a paved road.

Water temperature: 122 degrees F at the source. The swimming pool is maintained around 85 degrees F in the summer, and 94 degrees F during the winter. The two hot tubs are maintained between 102 and 104 degrees F.

Nearby attractions: Sequoia National Forest, Sequoia National Monument.

Services: A small store and lunch counter are at the hot springs. Buffet breakfasts, lunches, and dinners can also be arranged for groups. Other services are available in the adjacent town of California Hot Springs.

Camping: An RV park is located across the road, complete with forty-four hookups, showers, and flush toilets.

Map: California Highway Map.

Finding the springs: From California Highway 99, travel east on County Road J22/Hot Springs Road (at Earlimart, between Bakersfield and Visalia) for 19 miles through the small town of Ducor to Fountain Springs. Bear right here onto Hot Springs Road, following the signs for California Hot Springs. Continue another 18 miles to the resort.

The Hot Springs

California Hot Springs consists of a large reconstructed lodge overlooking a big swimming pool and two hot tubs, in the foothills of the Sierra Nevada, adjacent to Sequoia National Monument. The swimming pool and tubs are available for day use for $9.00 per adult, $4.00 per child. Tent camping and an RV park are located across the road. Discounted pool and tub use is available for those staying in the RV park and campground. A small store and lunch counter are located in the lodge. Open 9:00 A.M. to 5:00 P.M. Monday through Friday, 9:00 A.M. to 8:00 P.M. Saturday, and 9:00 A.M. to 6:00 P.M. Sunday. Closed Thanksgiving, December 16–26, and New Year's Day. Contact California Hot Springs at (661) 548–6582, or visit them on the Web at www.CAHotSprings.com.

The natural hot springs at this location were long known and enjoyed by the Native American tribes living in the area (Yokuts). Subsequent miners, ranchers,

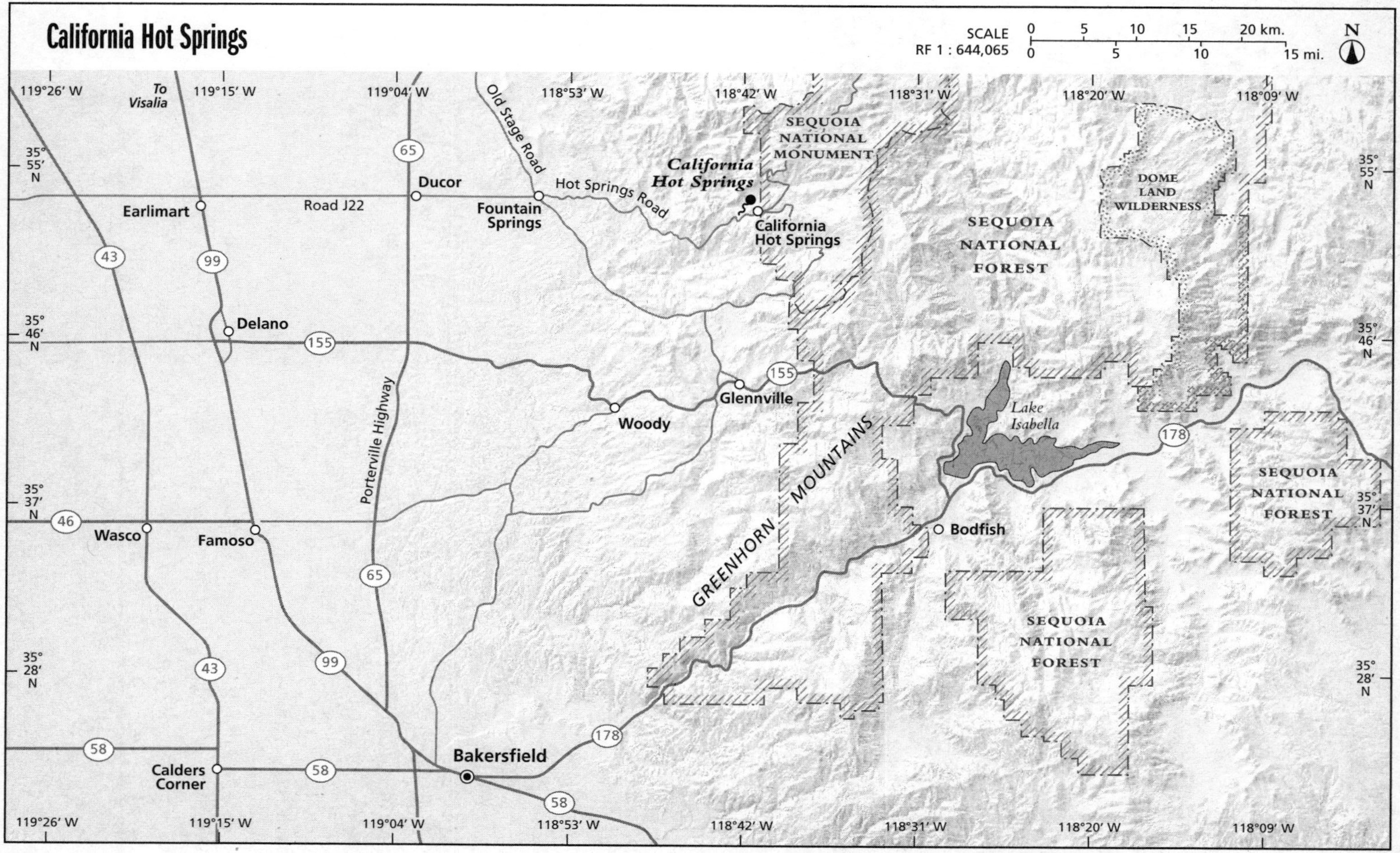
California Hot Springs
SCALE
RF 1 : 644,065
0 5 10 15 20 km.
0 5 10 15 mi.
N
119°26′ W
119°15′ W
119°04′ W
118°53′ W
118°42′ W
118°31′ W
118°20′ W
118°09′ W
35° 55′ N
35° 46′ N
35° 37′ N
35° 28′ N
To Visalia
Old Stage Road
Hot Springs Road
Road J22
Porterville Highway
SEQUOIA NATIONAL MONUMENT
California Hot Springs
SEQUOIA NATIONAL FOREST
DOME LAND WILDERNESS
Earlimart
Ducor
Fountain Springs
Delano
Glennville
Woody
Lake Isabella
GREENHORN MOUNTAINS
Wasco
Famoso
Bodfish
Bakersfield
Calders Corner
43
99
65
155
46
178
58

California Hot Springs

and homesteaders also used the hot springs for bathing. The California Hot Springs resort was founded in 1882 by Henry Witt. By 1902 he completed a large hotel immediately adjacent to the hot springs. Soon thereafter, guests came from all over California, riding the train to Bakersfield and Visalia and taking stage-coaches up to the resort. Because of its popularity, the resort was expanded and reached its zenith during the 1920s, when a commercial center, swimming pool, and therapeutic center were completed. Unfortunately, fire struck the hotel in 1932, followed by several more fires over the ensuing years. By 1968 the old resort was virtually abandoned following several attempts to resurrect it. Finally, in 1983 restoration on the resort began, which was completed in 1985.

MOJAVE DESERT REGION

One of the largest deserts in the country, the Mojave offers the traveler much. To the common traveler, who only sees it from Interstate 15 between Los Angeles and Las Vegas, the desert may seem empty and featureless. But to those who take the time to get off the main road and explore the region, it means much more. A wide variety of plant and animal life lives in the harsh climate of the Mojave, with its very hot summers and bitterly cold winters, often with exceedingly high winds. For years the Mojave Desert region was an area that travelers simply wanted to get through on their way to settlements on the coast or to points east. Later, however, the region's mineral wealth was discovered, and miners streamed in from all directions.

More recently the U.S. military has recognized the usefulness of the desert for its various training missions. Today huge tracts of the desert are owned and operated by the military, in the form of bases such as China Lake Naval Weapons Center, Fort Irwin Military Reservation (Army), and Edwards Air Force Base and Flight Test Center, among others. Outdoor enthusiasts recognize the recreational opportunities provided by the largely unpopulated and undeveloped desert. In 1994 over 1.4 million acres of the desert were set aside by the U.S. government as the Mojave National Preserve to protect the archaeological, historical, and natural resources in the area. The new preserve is roughly that land lying between Interstates 40 and 15.

45 Deep Creek

General description: A cluster of natural hot springs in an isolated canyon in the high desert of southern California. Recently discovered by many people, Deep Creek has become a favorite spot for those who like to go without clothing.

Location: Southern California, approximately 16 miles east of the town of Hesperia.

Primitive/developed: Primitive.

Best time of year: Fall, winter, and spring. Summer can be too hot. Avoid the shorter trail during high water levels (in early spring mostly), as the trail requires you to ford the river, which could be dangerous in high water.

Restrictions: None at the spring itself. To take the shorter trail you must park at a private ranch, which so far has permitted parking for a fee.

Access: Most vehicles will have no problem with the graded dirt roads to either trailhead. A hike of 6 miles one way is required along a gentle trail or 2 miles one way along an extremely steep trail.

Water temperature: Approximately 110 degrees F at the various sources, and varying in the pools depending upon the amount of creek water admitted.

Nearby attractions: Lake Arrowhead, Big Bear City and Lake.

Services: There are no services at this location but approximately 16 miles away in the town of Hesperia.

Camping: Camping is not permitted in the canyon, at the springs, or at the parking area for the longer trail. You can pay a fee at the Bowen Ranch to camp at the parking area there, however. There are campgrounds in the nearby San Bernadino Mountains at Silverwood Lake and Lake Arrowhead. Take Interstate 15 west to California Highway 138 east into the San Bernadino National Forest.

Map: USGS topographic, Lake Arrowhead, CA, quadrangle, 7.5-minute scale.

Finding the springs: Gentle 6-mile trail: From I–15, take the Bear Valley Road exit and turn right if traveling from the south; left if traveling from the north. Follow Bear Valley Road east for approximately 10 miles. Turn right on Central and drive 3 miles to Ocotillo Way. Turn left onto Ocotillo Way and continue for 2.2 miles. Turn right onto Bowen Ranch Road and follow 6 miles to Bowen Ranch. Park where you can, and walk to the top of the dam along a paved road that services it. The trailhead is to the left when facing the inside portion of the dam. A small metal sign is on the side of the hill where the trailhead begins. The trail goes steeply up the hill for the first few hundred yards, then levels out. Follow the trail for 6 miles, crossing the creek on a bridge after approximately 2 miles. The trail will lead right to the spring. Another way to reach the spring is from the Bradford Ridge Path, which begins where California Highway 173 crosses Kinley Creek.

Steep 2-mile trail: From I–15, take the Hesperia exit east onto Main Street. Follow Main Street for approximately 8 miles to Rock Springs Road (at the Y in the road) and go left. Follow Rock Springs Road for approximately 2.8 miles to Round-up Road; turn right. Follow Round-up Road for approximately 4.2 miles to Bowen Ranch Road; turn right. Follow this graded dirt road for 5.5 miles to the ranch itself and the parking area. Someone will generally be there to collect a parking fee and direct you to the trailhead. This trail is quite steep and slippery, and it's not recommended if you are not in good shape or don't have good balance.

The Hot Springs

The Deep Creek Hot Springs are quite a find, and will amaze you once you get there. Completely natural and undeveloped the springs have become rather popular for obvious reasons. The water is generally clear and an almost perfect temperature (averaging 105 degrees F), and there are several pools from which to choose. As with so many hot springs in this book, Deep Creek used to be relatively unknown but has become heavily visited. The visitors have done a good job of keeping this area pristine, free from trash and vandalism. As noted, many of the more recent (and more numerous) visitors to the springs prefer to go without clothing. This goes not only for in the pools, but outside them also. Be prepared when you set out to visit the springs, and remember that the mileages to the springs are one-way only. Do not attempt to visit these springs if you don't think you can walk the round-trip mileages. Also, bring plenty of water and food, and let someone know where you are going and when you expect to be back.

The San Bernadino Mountains offer high-elevation relief to high desert temperatures in the summer. Several lakes abound in the mountains. The region is largely controlled by the San Bernadino National Forest, but there are several small towns in the area, along with an abundance of year-round activities. To reach Lake Arrowhead, travel east on California Highway 18 off I–15 up into the mountains for approximately 10 miles. To reach ski and resort areas at Big Bear City and Lake, continue on CA 18 to Running Springs, and travel east for approximately 20 miles.

DEATH VALLEY REGION

46 Tecopa Hot Springs

General description: A group of rustic hot spring resorts in the low desert of eastern California near Death Valley.

Location: Southeastern California, approximately 58 miles north of the town of Baker and about 8 miles from the town of Shoshone.

Primitive/developed: The resorts are all developed.

Best time of year: Fall, winter, and spring. Summer is too hot.

Restrictions: The resorts are private and require that you either be an overnight guest or pay a fee for day use. Nude bathing is required and separate facilities are provided for men and women.

Access: Any vehicle can access the resorts, as all are immediately off the paved highway.

Water temperature: Varies depending upon venue chosen. The resorts' temperatures range, but most are around 106 degrees F.

Nearby attractions: Death Valley, East Mojave Scenic Area.

Services: All services can be found in the small town of Shoshone, 8 miles away.

Camping: There is a public campground on the outskirts of Tecopa and an RV park in the town of Tecopa Hot Springs.

Map: California Highway Map.

Finding the springs: From the town of Baker on Interstate 15, travel north on California Highway 127 for approximately 52 miles to the turnoff for Tecopa. Turn right (east) to the small town of Tecopa, then left to the town of Tecopa Hot Springs. The first resort you will come to is the Tecopa Hot Springs Resort on your right. Tecopa Hot Springs Campground and Pool is farther up the road on your right. At the end of town, Delight's Hot Springs Resort will be on your right, and Petersen's Tecopa Palms RV Park on your left.

The facility at Tecopa Hot Springs

The Hot Springs

This interesting no-frills town is hot spring heaven if you aren't looking for fancy hot spring resorts. Most of the hotels are older and have seen better days, and many are now closed. The resorts all have hot pools for use of their guests and in some cases for day use. The baths range from common warm pools to individual Jacuzzi-size private tubs.

Some of the resorts that were still open at the time of publication are Delight's Hot Springs Resort (760–852–4343), Tecopa Hot Springs Campground and Pools (760–852–4481), and Tecopa Hot Springs Resort (760–852–4420). For current information on local hot springs, contact the Death Valley Chamber of Commerce in Shoshone, (760) 852–4524.

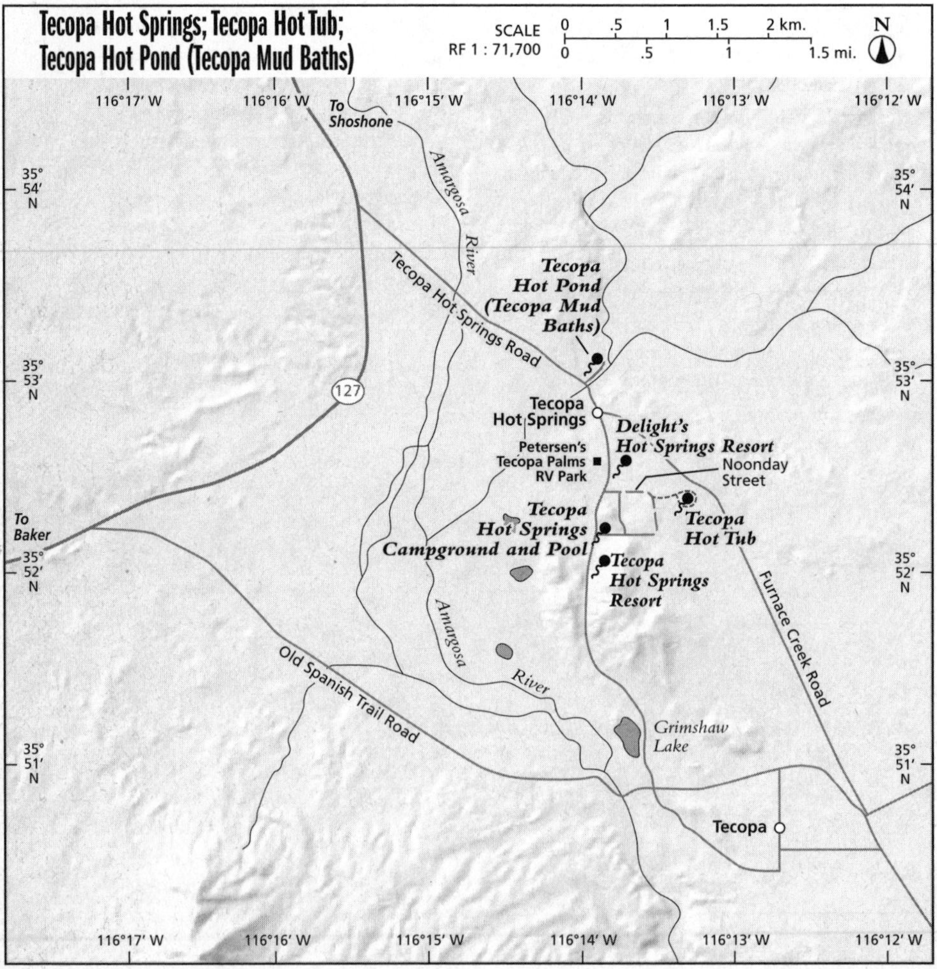

The county pool and bathhouse require nude bathing only and have separate facilities for men and women. There is no charge at this facility, and the pool is quite invigorating. The county also operates an RV park across the road from the springs.

47 Tecopa Hot Tub

See map on page 112.

General description: A small cement tub with hot water in the open desert immediately outside the town of Tecopa Hot Springs.

Location: Southeastern California, approximately 58 miles north of the town of Baker and about 8 miles from the town of Shoshone.

Primitive/developed: Primitive.

Best time of year: Fall, winter, and spring. Summer is too hot. Road may be impassable in wet weather.

Restrictions: The tub is located on Bureau of Land Management (BLM) land. There is no camping allowed immediately adjacent to the tub. Please respect the area by taking all trash with you.

Access: The tub is located approximately 1 mile from the town of Tecopa Hot Springs on a good dirt road, when conditions are dry. Most vehicles will have no trouble accessing the springs. Immediately after rains, however, the road can be impassable.

Water temperature: Water temperature in the tub is approximately 98 degrees F.

Nearby attractions: Death Valley, East Mojave Scenic Area, Tecopa Hot Springs.

Tecopa Hot Tub, outside the town of Tecopa Hot Springs

Services: All services can be found in the small town of Shoshone, 8 miles away.

Camping: Camping is not permitted immediately adjacent to the tub, but the surrounding BLM land is open for undeveloped camping. There is a public campground on the outskirts of Tecopa and an RV park at Tecopa Hot Springs.

Map: California Highway Map.

Finding the spring: From the town of Baker on Interstate 15, travel north on California Highway 127 for approximately 52 miles to the turnoff for Tecopa. Turn right (east) to the small town of Tecopa, then left to the town of Tecopa Hot Springs. In Tecopa Hot Springs, just north of the county hot springs, turn right onto Noonday Street, which is a dirt road. Follow this dirt road past a duck pond, and bear left as the main road curves to the right. Follow the road across a dry lake bed, and head toward a lone palm tree in the distance. The hot tub is beneath this tree.

The Hot Spring

The cement hot tub is at the end of a rather faint road east of town. The tub is fed by a pipe from an artesian hot well. The tub itself is approximately 6 by 6 feet and 3 feet deep, with a temperature of about 98 degrees F. The area around the pond is not altogether scenic, as many careless people have left trash and other debris. If you can block this junk out of your mind, the surrounding desert views are beautiful. The hot tub is fairly well known now, and getting it to yourself is not all that common during weekends. Other times, however, you may be able to find solitude here.

48 Tecopa Hot Pond (Tecopa Mud Baths)

See map on page 112.

General description: A collection of hot springs feeding a large pond in the open desert immediately outside the town of Tecopa Hot Springs, with several bathable spots.

Location: Southeastern California, approximately 58 miles north of the town of Baker and about 8 miles from the town of Shoshone.

Primitive/developed: Primitive. No improvement to the springs except a ladder into the hot water.

Best time of year: Fall, winter, and spring. Summer is too hot.

Restrictions: The pond is located on BLM land, and there is no camping allowed immediately adjacent.

Access: The warm pond is located approximately 1 mile from the town of Tecopa Hot Springs, a short distance off the paved highway. A short walk is required to reach the pond.

Water temperature: Water comes out of the ground at approximately 118 degrees F. The temperature in the pond itself varies depending upon where you are, but generally ranges between 104 and 108 degrees F.

Nearby attractions: Death Valley, East Mojave Scenic Area, Tecopa Hot Springs.

Services: All services can be found in the small town of Shoshone, 7 miles away.

Camping: Camping is not permitted immediately adjacent to the pond, but the surrounding BLM land is open for undeveloped camping. There is a public campground on the outskirts of Tecopa and an RV park at Tecopa Hot Springs.

Map: California Highway Map.

Finding the springs: From the town of Baker on Interstate 15, travel north on California Highway 127 for approximately 52 miles to the turnoff for Tecopa. Turn right (east) to the small town of Tecopa, then left to the town of Tecopa Hot Springs. Continue north out of town for approximately 1 mile, and keep an eye out for large ponds on both sides of the road. Park in a pullout at a BLM sign that restricts off-road driving on the mud hills, and walk the short distance (approximately 200 yards) to the hot pond. From Shoshone, travel south on CA 127 for approximately 7 miles and turn left at Tecopa Hot Springs Road. Continue on this road for approximately 1.7 miles to the pullout on the side of the road with the BLM sign (on your left).

The Hot Springs

Tecopa Hot Pond consists of a series of hot springs feeding a pond in the open desert adjacent to the small town of Tecopa Hot Springs. Several bathable pools are located at the edge of this pond, where the hot springs emerge from the ground. Volunteers have placed an aluminum ladder into one of these pools to provide easier access. The hot pond contains mud at the bottom and sides, which many users apply to their skin. The water is murky as a result of this mud.

Tecopa Hot Pond

49 Shoshone Hot Springs

General description: A swimming pool fed by a natural hot spring in the small town of Shoshone.

Location: Southeastern California, approximately 56 miles north of the town of Baker and at the east edge of Death Valley.

Primitive/developed: Developed, though rustic.

Best time of year: Fall, winter, and spring. Summer is too hot.

Restrictions: The pool is owned by the Shoshone Inn and RV Park for use by guests of either establishment or those paying a day-use fee.

Access: The pool is located in Shoshone on California Highway 127.

Water temperature: The spring's temperature is approximately 90 degrees F, and the swimming pool is slightly cooler.

Nearby attractions: Death Valley, East Mojave Scenic Area, Tecopa Hot Springs.

Services: All services can be found in the small town of Shoshone.

Camping: There is an RV park and campground immediately adjacent to the swimming pool.

Map: California Highway Map.

Finding the springs: From the town of Baker on Interstate 15, travel north on CA 127 for approximately 56 miles to the town of Shoshone. Keep an eye out for the Shoshone Inn on the left and the Shoshone RV Park farther up the road. The swimming pool is located behind the RV park on the old road through town.

The Hot Springs

A natural hot spring is harnessed to feed this large, warm swimming pool, for use by guests of the Shoshone Inn and RV Park. Day use is also available for a fee. Call the Shoshone Inn for further information at (760) 852–4335 or the RV park at (760) 852–4569.

Tecopa Consolidated Mining Company: Tecopa is one of many small desert communities owing their existence to mining. Silver-lead ores were discovered in the area in 1865 and mined until 1882. The mine apparently contained enough ore to warrant the construction of a ten-stamp mill and three furnaces, along with the digging of a tunnel over 1,000 feet into the mountain.

By the turn of the century, as copper became a more valued commodity, miners increasingly sought out the source of the metal. With the increased mining activity at Goldfield and Tonopah in the early 1900s, miners fanned out in the surrounding countryside in search of gold, silver, and copper deposits. In 1904 copper was discovered southwest of Death Valley Junction, and the town site established nearby was named Greenwater. By 1907 over 700 people lived in the town, and a telephone line was constructed, connecting it with the mining community of Rhyolite to the northwest. Rampant speculation followed the miners, with over thirty companies forming to take advantage of Greenwater's expected riches. By the summer of 1907, the town included a telephone, a telegraph, two newspapers, a bank, a boardinghouse, several stores, and many saloons. As the ore body quickly petered

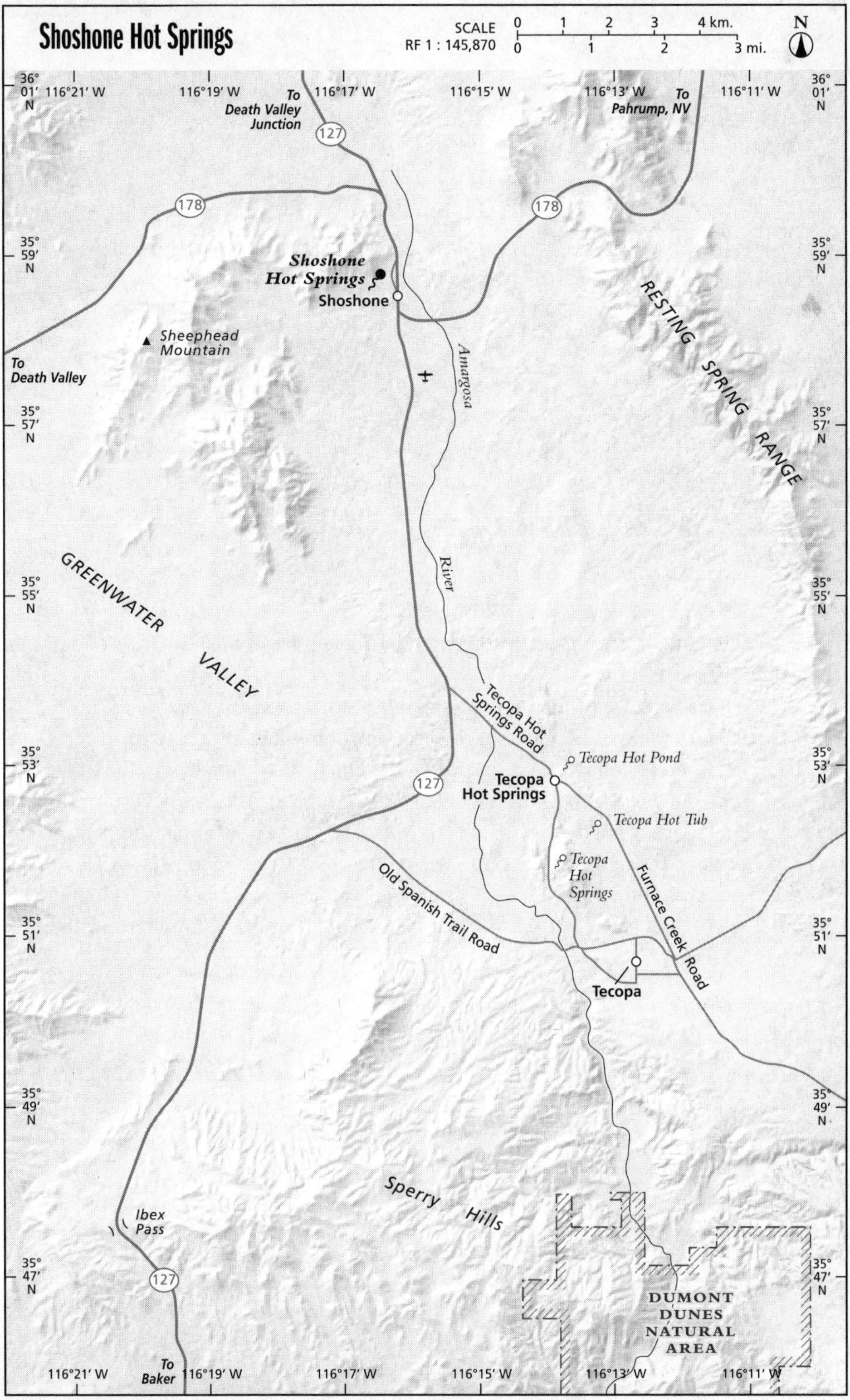
Shoshone Hot Springs
SCALE
RF 1 : 145,870
0 1 2 3 4 km.
0 1 2 3 mi.
N
To Death Valley Junction
To Pahrump, NV
127
178
178
Shoshone Hot Springs
Shoshone
Sheephead Mountain
To Death Valley
RESTING SPRING RANGE
Amargosa
River
GREENWATER VALLEY
Tecopa Hot Springs Road
Tecopa Hot Pond
Tecopa Hot Springs
127
Tecopa Hot Tub
Tecopa Hot Springs
Old Spanish Trail Road
Furnace Creek Road
Tecopa
Sperry Hills
Ibex Pass
127
DUMONT DUNES NATURAL AREA
To Baker
36° 01′ N
35° 59′ N
35° 57′ N
35° 55′ N
35° 53′ N
35° 51′ N
35° 49′ N
35° 47′ N
116°21′ W
116°19′ W
116°17′ W
116°15′ W
116°13′ W
116°11′ W

Shoshone Hot Springs

out, however, the town was all but deserted by September of the same year of its founding.

To take advantage of the supposed wealth of the Greenwater mines, the Tonopah and Tidewater Railroad began extending their line toward Greenwater. Once Greenwater's collapse came, however, the line had only made it to the Amargosa River. The line did reach the vicinity of Tecopa, giving the Noonday and Gunsite mines an outlet for their silver. The Tecopa Consolidated Mining Company built a railroad from the mines to the Tecopa station and the Tonopah and Tidewater Railroad, along which its ore was transported to smelters in Utah. The mines continued to operate from 1912 through 1928, producing over $3 million worth of silver and lead.

50 Saratoga Warm Springs

General description: A large natural pond fed by several warm springs in the southern part of Death Valley.

Location: Southeastern California, approximately 35 miles north of the town of Baker and 25 miles from the town of Shoshone.

Primitive/developed: Primitive. There has been no development to the springs.

Best time of year: Fall, winter, and spring. Summer is too hot.

Restrictions: The pond is within Death Valley National Monument. There is no bathing or camping allowed, nor vehicles permitted immediately adjacent to the pond.

Access: The pond is located several miles from California Highway 127, on largely well-maintained, graded dirt roads. Wet weather may make the last half mile impassable.

Water temperature: The spring's temperature is approximately 82 degrees F.

Nearby attractions: Death Valley, East Mojave Scenic Area, Shoshone, Tecopa Hot Springs.

Services: All services can be found in the small town of Shoshone.

Camping: There is no camping allowed at the springs, but several campgrounds are available in other parts of Death Valley. There is also BLM land several miles away where camping is permitted.

Map: USGS topographic, Owlshead Mountains, CA, quadrangle, 1:150,000 scale.

Finding the springs: From the town of Baker on Interstate 15, travel north on CA 127 for approximately 30 miles to Harry Wade Road (graded dirt road). Turn left (west) on this road and travel approximately 6 miles to a sign for Saratoga Springs, where you turn right (north). Follow this graded dirt road for another 4 miles toward a series of hills. At the base of the hills, the road will make a turn to the left. Follow it for another 0.75 mile to its end at a parking lot. Walk the short distance over a hill to the springs and pond.

The Hot Springs

This large natural pond, fed by several warm springs, is home to many species of birds and other wildlife. It is located in an isolated desert at the margin of the Amargosa River. Although no bathing opportunities exist at Saratoga Springs, it is

Saratoga Warm Springs in Death Valley

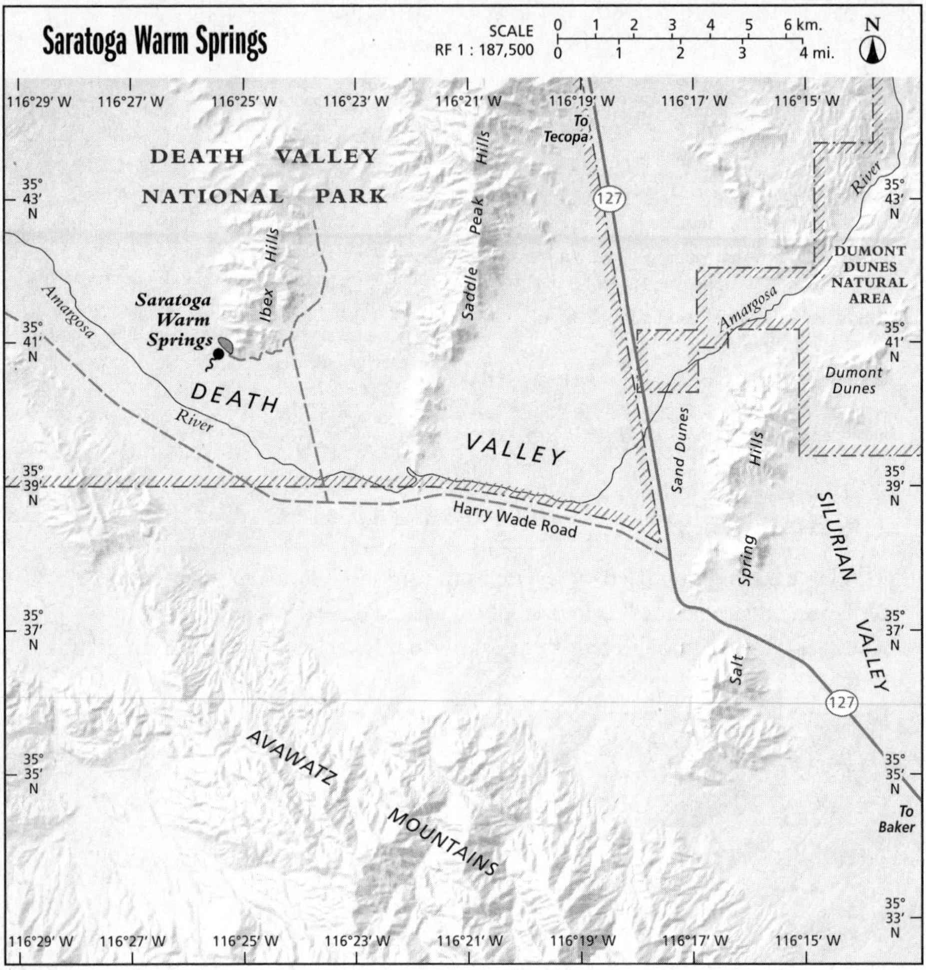

a beautiful and interesting place. The presence of water in this arid region made Saratoga Springs important to Native Americans, as well as early travelers and miners. The road to the springs is generally in good condition, though wet weather may make the last half mile or so difficult to impassable. Be sure to bring plenty of water when visiting the springs. The springs are located near what was known as the Old Spanish Trail, an early travel route through the arid southwest from New Mexico to settlements in southern California. The springs were also passed by the Harry Wade family, members of the ill-fated Manly party, which became trapped in Death Valley in 1849. The Wade family found their way out of Death Valley through this area, where they intersected with the Old Spanish Trail.

51 Keane Wonder Springs

General description: A very interesting collection of warm springs emanating from the side of the mountains in eastern Death Valley. Originally supplying water to the nearby Keane Wonder Mill, the springs are now left in a natural state. There are no bathing opportunities.

Location: Southeastern California, approximately 19 miles from Furnace Creek in Death Valley.

Primitive/developed: Primitive.

Best time of year: Fall, spring, and winter. Summer is far too hot.

Restrictions: The springs are within Death Valley National Park. No motor vehicles are allowed to the springs.

Access: Located approximately 0.5 mile down an unmarked trail. The trailhead is at the end of a fairly well-maintained, graded dirt road.

Water temperature: 93 degrees F at the source.

Nearby attractions: Bailey's Hot Springs, Death Valley National Park.

Services: There are no services at the springs. Nearest services are available at Furnace Creek, approximately 19 miles away, or in Beatty, Nevada, about 26 miles away.

Camping: There is no camping allowed at the springs or at the mill, but there are several National Park Service campgrounds in other parts of Death Valley.

Map: USGS topographic, Beatty, CA, quadrangle, 1:100,000 scale.

Finding the springs: From Beatty, Nevada, travel west for 19 miles on Nevada Highway 374 into California and Death Valley National Park. Turn left at the Beatty Cutoff toward Furnace Creek. Travel on this paved road for approximately 5 miles. Look for a sign for Keane Wonder Mill, and turn left on the dirt road. From Furnace Creek in Death Valley, travel north on California Highway 190 for 12 miles to the Beatty Cutoff, where you turn right. Travel for approximately 5 miles and look for the signs for Keane Wonder Mill, where you turn right. Travel on this graded dirt road to the parking lot at the mill. After looking at the mill area, walk a short distance back on the road and look for a faint trail leading along the base of the mountains on your right (northwest). This trail will be on your left when driving up to the parking lot. Follow this trail for approximately 0.5 mile as it leads you to the base of the mountains where the springs are located. Be sure to bring water!

Keane Wonder Springs in Death Valley

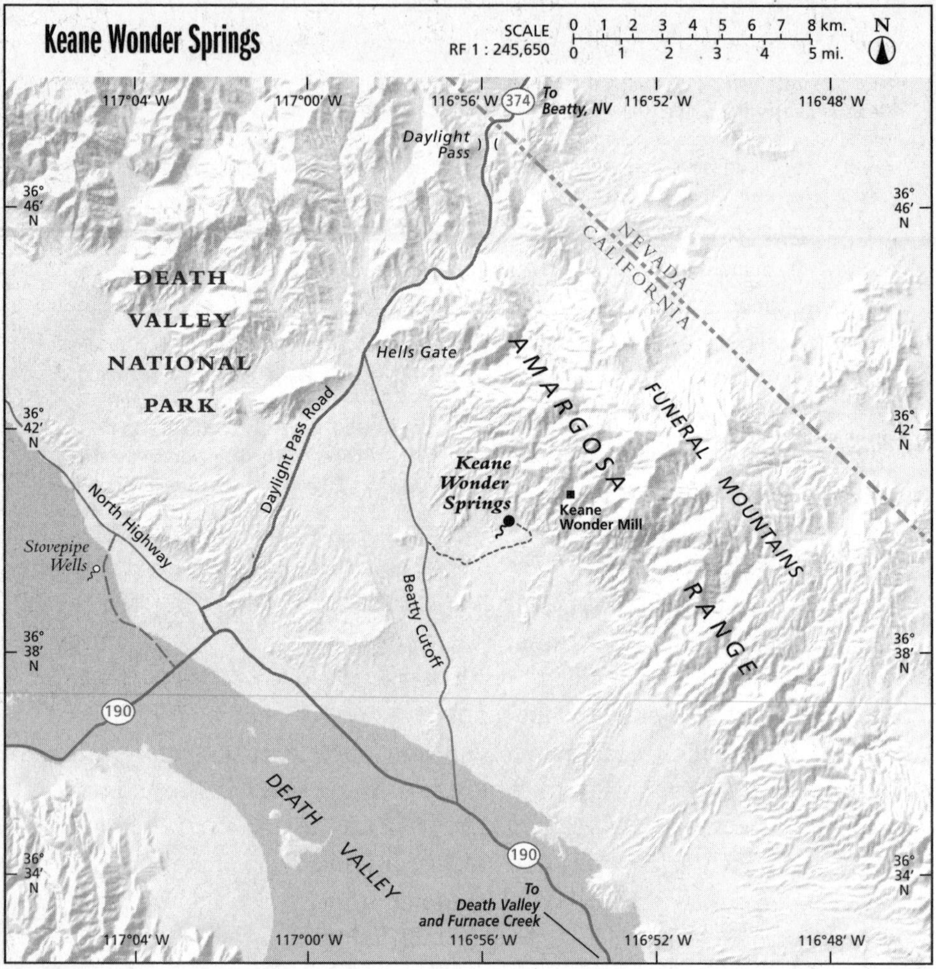

The Hot Springs

Keane Wonder Springs are a very interesting set of warm springs flowing out of the base of the Funeral Mountains in eastern Death Valley National Park. These springs were harnessed to provide water for the Keane Wonder Mill during its operation. A pipeline from this period still remains, though the water itself has been allowed to flow naturally again. There are several warm springs in the area, the largest of which is at the bottom of a shaft. Stay away from the opening of this shaft! There are no bathing opportunities at Keane Wonder Springs, but it is worth a visit if you are in this part of Death Valley.

SANTA BARBARA REGION

Long a haven for artists and movie stars, with spectacular Pacific coast scenery mixed with excellent amenities and seaside charm, Santa Barbara is understandably a sought-after location. Several beaches line the Santa Barbara region, from the University of California in the north to Carpinteria in the south. Depending upon what you want, there is bound to be a beach to your liking. Downtown, State Street offers a plethora of shopping, dining, and nightlife entertainment.

The towering Santa Ynez Mountains to the east offer a splendid backdrop for the city. The mountains also offer countless getaway opportunities for those tired of the crowded coast. Although the mountains are rugged and largely unpopulated, there are several roads leading up into them. Deep in the Los Padres National Forest, many of these roads are dirt and only minimally maintained. Campgrounds, picnic spots, and hiking and biking trails provide some of the outdoor recreation for the mountainous region. Although rather dry, there are a few year-round waterways through the mountains.

Big and Little Caliente Hot Springs are located in this rugged terrain, but can be reached by a few hours' drive from Santa Barbara. Most standard passenger cars should be able to make the trips. U.S. Highway 101 connects the city with other communities to the north and south, along with Gaviota State Park, within which the Las Cruces Hot Spring is located. Twenty-six miles from Santa Barbara, this hot spring is easily visited in a half day.

52 Big Caliente Hot Spring

General description: A natural hot spring, piped into a cement pool in the rugged mountains above Santa Barbara. Well known, Big Caliente experiences heavy visitation on weekends throughout the year.

Location: Southern California, approximately 26 miles north of Santa Barbara.

Primitive/developed: The spring itself has been developed and there are changing rooms and a bathroom, but otherwise the spring is in a primitive setting.

Best time of year: Spring and fall. Summer can be a little hot, and the road can be difficult to impassable in wet weather during winter.

Restrictions: The pool is on Forest Service property, and all rules must be obeyed. Because it is such a publicly visited spring, bathing suits are customarily worn.

Access: A high-clearance vehicle is recommended, though many passenger cars make the trip. Do not attempt the road in wet weather.

Water temperature: Approximately 110 degrees F at the source. The pool itself stays at about 105 degrees F, but can be lowered by diverting the source.

Nearby attractions: Pacific coast, Santa Barbara, Little Caliente Hot Spring.

Services: There are no services at this location, but they can be found approximately 26 miles away in Santa Barbara.

Camping: Camping is not permitted at the spring, but there are several developed Forest

Service campgrounds on the road to the spring and on the road to Little Caliente Hot Spring. Contact the Los Padres National Forest for further information and regulations, (805) 968–6640.

Map: USGS topographic, Cuyama, CA, quadrangle, 1:100,000 scale.

Finding the spring: From south of Santa Barbara, travel north on U.S. Highway 101, taking the Milpas exit (California Highway 144). Follow the signs for CA 144 through Santa Barbara, turning right on Mason, then left on Salinas, then right at a four-way traffic circle. After approximately 6 miles, CA 144 will intersect with California Highway 192, which is Stanwood Drive; turn left. Follow Stanwood for 1.2 miles to El Cielito and turn right. Be sure to stay on El Cielito for 0.5 mile to Gibraltar Road, where you turn right. Follow Gibraltar Road for another 6.5 miles to East Camino Cielo, where there is a Forest Service sign. Turn right on Forest Service Road 5N12, which is paved and windy for the first 6.8 miles, then dirt and windy the rest of the way to the spring. Follow FR 5N12 and all signs to Big Caliente, staying left 1 mile after the road turns to dirt. Five miles after the road turns to dirt, you will arrive at Juncal Campground, where you will turn left on Forest Service Road 5N15, with signs for Big Caliente. Continue for another 3 miles to Forest Service Road 5N16, where you turn right, following the sign to Big Caliente. Follow this road for another 2.5 miles to where the road dead-ends at the parking lot for the hot spring. The spring will be on your right as you enter the parking lot. The drive to the spring from Santa Barbara is long and slow. Allow several hours to get there and several to get back. Do not rush, as in many places the road is slippery, and there are steep drop-offs on one side.

Big Caliente Hot Spring

The Hot Spring

Despite its rather rugged location, Big Caliente has had many improvements made to it. The hot spring source is piped into a somewhat elaborate concrete tub built into the ground. The hot springs are also equipped with a concrete dressing room and latrines. The concrete tub is approximately 7 by 4 feet and 3 feet deep, ideal for several people to bathe in at once. The water is rather hot, and you may want to divert the water out of the pond for a while before bathing to allow it to cool off. A light trickle of water sprays over the spring from the source, creating a mild shower effect. The hot springs are relatively well known and are heavily visited on weekends, when bathing suits are universally worn. During the week you may be fortunate enough to have the spring to yourself. There are other smaller sources of hot spring water upstream from the main pool at Big Caliente. These other sources are primarily located below a trailhead at the far end of the parking area. The springs have a low flow rate, and the ponds they create require digging to make a workable soaking experience.

53 Little Caliente Hot Spring

General description: A less developed, more natural hot spring than Big Caliente, Little Caliente is farther out and may require a 2-mile hike or bike ride to reach it from the closest parking area if a gate is closed. Also popular, Little Caliente Hot Spring sees many visitors on weekends, but is less busy during the week.

Location: Southern California, approximately 29 miles north of Santa Barbara.

Primitive/developed: Primitive, except for the construction of a crude cement pool to capture the hot spring water.

Best time of year: Spring and fall. Summer can be a little hot, and the road can be difficult to impassable in wet weather during winter.

Restrictions: The hot spring is on National Forest Service property, and all rules must be obeyed.

Access: A high-clearance vehicle is recommended, though many passenger cars make the trip. Do not attempt the road in wet weather. The last 0.5 mile of the road to the spring is rather rough, and you will want a high-clearance vehicle at the least. If the gate at Mono Hill is closed, it is approximately 2 more miles of either hiking or biking to the spring.

Water temperature: Approximately 110 degrees F at the source, 105 degrees F in the upper tub, and 103 degrees F in the lower tub.

Nearby attractions: Pacific coast, Santa Barbara, Big Caliente Hot Spring.

Services: There are no services at this location, but many can be found approximately 26 miles away in Santa Barbara.

Camping: Camping is not permitted at the spring, but there are several developed Forest Service campgrounds on the road to the spring. Contact the Los Padres National Forest for further information and regulations.

Map: USGS topographic, Cuyama, CA, quadrangle, 1:100,000 scale.

Finding the spring: From south of Santa Barbara, travel north on U.S. Highway 101, taking the Milpas exit (California Highway 144). Follow the signs for CA 144 through Santa Barbara, turning right on Mason, then left on Salinas, then right at a four-way traffic circle. After approximately 6 miles CA 144 will intersect with California Highway 192, which is

Stanwood Drive; turn left. Follow Stanwood for 1.2 miles to El Cielito and turn right. Be sure to stay on El Cielito for 0.5 mile to Gibraltar Road, where you turn right. Follow Gibraltar Road for another 6.5 miles to East Camino Cielo, where there is a Forest Service sign. Turn right on Forest Service Road 5N12, which is paved and windy for the first 6.8 miles, then dirt and windy the rest of the way to the spring. Follow FR 5N12 and all signs to Big Caliente, staying left 1 mile after the road turns to dirt. Five miles after the road turns to dirt, you will arrive at Juncal Campground, where you will turn left on Forest Service Road 5N15. Continue for another 3 miles to Forest Service Road 5N16, which goes to Big Caliente. Continue straight here, following the sign to Little Caliente. Continue on FR 5N15 for approximately 3.5 miles, crossing a creek and reaching a gate at Mono Hill, which may be closed. If it is closed, park here and walk or bike the last 2 miles to the spring. After another mile you will reach Mono Campground, where you may want to park your car if it does not have high clearance. Stay on the main road uphill to another Forest Service sign for Little Caliente Spring, where you will turn right. Follow this road, which is in poor condition, for 1 more mile to the spring. After a mile the road will climb up a hill, and the springs will be to your right, emerging from a canyon with a little bit of greenery. Look for wooden steps and a metal post sticking out of the ground. As with the drive to Big Caliente, allow several hours each way, as the road is curvy, dirt, and slippery. Take it slow, as there are many blind curves and steep drop-offs.

The Hot Spring

Little Caliente is a pleasant place to visit in the fall and spring, when the weather is not too hot. The source is a small trickle of water that is piped into two separate

Little Caliente Hot Spring

tubs built out of concrete. Both tubs are rather primitive and don't detract from any wilderness experience you may be trying to enjoy, and both provide nice soaking opportunities. Again, these hot springs are heavily visited on weekends in the summer, and you should not expect any privacy during these times. During the week, however, you will find few people and may have it to yourself.

54 Gaviota State Park (Las Cruces) Hot Spring

General description: A natural, murky hot spring in a pleasant canyon with substantial vegetation, less than a mile off U.S. Highway 101 in southern California. From the parking area a 0.75-mile trail takes you to the spring.

Location: Southern California, approximately 20 miles east of the town of Lompoc.

Primitive/developed: Primitive.

Best time of year: Year-round. Summer can be a little hot, but the vegetation at the spring provides proficient shade and keeps it cool.

Restrictions: The hot spring is on state park land, and all rules must be obeyed. It is open to day use only, and there is a fee for parking.

Access: Any vehicle can make the trip to the parking area, as it is only a short distance off a major highway. A 0.75-mile hike is required to reach the spring.

Water temperature: Approximately 100 degrees F at the source, 90 degrees F in the small pond where the best bathing is. A larger pond with a waterfall measures about 80 degrees F.

Nearby attractions: Gaviota State Beach, Buellton.

Services: There are no services at this location, but they can be found approximately 20 miles away in the town of Lompoc or 31 miles away in Santa Barbara.

Camping: Camping is not permitted at the spring or the parking area. There are several state campgrounds to the south along the beach.

Map: California Highway Map.

Finding the spring: From Santa Barbara, travel north on US 101 to the exit for California Highway 1 toward Lompoc. Exit here, staying on the east side of the highway, and turn right on a frontage road paralleling the highway to the south. This road will lead you to the parking area for Gaviota State Park. Park here and pick up the trailhead to the spring. The trail is well marked and is only 0.75 mile to the spring. The way there is mostly uphill.

The Hot Spring

Despite its murky appearance, this hot spring provides for a great soak. The surrounding vegetation makes you feel like you're in a jungle, and it keeps the location cool. The main pool is fed by a small natural hot spring that maintains a temperature of approximately 100 degrees F. The water overflows out of this smaller pool down a little waterfall and into a larger pool, which is approximately 80 degrees F. This lower pool is less appealing due to the moss and algae growing in it and the large amount of leaves and other vegetation falling into it. So far, the hot spring has been kept clean and free from trash, thanks no doubt in large part to hardworking park rangers. Remember, the spring is only open during daylight hours, as the parking lot closes at dusk.

INLAND EMPIRE REGION

The fast-growing eastern Riverside and San Bernardino Counties region is the location for numerous hot springs. In the past many of these hot springs were the locations of lavish resorts and spas. As the popularity of these kinds of establishments waned, most of these springs were closed and remain off-limits today. A few, however, can still be visited.

55 Cahuilla Warm Spring

General description: A beautiful pond formed from a warm spring on the Cahuilla Indian Reservation, in eastern Riverside County.

Location: Southern California, immediately adjacent to the Cahuilla Creek Casino and approximately 30 miles east of the town of Temecula.

Primitive/developed: Primitive.

Best time of year: Fall, winter, and spring. Summer can be too hot.

Restrictions: The warm springs are on Indian reservation land. Obey all signs.

Access: Any vehicle can make the trip, as the hot springs are located immediately off a paved highway.

Water temperature: Approximately 98 degrees F at the source, cooling to about 90 degrees F in the pond.

Nearby attractions: Mount San Jacinto, the resort city of Palm Springs.

Services: There currently are no services at this location, but many can be found approximately 30 miles away in Temecula.

Camping: Camping is not permitted. There are many campgrounds in the Mount San Jacinto area, including in the state park and the national forest.

Map: California Highway Map.

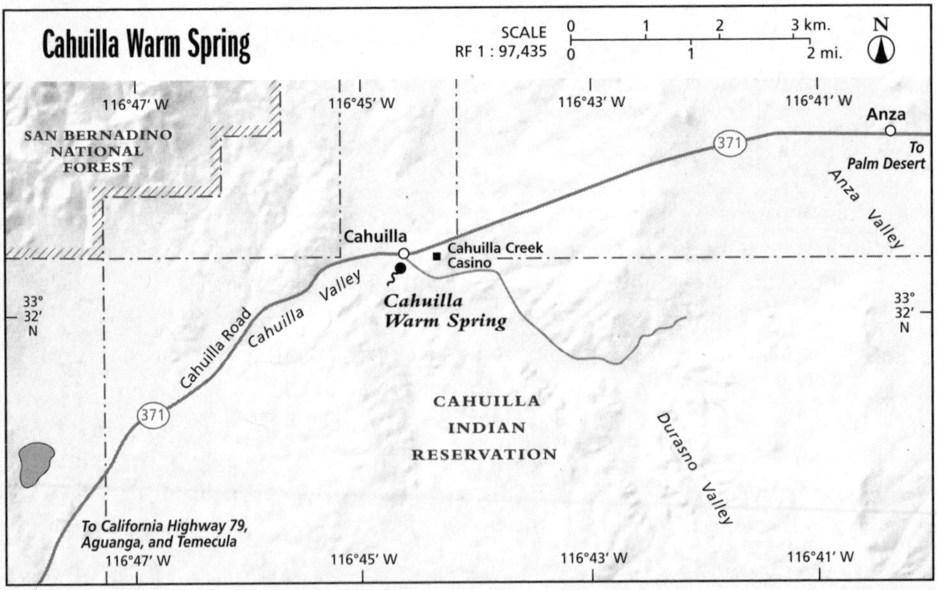

Cahuilla Warm Spring

Finding the spring: From Temecula, travel east on California Highway 79 for 19 miles to Aguanga and the turnoff for California Highway 371. Turn left and take CA 371 for approximately 12 miles to the Cahuilla Creek Casino. Immediately before reaching the casino (to the west), turn right at the sign for Santos Road and Tribal Road (although you won't be taking either of these roads). Make an immediate right on a small dirt road, and drive for a short distance to a small parking area and the pond.

The Hot Spring

Cahuilla Warm Spring consists of a small pond surrounded by green vegetation immediately adjacent to an Indian casino and right off a state highway. The ruins of a small swimming pool still exist, indicating that these springs at one time provided bathing opportunities. Over a hundred years ago, anthropologists visiting the Cahuilla Indians who lived here described them bathing in the warm springs frequently. These springs may be closed to the public in the future, so be sure to obey all signs.

56 Spa Resort Casino

General description: A new hot springs spa resort and hotel in Palm Springs.

Location: Southern California in the city of Palm Springs.

Primitive/developed: Developed.

Best time of year: Year-round, though summers can be quite hot.

Restrictions: This is a spa resort.

Access: In the city of Palm Springs.

Water temperature: The hot springs source temperature is 104 degrees F, though the water temperature varies in the hot tubs.

Nearby attractions: Mount San Jacinto, the resort city of Palm Springs.

Services: This is a full-service spa, with a hotel. All other services are available in Palm Springs.

Camping: Camping is not permitted. There are many campgrounds in the Mount San Jacinto area, including in the state park and the national forest.

Maps: California Highway Map; Palm Springs Map.

Finding the springs: The Spa Resort Casino is located in the heart of Palm Springs, at 100 North Indian Canyon Drive. The casino and hotel/spa are located across the street from each other. From the east on Interstate 10, exit at Ramon Road and head west to Indian Canyon Drive in downtown Palm Springs, where you turn right and drive a few blocks to the resort. From the west, exit I–10 at Gene Autry Trail and head south to Ramon Road, where you turn right. Continue to Indian Canyon Drive, where you turn right to the resort a few blocks away.

Spa Resort Casino, Palm Springs

Spa Resort Casino

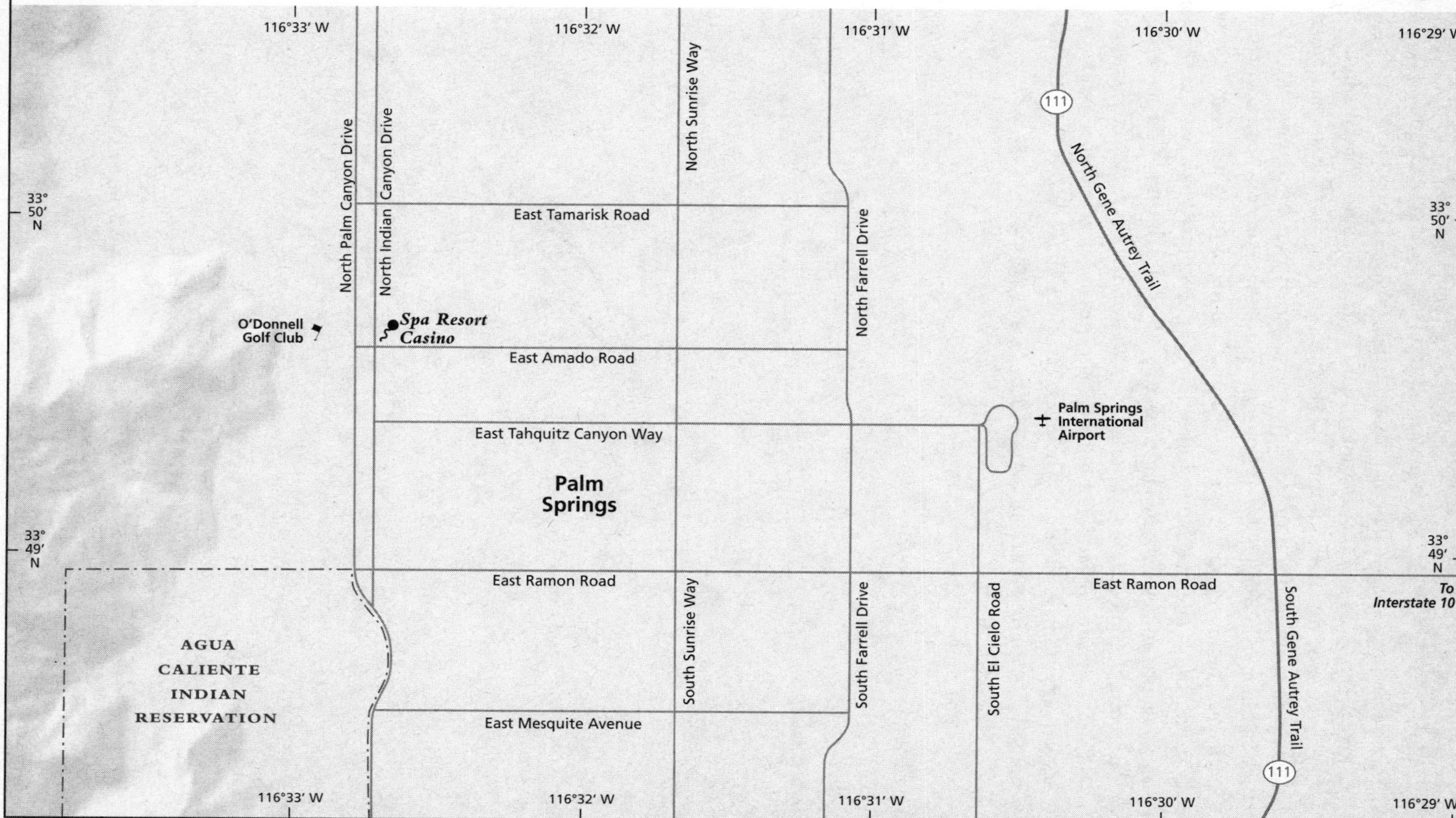

The Hot Springs

The Spa Resort Casino is based around the natural hot springs known as Agua Caliente. The owners of the resort, the Agua Caliente Band of Cahuilla Indians, take their name from the hot springs. Though the source for the springs is 104 degrees F, the water is controlled to provide a variety of temperatures in the tubs and outdoor swimming pools. A full-service spa, the resort offers a variety of packages. The most popular is known as the "Taking of the Waters," which consists of steam, sauna, and Eucalyptus inhalation rooms, followed by a bath in a private tub of natural mineral water. This service also includes the use of the locker room, fitness center, and outdoor swimming pools. The facility is separated into men's and women's sides. A variety of other spa services are available, as is lodging and several restaurants at the nearby hotel and casino. Call (760) 778–1772 for reservations and for more information, or visit www.sparesortcasino.com.

SAN DIEGO AND IMPERIAL COUNTIES DESERT REGION

The Imperial Valley is a dry, low desert region that is now an agricultural center, made possible by irrigation through a variety of canals drawing water from the Colorado River. The largest feature in the region is the Salton Sea, a lake with no outlet, unfortunately polluted by agricultural runoff and sewage. Anza Borrego Desert State Park lies to the west of the Imperial Valley, a low desert environment punctuated by mountain ranges and low hills. The Anza Borrego region is a desert lover's paradise. Several different desert regions intersect in the park, and a wide variety of biotas exist. Camping, hiking, biking, and off-highway driving are some of the more popular activities in the park.

The main means of access to the region is from Interstate 8, which runs from San Diego due east, south of Anza Borrego, across the Imperial Valley and eventually into Arizona. Highline Hot Well lies literally a few yards from the Interstate. Agua Caliente lies in the southern part of the state park, along County Road S-2. Palm Oasis is a picturesque warm pond shaded by palm trees, surrounded by desert sand. This region should be avoided during summer months, as temperatures can, and do, exceed 110 degrees F with regularity. Winter is the best time to visit both Agua Caliente and Highline Hot Well, as lower temperatures will make the soaking more enjoyable.

57 Highline Hot Well

General description: A large hot well piped into a rather elaborate concrete pool immediately off Interstate 8 in extreme southern California.

Location: Southern California, approximately 15 miles east of the town of El Centro.

Primitive/developed: The hot well itself is developed, but the surrounding area is undeveloped save for restrooms.

Best time of year: Fall, winter, and spring. Summer are far too hot, often exceeding 120 degrees F.

Restrictions: The well is on state land, and camping is not allowed at the pool itself. The pool is only open for use during the day.

Access: Any vehicle can make the trip, as the hot spring is located immediately off an interstate highway.

Water temperature: Approximately 120 degrees F at the source, cooling to about 105 degrees F in the pool.

Nearby attractions: Palm Oasis, Salton Sea, Colorado River.

Services: There are no services at this location, but approximately 15 miles away in El Centro.

Camping: Camping is not permitted at the pool itself, but there is a large campground across the road with many undeveloped spaces.

Maps: California Highway Map; Imperial County Map.

Finding the spring: From El Centro, travel east on I–8 for approximately 15 miles to the Van der Linden exit, where you exit and cross over the freeway. Turn right immediately as you pass over the freeway onto the frontage road (Evan Hughes Highway). Take the frontage road for approximately 1 mile to a campground on your left and a parking area on your right. Park here. The hot well is immediately downhill from the restrooms, up against the interstate.

The Hot Spring

Highline Hot Well is not the place to go if you want nature and seclusion. The pool is immediately off a major interstate highway, across the road from a popular campground, and has no views of the surrounding countryside. Despite this, the pool itself is excellent for a hot bath. The well that supplies the pool is approximately 120 degrees F and cools to an almost-perfect 105 degrees F for an invigorating soak. There is also a mild shower effect as water sprays over the pool. The main pool is deeper than most (4 feet) and large, about 6 by 6 feet. There is also a smaller pool adjacent to the main one, slightly cooler and not quite as inviting. The pool is well-maintained by campers who tend to stay at this location for weeks at a time during the winter.

Highline Hot Well

58 Agua Caliente Hot Spring

General description: A county-run park with a large indoor warm pool and an outdoor pool fed by a natural hot spring in the low desert of southern California.

Location: Southern California, within the Anza Borrego Desert State Park, approximately 95 miles from San Diego.

Primitive/developed: Developed.

Best time of year: The park is only open September through May.

Restrictions: This is a county park and campground, and the pools are open to campers and for day use for a fee.

Access: Any vehicle can make the trip, as the hot spring is located immediately off a paved highway.

Water temperature: Approximately 95 degrees F throughout the indoor pool, 90 degrees F in the outside pool.

Nearby attractions: Anza Borrego Desert State Park.

Services: There are no services at this location, but gasoline, food, and supplies can be found approximately 35 miles away in the small town of Ocotillo.

Camping: Developed campsites are available for $10 per night for tents, $14 for full RV hookups, and $12 for partial hookups.

Maps: California Highway Map; Anza Borrego Desert State Park Map.

Finding the spring: From San Diego, travel east on Interstate 8 to the exit for Ocotillo Wells and County Road S-2. Travel north on CR S-2 for approximately 35 miles to Agua Caliente County Park, where you will turn left and reach an entry kiosk. Pay fees here, and drive to the back end of the campground where the pools are located.

The Hot Spring

The large indoor warm pool is a great place for a communal soak when the weather is cool. The pool is equipped with Jacuzzi-like jets, and the temperature hovers around 95 degrees F. The park is equipped with showers, restrooms, and dressing rooms. This indoor pool is reserved for adults only. Kids are free to use the outdoor pool (with proper supervision), which is also pleasant and a little cooler (90 degrees F). Both are well cared for and kept clean. The park is owned by the county of San Diego but is within the larger Anza Borrego Desert State Park, which is one of the most beautiful desert parks, containing thousands of acres of fascinating country. The state park can be reached at (619) 767–4684. Agua Caliente County Park can be reached at (619) 565–3600.

59 Palm Oasis

General description: A beautiful little oasis formed by a well of warm water, located in the stark desert of southeastern California, near the town of El Centro.

Location: Southeastern California, approximately 16 miles from Brawley, 30 miles from El Centro, and 60 miles from Yuma, Arizona.

Primitive/developed: Primitive.

Best time of year: Winter, spring, and fall. Summer is too hot.

Restrictions: The warm springs are located on public land, but several U.S. Navy bombing ranges are nearby. Be sure to stay on the established road.

Access: The road to the oasis contains several sandy sections, not suitable for many passenger vehicles. High clearance is appropriate, and four-wheel drive is recommended.

Water temperature: Water emerges from the ground at approximately 95 degrees F, cooling off to about 90 degrees F in the small pool.

Nearby attractions: Highline Hot Well, Imperial Sand Dunes Recreation Area.

Services: None; nearest gasoline, food, and lodging can be found in Brawley, approximately 25 miles away.

Camping: Camping is not permitted within a half mile adjacent to the oasis, but is allowed in the surrounding desert. There are no developed sites, however. Campgrounds are located in the Imperial Sand Dunes Recreation Area nearby.

Map: California Highway Map.

Finding the spring: From El Centro, travel north on California Highway 86 for 14 miles to the town of Brawley. Turn east (right) on California Highway 78 and travel 15 miles, crossing the Highline Canal. At 0.5 mile past the canal (0.2 mile past Whitlock Road), look for a very small and faint dirt road on your right. Turn here on this sandy road and travel 1.6 miles toward a collection of palm trees.

The Hot Spring

This beautiful little oasis is formed from a well of hot water that bubbles out into a small pond. The water emerges from the ground at approximately 95 degrees F and cools off to about 90 degrees F in the pond. The pond itself is surrounded by several palm trees, offering ample shade. The pool is about 20 feet across and about 3 feet deep. For the most part, trash has been kept to a minimum here, and

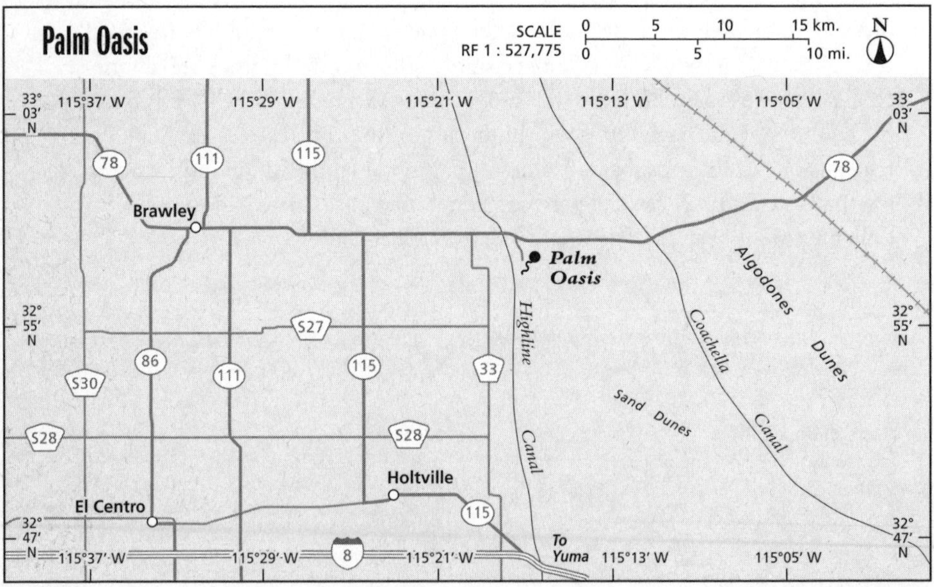

Palm Oasis

most visitors are respectful of the oasis. The Bureau of Land Management (which manages the land) asks that you do not camp within a half mile of the pond (so that wildlife can access it), nor park within 150 feet. The road to the spring has several sandy places that can be treacherous if you are not careful. Once stuck in this sand, it is quite difficult to get out. The pond is fairly well-known, so don't expect to have it to yourself.

NORTHERN NEVADA

Northern Nevada is one of the most geothermally active areas in the United States. There are numerous hot springs sprinkled across this part of the state. Many of these springs have been harnessed for geothermal power, though many more are open for you to discover and enjoy. Because the majority of land in Nevada (80 percent) is controlled by the Bureau of Land Management, it's a great place to go to get away from it all.

Northern Nevada is dominated by ranching and mining. The region is included in a physiographic region termed the Great Basin, so named because all water remains landlocked, never reaching the sea. Most of this water is deposited into groundwater or evaporates away. The region's most distinctive feature is its series of mountain ranges. The ranges all trend north–south, and many reach well over 8,000 feet in elevation. These mountains support completely different plant and animal biotas than the valley floor a few miles away. This varied topography is one of northern Nevada's strong points, allowing the traveler a quick escape from the desert heat on the valley floor.

Jackson Mountain (Macfarlane) Hot Springs

RENO AREA

There are several hot springs in the greater Reno area. Some of the springs, however, are either on private property, offer limited bathing opportunities, or are completely tapped by geothermal power companies. Before the city reached as far southwest as it does now, there was a collection of natural hot springs near the present-day Moana Lane. The Moana Hot Springs were the site of a large spa, which in the early 1900s could be reached by streetcar from downtown. Since then, however, the hot spring waters have been used in individual houses for space heating and in swimming pools.

If you are spending a quick getaway weekend in Reno—gambling, skiing, or just sightseeing—all three of the springs listed below are within a short drive of the city.

60 Steamboat Villa Hot Springs Spa

General description: A historic hot springs resort south of Reno immediately off U.S. Highway 395. Closed for years, the resort was just recently reopened. The many large-volume hot springs have provided bathing for centuries and now support a big geothermal plant on the other side of the highway from the present resort.

Location: Approximately 11 miles south of Reno.

Primitive/developed: Developed.

Best time of year: Year-round.

Restrictions: This is a privately owned resort.

Access: Immediately off the highway, this resort can be reached by any vehicle.

Water temperature: Varies depending on room.

Nearby attractions: Reno, Carson City, Mount Rose, Virginia City.

Services: Gas, food, and lodging can be found north and south along US 395.

Camping: None at the resort itself, but several Forest Service campgrounds are nearby, including Ophir Creek, south on US 395.

Maps: Nevada Highway Map; USGS topographic, Carson City, NV, quadrangle, 1:100,000 scale.

Finding the springs: From Reno, drive south on US 395 for approximately 11 miles. Two miles after passing the intersection with Nevada Highways 341/431 to Virginia City and Mount Rose, keep an eye out for a mission-style building on the east side (on your left). Turn left onto the paved road (Rhodes) leading to the resort, immediately off the highway. The resort is not well-signed, so keep your eyes open while traveling south.

The Hot Springs

Steamboat Villa Hot Springs is built on an extremely geothermal-active hillside. A large geothermal power plant was built recently on the west side of the highway, tapping the largest portion of the hot springs in the area. There is plenty of hot water left for the Steamboat resort, however. Its source is enclosed by a cement structure, with steam bellowing from it during most of the year. Other geothermal features

Steamboat Villa Hot Springs Spa

exist on the site, including fumeroles. The resort offers a variety of bathing rooms to the public, with temperatures varying in each of these rooms. The spa is a non-profit organization, which offers a drop in prices as well as memberships. The charge for a forty-five minute visit is $16. Massages are also available. Reservations are suggested. Hours as of this writing are noon to 8:00 P.M. every day except Wednesday. Phone ahead at (775) 853–6600 for current rates, hours, and details, or write 16010 South Virginia Street, P.O. Box 18106, Reno, NV 89511.

A little history: Located close to emigrant pathways and nearby settlements, these hot springs have been utilized continuously since prehistoric times. During the westward emigration of the mid-nineteenth century, the hot springs lay on a commonly traveled route from the Truckee Meadows to the Carson Valley and beyond. One of the first hot springs to be exploited in the West, Steamboat had a hospital and bathhouse constructed at the site as early as 1860. Felix Monet was the first to exploit the springs, acquiring the property in the late 1850s and building the bathhouse in 1860. By 1861 a traveler described the area in the following way: "The ground trembles here and scalding water sullies forth from cracks in the earth. Jets of steam engulf the land and the air is heavy with the scent of brimstone and sulfur."

The springs were so named because the steam emanating from within sounded like the puffing of a steamboat. With the discovery of vast amounts of silver in the Comstock Lode and the establishment of the town of Virginia City (in the mountains to the east), the resort served as a terminal for the Virginia & Truckee Railroad beginning in 1871. A small town sprang up in the immediate vicinity, including a post office in 1880. Many Virginia City residents visited the fancy hot spring resort. Most notably, the springs were profiled by Virginia City humorist Mark Twain in his piece entitled "Curing a Cold." The springs passed through the hands of several owners through the years, the name changing between Reno Hot Springs, Mount Rose Hot Springs, and Radium Hot Springs, among others. In 1909 Dr. Edna Carver came to the area and in the following years developed a spa. Thousands of people visited Steamboat Springs over the ensuing years. The springs reportedly became a popular spot for prizefighters to come to train and benefit from the hot water and steam therapy.

The resort eventually closed, and around the same time a large geothermal plant was opened on the west side of US 395. The vast energy produced from the hot springs has been utilized in a variety of ways in the recent past, from geothermal energy to a flameless source of heat in the manufacture of plastic explosives. Over the past few decades, various attempts have been made to resuscitate the hot springs resort, most failing. Today, however, they are open to the public again.

61 Patua (Hazen) Hot Springs

General description: A collection of very hot springs in a flat adjacent to the town of Fernley. Currently, the hot springs provide no bathing opportunities, but this may change.

Location: In northern Nevada close to the town of Fernley, off U.S. Highway 50.

Primitive/developed: Primitive.

Best time of year: Year-round, though summer is hot. During wet weather the area may be muddy.

Restrictions: None currently.

Access: Several dirt roads formerly provided access to these springs, but they no longer do, as crossings over the railroad tracks were removed. You must now drive a short distance down a fairly good dirt road and walk about 0.25 mile to the springs themselves.

Water temperature: Varies depending on spring, though the official source temperature is 187 degrees F. Be careful!

Nearby attractions: Lahontan Reservoir, Reno.

Services: Gas and food can be found in Fernley, approximately 6 miles away.

Camping: No camping is available at or near the springs, but campgrounds can be found at the Lahontan State Recreational Area, approximately 10 miles away.

Maps: USGS topographic, Reno, NV, quadrangle, 1: 100,000 scale; Hazen, NV, quadrangle, 1: 24,000 scale.

Finding the springs: From Reno, travel east on Interstate 80 for 30 miles to Fernley, taking the second exit (number 46). Travel south on this road (Alternate U.S. Highway 95) to the intersection with Alternate U.S. Highway 50. Turn left (east) on Alternate US 50, and go 6 miles. Keep an eye out for a small dirt road on the left (north) near a group of trees at mile marker 6. Take this small dirt road for approximately 0.6 mile to the railroad tracks. This is the old railroad siding of Darwin. Park here. Cross the railroad tracks on foot (take care to watch for trains!), and head north a few hundred yards to a collection of small hills nearby. The hot springs are on the other side of these hills.

The Hot Springs

Patua Hot Springs consist of several sources of very hot water forming small, shallow pools. The water has been used for many purposes in the past, but currently they are left in a natural state. Previously water was diverted into a concrete

Patua (Hazen) Hot Springs

bathing tub, but it was subsequently demolished. Currently no bathing opportunities exist, but this may change in the future. Patua Hot Springs have been known by several other names, including Hazen and Fernley. These springs are in a very beautiful setting near the Fernley Wildlife Management Area and are worth a visit. They are also in an area of extensive geothermal activity, from the Soda Lake area to Brady's Hot Springs.

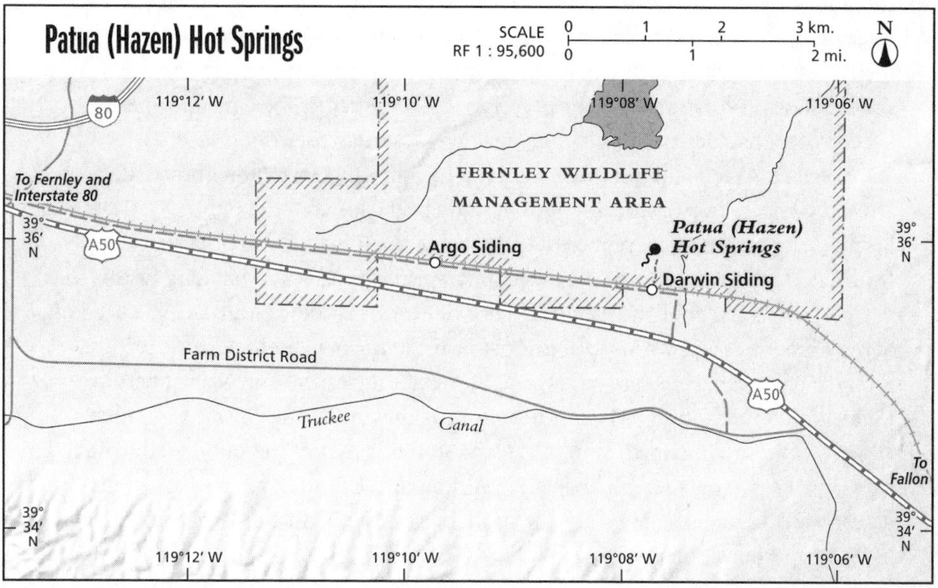

BLACK ROCK DESERT REGION

Rich in history, prehistory, natural beauty, and geothermal resources, this part of Nevada is a must-visit for those who truly enjoy the peaceful solitude only the desert can offer. Only a few hours from the bright lights of Reno, this high desert setting makes you feel as if you're in another world. Located near the margins of the Black Rock Desert Playa, most of these springs are a two- to three-hour drive from Reno. The nearest town is Gerlach, a small railroad town with only the most basic of services and a small hotel and casino.

The Black Rock Desert is the remains of a huge prehistoric lake that covered a large part of northern Nevada during the Pleistocene. Ringed by imposing mountain ranges, the area was filled with water as recently as 10,000 years ago from Lake Lahonton, as the ancient lake was known. Large animals, all of which are now extinct, roamed this country during the Pleistocene, more commonly known as the Ice Age. Huge wooly mammoths, saber-toothed cats, horses, bison, ground sloths, camels, and many other animals at one time lived in this area. The men who lived here during this time hunted these animals in a much different fashion than more recent hunters. Occasionally evidence of these ancient animals turns up in the Black Rock Desert, the most notable of which is an intact skeleton of a wooly mammoth found on the Black Rock Desert Playa a few years ago.

As you will be far from the conveniences of civilization, come prepared on this trip. Bring more water than you plan to consume, plenty of food, a basic automotive tool kit, a shovel, first-aid supplies, and warm clothing. Also be sure to notify someone of your trip destination, when you plan on leaving, and when you plan on returning. While the majority of the land you will be driving on is owned by the Bureau of Land Management, there are areas of private property, which you should stay out of without prior permission. Please remember to stay on established roads, pack out all trash, and leave the desert as you found it.

Gerlach Area: Though there are numerous hot springs in the immediate area around Gerlach, two of the best have recently been closed to the public. Gerlach Hot Springs, run by the town, reportedly closed due to an inability to obtain permits from the Health Department. Great Boiling Springs, a resort with a long history, has been closed to the public for a longer period of time, and the entire site is fenced off. Several other hot and warm springs exist near the town, including Mud Springs, immediately west, which are largely used for watering cattle. The nearest bathing opportunities are at Trego Hot Springs, approximately 20 miles away. Fly Ranch, about 15 miles to the northwest, is the largest in this part of the state, producing a substantial reservoir used for irrigation. Although the hot springs and associated geyser were open to the public in the past, today they are off-limits and only accessible with special permission.

John Charles Fremont—the pathfinder: During his historic expedition of 1843–1844, Captain John Charles Fremont of the U.S. Topographic Corps camped at the Great Boiling Hot Springs, near the present-day town of Gerlach. Until recently the spring could still be visited, but today it is off-limits. Fremont and his party were exploring the Great Basin, searching for the source for the legendary San Buenaventura River. The maps and descriptions of the country in which they traveled would be utilized by hundreds of later emigrants to California and Oregon. Fremont described the hot springs as "the most extraordinary locality of hot springs we had met during the journey" and recorded temperatures as high as 208 degrees F. The party had been away from home for over a year when they reached the hot spring, after which they traveled south to Pyramid Lake. As with many other places throughout the West, Fremont gave the hot spring its name. Fremont, incidentally, also named Pyramid Lake, as the small pyramid-shaped island near the south shore reminded him of the great edifices in Egypt.

62 Trego Hot Springs

General description: Approximately four hours from Reno, Trego Hot Springs consists of a small, shallow, silty, warm source pond that flows into a ditch, where the water cools. The spring lies on the edge of the Black Rock Desert Playa, adjacent to the Western Pacific Railroad. Visiting this spring makes for an excellent camping trip and can be linked to other trips listed in this book.

Location: Northwestern Nevada, approximately 120 miles north of Reno.

Primitive/developed: Primitive.

Best time of year: Spring and fall. During winter roads can become muddy and impassable in passenger cars, and summer can be hot.

Restrictions: None.

Water temperature: 100 degrees F at the source at the railroad tracks, about 95 degrees F in the pond, and cooler in the ditch.

Access: During dry periods most passenger cars can make the trip. If roads are wet, four-wheel drive is mandatory.

Nearby attractions: Black Rock Desert Playa, Pyramid Lake.

Services: None; nearest gasoline, food, and lodging is in Gerlach, about 20 miles away to the south.

Camping: Plenty of undeveloped space near the spring.

Map: USGS topographic, Gerlach, NV, quadrangle, 1:100,000 scale.

Finding the springs: From Reno, take Interstate 80 east for 35 miles, exiting onto Nevada Highway 447 north. Travel on NV 447 through Wadsworth for 16 miles to Nixon. Immediately north of Nixon on NV 447 is Pyramid Lake. Continue north on NV 447 for 56 miles to the town of Gerlach, where you may want to gas up if you plan on being out for more than the day. From the only gas station in town (Bruno's Texaco), backtrack on NV 447 across the dry lake bed for 2.7 miles to the first dirt road on the left. Take this graded road east for 15.6 miles to a secondary dirt road on the left. Follow this road approximately 1 mile to the spring, bearing right at 0.4 mile and left at another 0.3 mile. Another road a little farther down the main dirt road also leads directly to the spring.

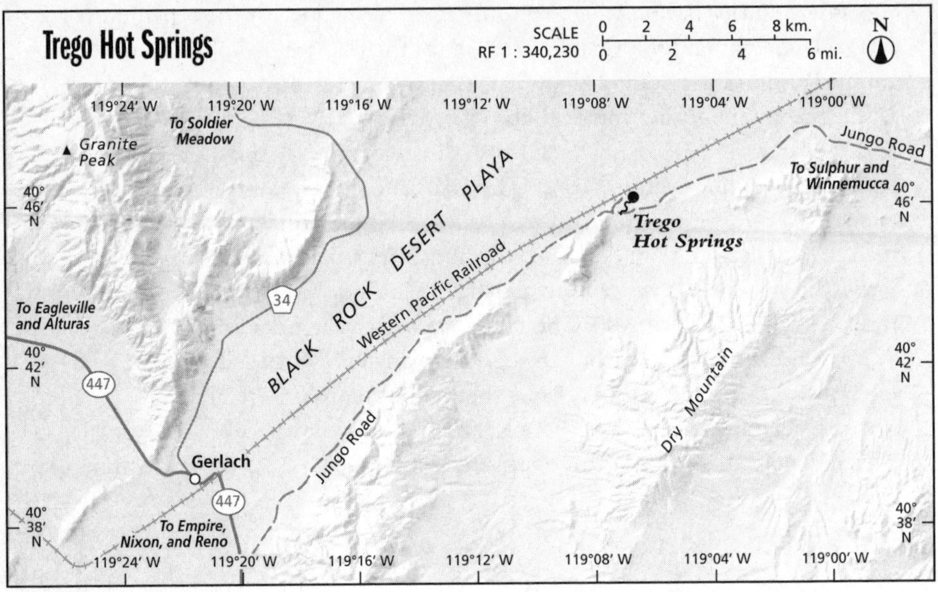

The Hot Springs

Trego Hot Springs consists of a small pond and ditch formed by a series of hot springs bubbling up immediately next to railroad tracks. The source is approximately 187 degrees F. The pond is about 2 to 3 feet deep, with a silty bottom into which you sink above your ankles. The water in the pond is approximately 100 degrees F. The hot water flows out of the pond and into a ditch, with the temperature decreasing the farther it gets from the pond. Depending upon the time of year you visit, you may want to sample each part of this spring to find the right temperature to suit your desires.

The Nobles Trail: Trego Hot Springs was a campsite along the emigrant trail known as Nobles Cut-off, used during the early 1850s. Beginning in 1847, the Applegate Trail diverged from the main emigrant trail at Lassen's Meadows on the Humboldt River (present-day Rye Patch Reservoir), traveling west to Rabbit-hole Springs and then north to cross the Black Rock Desert. Traveling along the western edge of the Black Rock Range, the trail headed west again at Soldier Meadows through High Rock Canyon, and eventually to Oregon. Prominent landowner and explorer Peter Lassen blazed a divergent trail off Applegate Trail near Goose Lake south to his ranch in northern California. Lassen's trail, far from a shortcut to California, actually led travelers 200 miles out of the way from the more heavily traveled Truckee and Carson River routes. The Nobles Trail was a shortcut to the much longer Lassen/Applegate Trail to northern Cali-

Trego Hot Springs

fornia and was used for the first time in 1852. In 1853 the trail changed its course slightly and passed through what is now known as Trego Hot Springs and the present-day town of Gerlach.

63 Jackson Mountain (Macfarlane) Hot Springs

General description: A hot spring bubbling out of the top of a ridge of travertine, forming two small pools. In an equally scenic setting to that of Trego, this hot spring also lies on the east side of the Black Rock Desert Playa.

Location: In northwestern Nevada, approximately 40 miles northeast of Trego Hot Springs and about 160 miles northeast of Reno. The spring is also approximately two hours northwest of Winnemucca, by a different road.

Primitive/developed: Primitive.

Best time of year: Spring and fall. Roads can become difficult during wet winters, and summer can be hot.

Restrictions: None.

Access: When the roads are dry, most passenger vehicles can make the trip. A high-clearance vehicle is recommended, and four-wheel drive is required when the road becomes wet or washed out.

Water temperature: 170 degrees F at the source.

Nearby attractions: Black Rock Desert Playa, Sulphur (site of old railroad town).

Jackson Mountain (Macfarlane) Hot Springs

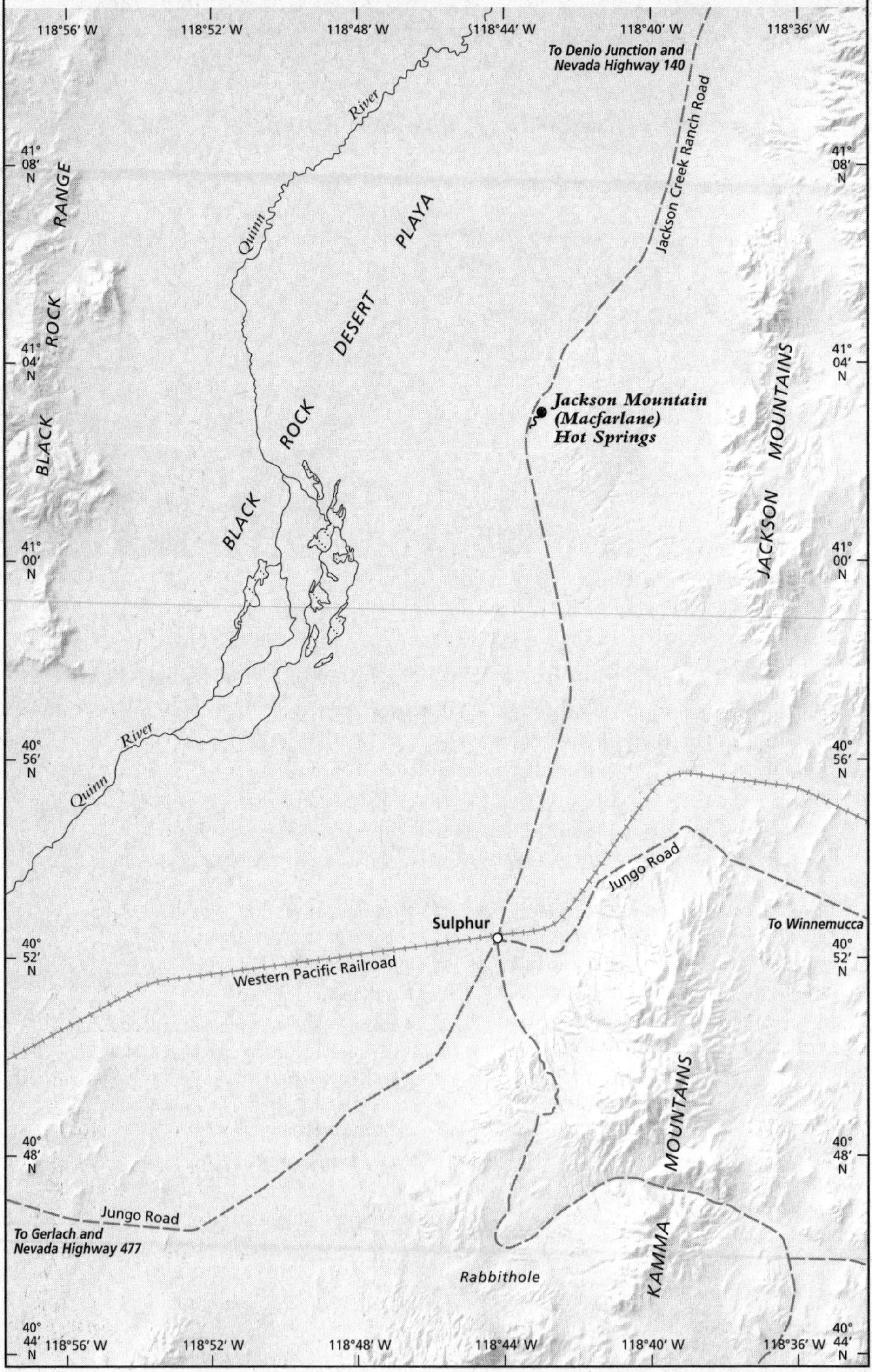

Services: None; nearest gasoline, food, and lodging is in Winnemucca, 68 miles to the southeast, or Gerlach, about 50 miles away to the southwest.

Camping: Undeveloped space for a few vehicles near the springs, and plenty of open space in the immediate vicinity.

Map: USGS topographic, Jackson Mountains, NV, quadrangle, 1:100,000 scale.

Finding the springs: From Reno, take Interstate 80 east for 35 miles, exiting onto Nevada Highway 447 north. Travel on NV 447 through Wadsworth for 16 miles to Nixon. Immediately north of Nixon on NV 447 is Pyramid Lake. Continue north on NV 447 for 56 miles to the town of Gerlach, where you may want to gas up if you plan on being out for more than a day. From Gerlach (Bruno's Texaco), travel on NV 447 south for 2.7 miles to a graded dirt road on the left. Take this road for 41 miles to the old railroad town of Sulphur. Travel north (turn left) out of Sulphur, across the railroad tracks on a graded dirt road with a sign to Denio. Continue on this road for 13.5 miles, finding the hot spring on the right, directly off the road. To reach Winnemucca, continue on the main graded road straight through Sulphur (instead of turning left to Jackson Mountain Hot Springs).

The Hot Springs

Jackson Mountain (or Macfarlane) Hot Springs consists of a small source of hot water on the top of a ridge of travertine. The source (about 170 degrees F) trickles down the ridge into a small pool and eventually into a small pond. At one time this pond may have offered bathing opportunities, but at present it serves more as a watering trough for cattle. Perhaps some dedicated volunteers may one day improve some part of the spring enough to offer a soak. The breathtaking scenery of the Black Rock Desert makes up for the limited bathing opportunities.

Prehistoric inhabitants: Native Americans have inhabited the Black Rock Desert area as far back as 10,000 years ago and up to as recently as 150 years ago. Several bands of the Northern Paiute Indians have called the Black Rock Desert home. The springs found in several places around the lake were no doubt a source of reliable water for these people. Evidence of prehistoric occupation of the Jackson Mountain Hot Springs can be found if one looks closely. In the area immediately surrounding the spring, small pieces of a rock known as chert can be found. Hundreds of these rocks are what archaeologists call "flakes." The broken edges of this material are very sharp, and made for excellent tools such as spear points, hide scrapers, choppers, and various other implements.

Remember that these flakes are archaeological resources and should not be taken from their place. The hot spring is on federal land, and the removal of artifacts from anywhere on federal land is a crime. These resources need to remain where they are for generations to come, so that they too can get a glimpse of how our prehistoric predecessors lived.

Jackson Mountain (Macfarlane) Hot Springs

64 Black Rock Hot Springs

General description: An immense pool of aqua blue water on the northern reaches of the Black Rock Desert. The spring is incredibly hot, and all precautions should be taken to avoid serious injury.

Location: Northern Nevada, approximately 30 miles north of Gerlach.

Primitive/developed: Primitive.

Best time of year: The springs can only be reached when the playa is completely dry. This will usually be during the months of August, September, and early October. Do not under any circumstances try to get there when there is standing water on the playa or if it is wet in any way.

Restrictions: None.

Access: A high-clearance vehicle is necessary, as the last few hundred yards to the springs are a little rough. There is substantial sand at the margins of the playa, so four-wheel drive is recommended. No vehicle can make the trip if the playa is wet, and vehicles have become stuck for days in its sticky surface. The sink of the Quinn River is to the east of where you will be driving, so don't veer off onto parts of the playa to the east. Inquire in Gerlach for conditions on the playa immediately prior to venturing out on its surface.

Water temperature: 150 degrees F at the source, cooling off as the water flows from the main source.

Nearby attractions: Black Rock Desert Playa.

Services: None; nearest gasoline, food, and lodging can be found in Gerlach, approximately 30 miles away.

Camping: Camping is permitted; just be sure to come prepared, as there are no services of any kind at this remote location.

Map: USGS topographic, Gerlach, NV, quadrangle, 1:100,000 scale.

Finding the springs: From Gerlach, travel northwest out of town on Washoe County Road 34. As the road bends to the north, around the playa, keep an eye out for a dirt road marked by two stone pillars near the edge of the playa. This road will be on your right, approximately 3 miles after leaving Gerlach. Drive on this dirt road for a few hundred yards to the playa surface. You will then see tire tracks leading north onto the dry lake. Follow these tracks in a northerly direction, staying on the most distinct path. As you travel north, you will see the large black rock from which the desert derives its name. Head toward this rock, following the tracks that lead you in that general direction. Do not stray from the tracks, and do not veer too far from north. The drive across the playa is approximately 25 miles to the spring. As the tracks leave the playa on the north side, immediately below the black rock, they will continue through hummocky terrain to the hot spring itself.

The Hot Springs

Another campsite along the Lassen, Applegate, and Nobles Trails, the Black Rock Hot Springs is a wonder of the region. The spring itself is a massive pool of water, extending to unknown depths. This water is extremely hot, and all precautions should be taken here. Keep a close hold on children and pets. An emigrant party in the 1850s was unable to stop one of their dogs from jumping in, and the dog was boiled to death in a matter of minutes. A shepherd's wagon lies adjacent to the spring, which some people have covered with tarps for protection from the sun. Although the spring itself is extremely hot, the water flows out onto a small marshy area where it cools off considerably.

Black Rock Hot Springs

Black Rock Hot Springs is far from civilization, can only be reached a few months out of the year, and requires driving that follows little more than tire tracks. The spring, nevertheless or because of these factors, is a fantastic place to visit. The entire Black Rock Desert spreads out before you, and the brilliantly colored water dazzles your eyes. Be sure to plan ahead for the trip to this spring, and inquire locally for conditions of the playa before you depart.

65 Double Hot Springs

General description: Another fantastic hot spring on the margins of the Black Rock Desert Playa, Double Hot Springs is even farther away than Black Rock and more difficult to reach. The spring does, however, offer ample bathing opportunities.

Location: Northern Nevada, in the Black Rock Desert, approximately 35 miles north of Gerlach.

Primitive/developed: Primitive.

Best time of year: The spring is best accessed from Black Rock Hot Springs first, and therefore should only be visited in August, September, and early October.

Restrictions: None.

Access: Four-wheel drive is recommended and may be absolutely required. The road from Black Rock Hot Springs to Double Hot Springs can be difficult.

Water temperature: 140 degrees F at the source, cooling off to varying temperatures. Some reports place the temperature of the hottest portions of the spring as high as 202 degrees F.

Nearby attractions: Black Rock Desert Playa.

Services: None; nearest gasoline, food, and lodging can be found in Gerlach, approximately 35 miles away.

Camping: Camping is permitted, but be sure to come prepared, as there are absolutely no services of any kind and you will be a long drive from civilization.

Map: USGS topographic, High Rock Canyon, NV, quadrangle, 1:100,000 scale.

Finding the springs: From Gerlach, travel northwest out of town on Washoe County Road 34. As the road bends to the north, around the playa, keep an eye out for a dirt road marked by two stone pillars near the edge of the playa. This road will be on your right, approximately 3 miles after leaving Gerlach. Drive on this dirt road for a few hundred yards to the playa surface. You will then see tire tracks leading north onto the dry lake. Follow these tire tracks in a northerly direction, staying on the most distinct path. As you travel north, you will see the large black rock from which the desert derives its name. Head toward this rock, following the tracks that lead you in that general direction. Do not stray from the tracks, and do not veer too far from north. The drive across the playa is approximately 25 miles. As the tracks leave the playa on the north side, immediately below the black rock, they will continue through hummocky terrain to Black Rock Hot Springs. From Black Rock Hot Springs, continue on the same road northwest, roughly paralleling the edge of the playa. Follow this increasingly difficult road for approximately 5 miles to another expanse of dark green vegetation, which marks the location of Double Hot Springs.

Double Hot Springs

The Hot Springs

Similar to Black Rock Hot Springs, Double Hot Springs also has an extremely hot source that travelers should be wary of. There are also numerous seeps in the surrounding area, making the terrain rather marshy. Explore the entire area to find a place to bathe, but remain careful of the hot water. The evidence for prehistoric occupation of this site abounds. As you will quickly realize, however, people have been visiting this spring for generations, as is evidenced by the varying type of garbage left by different groups. Older refuse can be discerned among the more recent debris. As always, do not leave any garbage yourself, and refrain from removing any artifacts from the area.

Along with Black Rock Hot Springs and Double Hot Springs, there are several other hot springs in the immediate area, although none provide any real bathing opportunities. Almost without exception, all of these springs lie along a geological fault line running roughly north–northwest to south–southeast, along the base of the Black Rock Range to the Trego Hot Springs area. This fault also extends into the Soldier Meadow region, where there are several other hot springs (see the next three entries), making the fault approximately 35 miles long. An earthquake of approximately 4.1 magnitude in 1936 was attributed to this fault line.

66 Soldier Meadows Hot Springs

General description: A series of hot spring ponds formed by many seeps, located in a remote desert setting. These hot springs are in an extremely geothermally active valley, offering several choices in a short radius.

Location: Northwestern Nevada, approximately 60 miles northwest of Gerlach and 170 miles from Reno.

Primitive/developed: Primitive.

Best time of year: Spring, fall, and winter. Summer can be hot.

Restrictions: None.

Access: This long trip is best made in a high-clearance vehicle, though some vans and passenger cars can make it. During wet periods you may need four-wheel drive. The road is of varying quality and can be washed out in places, making for sandy spots. In winter and spring the secondary roads can become muddy.

Water temperature: Ranging from 100 to 115 degrees F, depending upon the spring chosen.

Nearby attractions: High Rock Canyon (historic inscriptions), Black Rock Desert Playa, Summit Lake.

Services: None; nearest gasoline, food, and lodging can be found in Gerlach, approximately 60 miles away. A nearby guest ranch could provide a place to stay, though these springs are best enjoyed by camping adjacent to them.

Camping: Plenty of undeveloped space to camp; just remember to camp away from the springs themselves, and respect other people's privacy.

Map: USGS topographic, High Rock Canyon, NV, quadrangle, 1:100,000 scale.

Finding the springs: From Gerlach, travel north through town on Nevada Highway 447 until you come to a fork in the road just outside of town (you pass Gerlach Hot Springs, now closed, on your right). Take the right fork, which is Washoe County Road 34. Travel north on CR 34 along the west side of the Black Rock Desert Playa (immediately after the intersection with NV 447 and CR 34, you pass Great Boiling Hot Springs, also now closed, on your right) for 12.2 miles. Turn right on to a dirt road with a sign for Soldier Meadows Guest Ranch. Travel along this dirt road for 43.3 miles to a fork in the road, with a sign pointing toward the Soldier Meadows Guest Ranch. Take the left fork, where you will immediately be met with a choice of three roads. Take the middle road (the least developed of the three choices). There will be some springs seeping onto the road, sometimes making it wet and muddy. Follow this road for approximately 0.6 mile (the road will cross another more major road), until you come to a small hill. Continue on the same road up and around this hill for another 0.3 mile until you spot the hot spring seeps on the other side. Park here and select the pond that you prefer.

The Hot Springs

Settled in a small valley, these springs have views of the Soldier Meadows area and of the majestic Black Rock Range to the east (which are usually snowcapped in the winter). The pond offering the best soaking opportunity is approximately 5 by 5 feet and about 4 feet deep, with clear water, a sandy bottom, and often covered with reeds. The other ponds nearby (within 50 yards) are hotter and shallower but can also provide for a good soak. Just be sure to check the temperature before getting in. Camping is permitted and is ideal at this location. There are over fifty distinct hot springs in this geothermally active valley. Most of these springs are also large in volume and temperature, though there are fewer bathing opportunities.

Fort McGarry: The valley in which these hot springs are found was named for soldiers stationed at an army post established in the early 1860s. The camp originated as an outpost deep in the heart of Northern Paiute territory, at a time of heightened Indian-white conflict during and immediately after the Civil War. In 1865 Camp McGarry was established as a winter camp to protect travelers passing through this part of Nevada, utilizing the Lassen-Applegate Trail. Following a silver discovery in Idaho, regular freight wagon trains traveled from Chico and other California towns north to Silver City, Idaho, passing through this area. Protection was needed along this stretch of the trail, so the army established a fort near Summit Lake (now the Summit Lake Indian Reservation). In the winter they moved the fort south to Soldier Meadows because it was quite a bit warmer due to the lower elevation and warm water from the nearby hot springs. Stone officers quarters, stables, and other structures were constructed, several of which remain in use today.

The fort was later abandoned by the army, but then utilized by cattle ranchers, most notably the firm Miller and Lux, which grazed cattle over an immense area. Cattle barons Henry Miller and Charles Lux in the late 1800s began putting together the Pacific Livestock Company, which operated until 1928. Later owners of Solider Meadows continued to run both cattle and sheep for many years. The current owners, the Estill family, also continue to raise cattle on the land, and today Soldier Meadows Ranch operates as a working cattle ranch as well as guest ranch, complete with overnight accommodations, camping, trail rides, and other attractions. Contact the ranch for further information: Soldier Meadows Guest Ranch, P.O. Box 655, Eagleville, CA 96110; (530) 279–4881; reservation information, (530) 279–2024.

67 Soldier Meadows Warm Pond

General description: A large, warm, 5-foot deep pond in the Soldier Meadows area.

Location: Northwestern Nevada, approximately 60 miles northwest of Gerlach and about 160 miles from Reno.

Primitive/developed: Primitive.

Best time of year: Spring and fall. Roads can be wet and muddy in winter, and summer can be hot.

Restrictions: The nearby guest ranch asks that you do not camp at the warm spring itself; please honor that request. There is plenty of undeveloped camping in the immediate vicinity, however.

Access: High-clearance vehicle recommended for most of the year. During wet periods you may need four-wheel drive.

Water temperature: Approximately 95 degrees F, depending upon which part of the pond you are in. In places along the margins of the pond, extremely hot water bubbles up through the mud—be careful!

Nearby attractions: High Rock Canyon (historic inscriptions), Black Rock Desert Playa, Summit Lake.

Services: None; nearest gasoline, food, and lodging can be found in Gerlach, approximately 60 miles away.

Camping: Not allowed at the warm spring itself. There are plenty of other springs nearby where camping is permitted. Just remember to camp away from the springs themselves, and respect other people's privacy.

Map: USGS topographic, High Rock Canyon, NV, quadrangle, 1:100,000 scale.

Finding the spring: From Gerlach, travel north through town on Nevada Highway 447 until you come to a fork in the road just outside of town. Take the right fork, which is Washoe County Road 34. Travel north on CR 34 along the west side of the Black Rock Desert Playa for 12.2 miles. Turn right on a dirt road with a sign for Soldier Meadows Guest Ranch. Travel along this dirt road for 43.3 miles to a fork in the road, with a sign pointing toward the Soldier Meadow Guest Ranch. Take the left fork, where you will immediately be met with a choice of three roads. Take the middle road (the least developed of the three choices). There will be some springs seeping onto the road, sometimes making it wet and muddy. Follow this road for approximately 0.6 mile (the road will cross another more major road), until you come to a small hill. Continue on the same road up and around this hill for another 0.3 mile until you spot the Soldier Meadows Hot Springs seeps on the other side. From Soldier Meadows Hot Springs, continue on the road, following the road around the other side of the creek formed by the hot spring seeps until it meets up with another road. Follow this road to the left for about 0.5 mile to a large parking and horse tie-up area adjacent to the warm pond. This road is usually wet in places, where the many hot seeps in the area flow across the road. Tread carefully.

The Hot Spring

The warm pond is approximately 30 by 30 feet and 5 feet deep in the deepest part. The water is approximately 95 degrees F, varying in temperature depending upon where you are in the pond. The Soldier Meadows area is geothermally active, and

Soldier Meadows Warm Pond

there are a number of hot springs near this warm pond. Aside from the other two springs described in this vicinity (Soldier Meadow Hot Springs and Hot Creek), the other springs offer limited bathing opportunities due to lack of depth or excessive temperatures. Camping is not permitted at this spot, and the local guest ranch asks that you camp at one of the many other hot springs in the area.

68 Soldier Meadows Hot Creek

General description: Similar in setting to Soldier Meadows Warm Pond and Hot Springs, this location offers several additional bathing opportunities, with quite a variance in temperatures. All three springs are only a few miles apart and can easily be visited in a day.

Location: Northwestern Nevada, approximately 165 miles northwest of Reno.

Primitive/developed: Primitive.

Best time of year: Spring and fall. Roads can be wet and muddy in winter, and summer can be hot.

Restrictions: None.

Access: High-clearance vehicle recommended for most of the year. During wet periods you may need four-wheel drive.

Water temperature: Varies with spring chosen and place in the creek, though generally around 105 degrees F.

Nearby attractions: High Rock Canyon (historic inscriptions), Black Rock Desert Playa, Summit Lake.

Soldier Meadows Hot Creek

Services: None; nearest gasoline, food, and lodging can be found in Gerlach, approximately 60 miles away.

Camping: Plenty of undeveloped space. Just remember to camp away from the springs themselves, and respect other people's privacy.

Map: USGS topographic, High Rock Canyon, NV, quadrangle, 1:100,000 scale.

Finding the spring: From Gerlach, proceed north through town on Nevada Highway 447. At the fork in the road out of town, take the road on the right, which is Washoe County Road 34. Proceed north for 12.2 miles to a dirt road on the right with signs to the Soldier Meadows Guest Ranch. Take this dirt road for approximately 43.3 miles to a fork in the road with another sign to the guest ranch. Take the left fork where you are immediately met with a choice of three roads. Take the road on the left, and follow it for 0.5 mile to a BLM sign indicating the road to High Rock Canyon and Lake. Bear left at this intersection and continue for approximately another 2 miles where you will take the road off to the right. Follow this less-developed road uphill for approximately 0.8 mile until you come to a small green valley where several hot springs form a pleasant creek.

The Hot Spring

The bright green oasis formed by the springs in this area is an abrupt change from the stark, drab colors of the surrounding desert. Several pools have been formed by individuals building dams in the creek, often where the hot water emerges from the ground. These pools vary in depth and temperature, ranging from 90 to 105 degrees F. Many of the springs offer the bonus of a kind of natural hydrotherapy as the hot creek water flows through the ponds. Located on BLM land, camping is permitted at the springs. Just be sure to camp a fair distance from the creek, pack out whatever you pack in, and do not wash dishes, or yourself, in the creek.

High Rock Canyon—a historic passageway: Along the Applegate-Lassen Trail, the Soldier Meadows region was undoubtedly a welcome campsite for weary emigrants. Between 1846 and the early 1860s, many pioneers traveled along the Lassen-Applegate Trail through this part of northern Nevada in hopes of reaching California. The pioneers left the main trail at the Humboldt River (at present-day Rye Patch Reservoir) and headed north toward the Black Rock Desert. Most of the trip was made without water and feed for the animals. The travelers found their first reliable water and grass at Black Rock Hot Springs, where there is about twenty acres of meadow. From there they went on to Mud Meadows, where the next water was found. After reaching Soldier Meadows, the trail went through Fly Canyon, down a wagon slide. Beyond the hot creek described above, the trail entered the narrow, perilous High Rock Canyon on its way to Massacre Lake and the Surprise Valley to points beyond in either Oregon (in the case of the Applegate Trail) or California (the Lassen Trail).

There are places where the trail is still visible today. Most notably, a few of the emigrants of the 1850s left behind a reminder of their passage on the walls of the great canyon. A traveler from Wisconsin left the most well-preserved inscription: "George N. Jaquith July The 16th 1852 from WIS." This historic graffiti can still be clearly read on the wall of High Rock Canyon. To reach High Rock Canyon, continue west on the secondary road past the turnoff for the hot creek, into the mountains. A BLM sign will point you the way once you reach High Rock Lake. The road through High Rock Canyon, however, is one of the most difficult roads described in this book, and it should only be tried by those familiar with off-road driving and with the proper vehicle. You will need substantial clearance, and I highly recommend having four-wheel drive. Prepare for the worst on this drive, bringing along plenty of provisions and notifying someone of your trip.

THE DENIO REGION

Close to the Black Rock Desert lies a region almost as geothermally active and closely related geologically. Perhaps even more remote than the Black Rock Desert area, the Denio region beckons the desert traveler. Services used to be available in Denio Junction, but the gas station, store, and hotel closed recently, and no services of any kind are available there anymore. Nearby Denio offers food but no gas. The nearest gas is in Fields, Oregon, 24 miles away. Keep this in mind when visiting the nearby hot springs.

The Denio region has changed little through time, the largest industry by far remaining cattle ranching. Most of the land in this area is managed by the Bureau of Land Management and is open to your enjoyment and exploration. The Denio region is slightly more watered than the Black Rock Desert region, and contains several small lakes in the mountains near the Oregon border. The main road through the area is Nevada Highway 140, which connects points in southern Oregon with U.S. Highway 95 and Winnemucca. The Sheldon National Wildlife Refuge borders the region on the west, offering an abundance of wildlife viewing. The region also contains the headwaters of several creeks and watersheds described in this book. The Quinn River, which eventually disappears on the Black Rock Desert Playa, emerges from the mountains east of Denio, draining a substantial portion of this region.

69 Baltazor Hot Spring

General description: A medium-size hot spring along with several seeps adjacent to a small homestead in an isolated part of Nevada. Limited bathing is provided, but the hot spring is located near another one that provides one of the best natural baths in the state (the Bog).

Location: Extreme northwestern Nevada, approximately 270 miles northeast of Reno.

Primitive/developed: Primitive.

Best time of year: Year-round.

Restrictions: None.

Access: Most passenger cars can make the trip.

Water temperature: Varies from 130 to 150 degrees F depending upon the spring. At the hottest portion of the largest source, temperatures up to 200 degrees F have been reported.

Nearby attractions: Sheldon National Wildlife Refuge.

Services: None; nearest gasoline, food, and lodging can be found in Fields, Oregon, approximately 30 miles away.

Camping: Plenty of undeveloped space at the spring. The spring is, however, immediately off the highway and offers little privacy.

Map: USGS topographic, Denio, NV, quadrangle, 1:100,000 scale.

Finding the spring: From the town of Denio Junction, travel west on Nevada Highway 140 for approximately 4.8 miles. On your left you will see an abandoned building and grassy field. Turn off the highway at the only road to the ruins, passing through a cattle gate (close it behind you), and continue 100 yards or so. Some of the smaller seeps can be found to the

Baltazor Hot Spring

left of the structure, where they eventually feed into the grassy fields. To reach the larger hot spring, follow a faint road past the ruins for approximately 0.4 mile to its end in a grassy field, where you will see the spring itself. Be careful not to drive into the spring! This road is a little rough, especially when wet, and is such a short distance that it can be walked if your vehicle can't handle it.

The Hot Spring

Located on the edge of a mostly dry lake, these hot springs at one time served to water grasses supporting large numbers of cattle. A small, hand-built home lies in partial ruins adjacent to the springs, and obviously used them for a variety of purposes. The larger of the two hot springs is extremely hot, approximately 181 degrees F. DO NOT GO IN! The water from this large spring does, however, flow out toward the grassy fields and can be diverted to cool for a bathing experience. The other smaller seeps are cooler and also flow toward the grassy field and could potentially be diverted for soaking. Just be careful because of the very hot water temperatures! In addition, please do not litter or damage, remove objects from, or otherwise vandalize the homestead at this location. The structure itself is most likely private property and will undoubtedly be fenced off if problems arise.

70 The Bog

General description: A fantastic hot pond formed by hot spring water flowing down a small creek.

Location: Extreme northwestern Nevada, approximately 260 miles northeast of Reno.

Primitive/developed: Primitive, except for the channelization of the creek.

Best time of year: Year-round.

Restrictions: None.

Access: Most passenger cars can make the trip.

Water temperature: Approximately 98 degrees F in the pond. The source is approximately 131 degrees F.

Nearby attractions: Sheldon National Wildlife Preserve.

Services: None; nearest gasoline, food, and lodging can be found in Fields, Oregon, approximately 38 miles away.

Camping: Plenty of undeveloped space. Just remember to camp away from the springs themselves, and respect other people's privacy.

Map: USGS topographic, Denio, NV, quadrangle, 1:100,000 scale.

Finding the spring: From the town of Denio Junction, travel west on Nevada Highway 140 for approximately 9.2 miles to a graded dirt road on your right, called Hot Bog Road. The dirt road will be immediately after you pass the edge of a hill, on the north side of the highway—you will not have much notice. Drive north for approximately 4.2 miles on the dirt road past a reservoir and ranch until you come to a secondary road on your left. Turn left (west) on this smaller road, and drive approximately 0.2 mile to the hot springs ditch and pond.

The Bog

The Hot Spring

The Bog was formed from the diversion of hot spring creek water into a channel, forming a small pond. The hot spring water originally rushed through a culvert from this channel into the pond, forming a Jacuzzi effect. The culvert is gone today, however. Different portions of the pond are different temperatures, though it's all around 98 degrees F. The pond ranges in depth from 2 to 4 feet, with a sandy and somewhat mossy bottom. You can park immediately adjacent to the pond itself; just be sure to leave no trash behind.

The spring has been used for over a century for the watering of stock and for supplying water for the growing of hay. The spring has also been utilized for domestic water usage and for mineral baths at the Bog Hot Springs Ranch, located downstream from the pond described here.

71 Bog Warm Spring

General description: A series of geothermal seeps upstream from the Bog.

Location: Extreme northwestern Nevada, approximately 260 miles northeast of Reno.

Primitive/developed: Primitive.

Best time of year: Year-round.

Restrictions: None.

Access: Most passenger cars can make the trip.

Water temperature: Varies from 90 to 110 degrees F.

Nearby attractions: Sheldon National Wildlife Preserve.

Services: None; nearest gasoline, food, and lodging can be found in Fields, Oregon, approximately 38 miles away.

Camping: Plenty. Just remember to camp away from the springs themselves, and respect other people's privacy.

Map: USGS topographic, Denio, NV, quadrangle, 1:100,000 scale.

Finding the spring: From the town of Denio Junction, travel west on Nevada Highway 140 for approximately 9.2 miles to a graded dirt road on your right, called Hot Bog Road. The dirt road will be immediately after you pass the edge of a hill, on the north side of the highway—you will not have much notice. Drive north for approximately 4.2 miles on the dirt road past a reservoir and ranch until you come a to a secondary road on your left. Turn left (west) on this smaller road, and drive approximately 0.2 mile to the Bog hot springs ditch and pond. From the wide parking area at the Bog, take a smaller dirt road to the north, or on your right (when facing the Bog). This road is a little rough, so those with passenger cars may opt to walk the short distance. Continue on this dirt road for approximately 0.5 mile, following the creek on the left. After 0.5 mile there will be numerous seeps of hot water in the creek, though there will be few pools.

The Hot Spring

These warm and hot springs are the source for the Bog downstream, though they vary widely in temperature. Explore this area to find the temperature you desire. As always, be extremely careful, and test the water before getting in. You may also

Bog Warm Spring

need to be creative in your choice of bathing spots, as there are no well-defined pools. Most of the water flows down the creek in a wide, shallow channel, but portions of it are the perfect temperature. If you are really ambitious, you may want to make a small dam for this water and create a makeshift pond. These springs offer the advantage of more privacy if the Bog is occupied.

72 Virgin Valley Hot Spring

General description: A man-made pool fed by natural hot spring water at a relatively popular campground in an isolated part of northern Nevada.

Location: Northwestern Nevada, approximately 250 miles northeast of Reno.

Primitive/developed: Minimally developed, utilizing natural hot spring water.

Best time of year: Year-round.

Restrictions: Bathing suits are required, and camping is not allowed within 50 feet of the warm pond.

Access: Most passenger cars can make the trip.

Water temperature: Varies within the pond, though averages 90 degrees F.

Nearby attractions: Sheldon National Wildlife Preserve.

Services: None; nearest gasoline, food, and lodging can be found in Fields, Oregon, approximately 50 miles away.

Camping: There is a state campground at the spring where camping is free. The campground has plenty of space, pit toilets, and a beautiful location. Camping is not permitted within 50 feet of the warm pond.

Map: USGS topographic, Virgin Valley, NV, quadrangle, 1: 24,000 scale.

Finding the spring: From the town of Denio Junction, travel west on Nevada Highway 140 for 25 miles. Turn left at the sign to Virgin Valley and the Royal Peacock Mine. Travel on this graded dirt road for approximately 2.7 miles to the campground where the warm pond is located.

The Hot Spring

The campground at Virgin Valley is a popular destination for outdoor enthusiasts in northern Nevada. Unless you are here on a weekday in the off-season, don't expect to have the place to yourself. A couple of old buildings, one a bathhouse, remain adjacent to the spring but are closed to public use today. The warm pond is approximately 30 by 30 feet and has a nice sandy bottom. The temperature hovers around 85 to 90 degrees F depending on the time of year. A recently added stone patio and small step ladder make access into the pond easier. This pond serves as a welcome oasis to those traveling in the desert backcountry for extended periods, and makes for an excellent stopover. I recommend also visiting the Bog, Bog Warm Spring, and Baltazor Hot Spring if you are in this area.

Virgin Valley Hot Spring

For those who are bird-watchers, the Sheldon Preserve offers an abundance of wildlife. The ponds you pass on your way to the campground are generally full of birdlife, often with a wide variety of species. In addition, the canyons south of the campground also contain reliable water sources and generally support a variety of birds and other animals.

73 Dyke Hot Springs

General description: An interesting series of hot spring sources flowing into a large warm pond in an isolated portion of northern Nevada. The hot spring water has been diverted into an old bathtub in one place, offering a very hot bath to those willing to partake.

Location: In northwestern Nevada, approximately 80 miles northwest of Winnemucca.

Primitive/developed: Only slightly developed, as a bathtub has been brought in and the pond was formed by a bulldozer.

Best time of year: Year-round.

Restrictions: None.

Access: Most passenger cars can make the trip. The roads can become muddy in wet weather, and four-wheel drive may be necessary in the winter.

Water temperature: 150 degrees F at the source, approximately 115 degrees F in the hot tub, and 80 degrees F in the pond.

Nearby attractions: Black Rock Desert Playa, Summit Lake.

Services: None; nearest gasoline, food, and lodging can be found in Fields, Oregon, approximately 60 miles away.

Camping: Plenty of undeveloped space.

Map: USGS topographic, Jackson Mountain, NV, quadrangle, 1:100,000 scale.

Finding the springs: From Denio Junction, travel south on Nevada Highway 140 for approximately 26 miles. Turn right onto Big Creek Road, which is a well-maintained graded road. Travel approximately 6.5 miles until the road dead-ends at Woodward Road. This is also a fairly well-maintained road, but can become slippery in wet weather. Turn left here and drive past a ranch at about 2 miles, continuing for another 1.8 miles to a faint road on the left. Turn here and drive approximately 100 yards to the pond formed by the hot springs. The hot springs themselves are immediately off the main road and form a small ravine leading to the pond. The bathtub is in the ravine.

The Hot Springs

Although located on the northern margins of the Black Rock Desert, Dyke Hot Springs is much easier to reach from the Denio region and is therefore placed in this section. The springs emerging from the ground adjacent to the road are extremely hot. From the sources this water flows down two separate ravines. When facing the springs from the road, the bathtub is in the ravine on your left. It is hidden from the road and requires a little bit of searching to find. The hot water in this tub can be very hot. To get the right temperature, divert some water into the tub with the pipe provided, and wait for it to cool down to your desired temperature. The other ravine has few soaking opportunities, as the water is too hot and has not been diverted or dammed up in any place. Both of these ravines flow into a man-made pond used by cattle. This pond is rather murky and not very appeal-

Dyke Hot Springs

ing for swimming. It does have thousands of frogs, which you will undoubtedly hear when you approach the pond. Again, as always, keep your car on established roads, and pack out all your trash.

Short history of the Quinn River region: It was somewhere in this northern portion of the Black Rock Desert where one of the long-standing mysteries of the region took place. Well-known settler Peter Lassen (for whom Mount Lassen and the Lassen Trail were named) and another man in his party were killed in this area in the spring of 1858. One of his party escaped after being wounded, but because the attack was carried out at night, no one to this day is sure who killed Lassen. Some suspect that it was the hostile Pitt River Indians, while others claim that it was the work of white men.

Another famous man, this time Indian, also gained fame in this region. "Black Rock Tom," a Northern Paiute, was well-known for his exploits in raiding and attacking white settlements. Black Rock Tom's white horse was of equal fame: "All hunters of Indians, who came to an engagement anywhere between this and Owyhee, and almost all parties attacked on that road, during the past season, remarked, a white horse of extraordinary qualities, the rider of which seemed to take great pride in his efforts to witch the world with noble horsemanship. The white horse was ever spoken of as a wonder of strength and fleetness. His rider, a stalwart Indian, delighted to dally just out of musket range from the white men, caricoling most provokingly, and darting off, occasionally, with the fleetness of the wind" (Wheeler, Sessions, *The Nevada Desert.* Caldwell, ID: Caxton Printers, 1982). The rider was Black Rock Tom. During renewed hostilities in the mid-1860s, Black Rock Tom was involved in attacks throughout northern Nevada.

After several raids throughout the Black Rock Desert and Quinn River areas during 1865, several reports of a white horse again surfaced. In September an Indian camp was attacked, and some reported seeing that "one horse, which had often before attracted notice, was again conspicuous on this occasion—a white animal that defied all efforts to approach his rider."

One of Black Rock Tom's more well-known attacks was on the road between the Black Rock Desert and Rabbithole Spring. Following this gruesome attack, a party of forty-six soldiers, four volunteer citizens, and eight Paiute guides went after Black Rock Tom's band. During the ensuing battle, which took place in the Black Rock Desert, Tom's band was almost completely annihilated (see the Paradise Valley War of 1865 in the next section, Paradise Valley Hot Spring). Black Rock Tom, however, managed to escape. Later the next year, however, Tom met his death in the area of the Humboldt Sink (near present-day Lovelock).

Evidence of prehistoric inhabitants also abounds in this part of the Black Rock Desert. As with other artifacts, these are protected by federal laws and must only be enjoyed in place, not removed. The artifacts described here were most likely made by the Northern Paiute people who lived in this area from approximately A.D. 1400. Archaeological studies and ethnographic information indicate that the first inhabitants of this region were supplanted by the Northern Paiutes about 500 years ago. The original inhabitants, who may have been here as far back as 9500 B.C., are termed the Lovelock Culture by archaeologists. These people also left clues to their habitation, with fish traps, petroglyphs, habitation sites, and other artifacts. John Charles Fremont indicates seeing "poor looking Indians" who lived in caves on the east side of Pyramid Lake, unrelated to the Northern Paiutes. Several oral histories conducted with Northern Paiutes also describe another group of Indians living in the Pyramid and Winnemucca Lake area who were not related to the current inhabitants. These people may have represented this earlier culture.

NORTH-CENTRAL NEVADA

The region bounded by portions of the Humboldt National Forest on the east and west is often referred to as the Owyhee, after the rivers that drain the area. For the sake of organization, this section of the book will also include those hot springs adjacent to Interstate 80 in the central part of the state. Most of the area included in this section served as ranching country, supporting nearby mining towns. Paradise Valley, for example, grew up solely as a food supplier to the mining town of Unionville to the south. As with other portions of northern Nevada, this region is wide-open country with thousands of acres to explore. The vast majority of the land is operated by the Bureau of Land Management, and there are few towns of any size. Although north-central Nevada has seen considerably more mining than previous regions described, ranching still remains a dominant activity. Access is slightly easier with I–80 bordering the region to the south, providing an east–west corridor to Reno and Elko. All manner of services can be located in Winnemucca and Battle Mountain, but come prepared if you plan on venturing far from the interstate.

Stony Point Hot Springs

PARADISE VALLEY AREA

74 Paradise Valley Hot Spring (Little Humboldt)

General description: A large travertine-lined pit with extremely hot water, diverted and cooled off into a plastic tub on the bank of the Little Humboldt River. A wonderful bathing opportunity awaits, if the water in the tub is allowed to cool off.

Location: Northern Nevada, approximately 50 miles northeast of Winnemucca.

Primitive/developed: Primitive, except for the diversion of water to the plastic tub.

Best time of year: Year-round.

Restrictions: None.

Access: Most passenger cars can make the trip.

Water temperature: 130 degrees F at the source, 115 degrees F in the tub.

Nearby attractions: Historic town of Paradise Valley, Chimney Dam Reservoir.

Services: None; nearest gasoline, food, and lodging can be found in Winnemucca, approximately 50 miles away. Some services can be found in Paradise Valley, 18 miles away, but don't count on getting supplies in this small farming and ranching center.

Camping: This is private property, but it is unclear as to whether camping is permitted or not at the spring. There is plenty of undeveloped space in the immediate vicinity, however.

Map: USGS topographic, Osgood Mountains, NV, quadrangle, 1:100,000 scale.

Finding the spring: From Winnemucca, travel north on U.S. Highway 95 for 22 miles. Turn onto Nevada Highway 290 northeast for 18 miles to the town of Paradise Valley. Drive through town and turn right (east) after the small market, following signs to Chimney Reservoir. Drive on this graded dirt road for approximately 10.6 miles (keeping right at a Y in the road), where you will turn right onto a smaller dirt road with a cattle gate across it. Open the cattle gate, drive through it, and close the gate behind you. Drive on this small dirt road for 0.2 mile to the spring.

The Hot Spring

A large hot spring source emerging from travertine-surrounded ground is diverted at 130 degrees F into a plastic tub. Do not go in the source! Also, check the water temperature in the plastic tub before getting in, as it can often be extremely hot. This hot spring is on private property, so please respect all signs, be sure to remove all trash, and generally leave no trace. The town of Paradise Valley is an interesting remnant of old Nevada, preserved well in several cases. The Chimney Dam Reservoir, east down the road from the hot spring, also provides many recreational opportunities. To reach the reservoir, stay on the graded dirt road, past the turn for the hot spring, for a few short miles.

The Paradise Valley War of 1865: The troubles between the Northern Paiute Indians and white settlers did not end with the conclusion of the Pyramid Lake War. Following several small, isolated conflicts, a band of Paiutes who frequented the Smoke Creek Desert (north of Pyramid Lake), led by "Smoke Creek Sam," wreaked havoc on many of the white settlements in the general area. Stage stations

Paradise Valley Hot Spring (Little Humboldt)

throughout the area and a few individual homesteads were attacked, with several whites losing their lives. In 1865, in response to these attacks, Captain A. B. Wells, heading fifty men of the Nevada Volunteers, marched to Winnemucca Lake to take revenge. A large group of Northern Paiutes was indeed camping on the shores of the shallow lake, and Wells attacked. The Indians, however, were not from the Smoke Creek band, but were instead Numaga's people, who had not taken part in any of the recent attacks. Many of the killed were reported to be women, children, and the elderly. The actual makeup of the camp is still being debated today, and no one is quite sure who these Nevada Volunteers fought in March of 1865.

In response to this massacre and a few other attacks, a Paiute war party took its revenge on the Granite Creek Station, north of present-day Gerlach. The station, whose remains can still be seen today, was burned and its inhabitants killed and mutilated. Following this attack, bands of Paiutes, along with allies from the Bannock and Shoshone tribes, continued attacking white outposts in the country. Many of these attacks were directed at settlers in the Paradise Valley region, which by this time already boasted a fair-size town. The attacks were so severe that an improvised fort was constructed at one of the ranches, behind which over seventy settlers took cover. A halfhearted attack was made by the Indians on this fort, but with little effect. The commander of federal troops in Nevada, Colonel Charles McDermitt, sent more than a hundred troops, led by Captain Wells, to the Paradise Valley region. Despite several attempts, these troops were largely ineffective, and the Paiutes held a reign of terror over a vast territory. The Indians attacked whites from south of the Humboldt River, near Unionville, to as far north as the Quinn and Little Humboldt Rivers. The vastly important overland route to California passed along the Humboldt River (present-day Interstate 80) and was in danger of being closed down because of these Indian attacks. Colonel McDermitt himself, in fact, was killed by an Indian war party in August of 1865.

A friendly band of Paiutes, living at the mining town of Unionville, decided to help the whites in their war against the hostile Indians. It was under this competent guidance that the federal troops were finally able to put an end to the hostilities. The most warlike of the bands were brought to battle in the Black Rock Desert region and put to flight after a sound defeat. The last hostile band, that of Black Rock Tom's, was also later subdued (see Short history of the Quinn River region in Dyke Hot Springs).

The following hot springs are all located in the heart of these conflicts, and were themselves utilized by Indians and whites alike for campsites and temporary settlements.

75 Midas Hot Spring

General description: A completely natural hot spring pool in an uninhabited part of northern Nevada.

Location: Northern Nevada, approximately 70 miles northeast of Winnemucca.

Primitive/developed: Primitive.

Best time of year: Spring, summer, and, fall. Roads can be muddy in winter.

Restrictions: None.

Access: High-clearance vehicle recommended. Some sturdier passenger cars and vans should also have no problems. Four-wheel drive may be needed in wet weather.

Water temperature: 105 degrees F at the source, a little cooler in the pool itself.

Nearby attractions: Historic mining towns of Midas and Tuscarora, Willow Creek Reservoir.

Services: None; nearest gasoline, food, and lodging can be found in Winnemucca, approximately 70 miles away. Some services (gas and food) can be found in Golconda, approximately 60 miles away.

Camping: There does not appear to be any restrictions against camping near the spring, though this will definitely be undeveloped camping.

Map: USGS topographic, Tuscarora, NV, quadrangle, 1:100,000 scale.

Finding the spring: From Winnemucca, travel east on Interstate 80 for approximately 16 miles to the town of Golconda. In Golconda, take Nevada Highway 789 (paved) for approximately 15.3 miles to where the highway turns to dirt. Follow the main road with signs leading to Midas (the middle road in the three-way split). Travel another 27.5 miles to the turnoff for the town of Midas. If you want to visit this interesting partial ghost town, turn left here. Continue straight on the main road to get to the hot spring. Continue for another 4 miles on the main road until you run into a road on your left with signs pointing to Rock Creek. Turn left (north) here and travel 3.6 miles on this less-developed dirt road to another dirt road on your right with a sign indicating Rock Creek. Turn right (east) here and travel another 3.6 miles until you reach the hot spring on your right.

Midas Hot Spring

The Hot Spring

A totally natural hot spring pond, Midas has not had any damming or reinforcement of the source, and none are necessary for bathing purposes. Unnamed on the topographic map, this spring is located in high-desert grazing country far from civilization. The hot water bubbles up through sand into a small pond approximately 5 by 5 feet and about 5 feet deep. The water is a warm 100 degrees F, pleasant on a cool day but perhaps not quite warm enough on a cold winter day. The water from the spring overflows onto a small plain, where cattle drink it. The area has the distinct imprint of cattle, but before the cattle came, this spring was obviously used by Native Americans as a small campsite. The spring may have been used as a stopover place, or it may have been a temporary village site. Evidence for this prehistoric occupation can be readily seen around the spring. As always, leave any artifacts where you find them.

An interesting side trip can be made to the partial ghost town of Midas. Several houses have been built in the canyon below the site of the mines themselves, many with year-round residents. Further up the canyon, well-preserved remains of many of Midas's mines can be found immediately off the road. Ore carts, tracks, a mill, and several outbuildings lie largely untouched in this historic canyon. Although mining has continued in adjacent areas, the Midas mines are completely abandoned today. This is one of the best ghost towns in this part of the state, and it deserves a visit. Please respect these remains by not disturbing any of them and leaving everything how you found it. In addition, respect the privacy of the home owners in the canyon by not trespassing, obeying all signs, and keeping quiet near the houses.

The equally interesting, and larger, partial ghost town of Tuscarora is located east of Midas, along the main road from Golconda. Discovered in 1867, with its largest production in the late 1870s, Tuscarora was typical of Nevada mining camps. Remains of several old buildings, a large smokestack, and a plethora of mining artifacts exist at this small town. Tuscarora currently has a post office and a few year-round residents. To reach the town, drive east on the main graded dirt road you took from NV 789, past the turnoffs for Midas and Midas Hot Spring. Follow the signs to Willow Creek Reservoir, and stay on the main road past the reservoir for over 20 miles, following the signs to Tuscarora.

76 Stony Point Hot Springs

General description: Several hot springs flowing into a pond in Rock Creek, near its confluence with the Humboldt River. Though no bathing opportunities exist here, wildlife is abundant, as is history in the form of the California Trail.

Location: North-central Nevada, approximately 12 miles north of Battle Mountain.

Primitive/developed: Primitive.

Best time of year: Spring, summer, and fall. Roads can be muddy in the winter.

Restrictions: None; just stay on established roads, and obey all NO TRESPASSING signs.

Access: The springs are located along a fairly well-maintained, graded dirt road. Sturdier passenger cars can make the trip. During wet weather, four-wheel drive may be necessary.

Water temperature: 122 degrees F at the source, but the hot water quickly mixes with water from Rock Creek, cooling considerably.

Nearby attractions: Tuscarora.

Services: None; nearest gasoline, food, and lodging can be found in Battle Mountain, approximately 12 miles away.

Camping: There does not appear to be any restrictions against camping near the spring, although there aren't any campgrounds, nor are there any really good places.

Map: USGS topographic, Battle Mountain, NV, quadrangle, 1:100,000 scale.

Finding the springs: In the town of Battle Mountain (off Interstate 80 at exit 229), follow Front Street (the main road through town) to Reese Street. Turn north on Reese Street, crossing the railroad tracks. Stay on this paved road for approximately 10 miles to another set of railroad tracks, which you will cross. On the other side of the tracks, make an immediate right turn on another paved road. This road becomes a graded dirt road soon thereafter. Follow this road for approximately 4.5 miles past a few industrial facilities. The road will wind around these facilities; just stay on the main road. Follow the signs to the Dyno facility, and when you get to the fence of this large facility, look for a small sign for the California Trail. Follow this dirt road as it winds its way between the facility and the railroad tracks. Travel for another 1.6 miles along this dirt road after passing through the facility. At this point, look for a small California Trail marker (a small section of railroad track on a post with a little plaque on it). Park your car here, off of the dirt road, and cross the railroad tracks. The hot springs are on the other side of the tracks, feeding a large pond in Rock Creek.

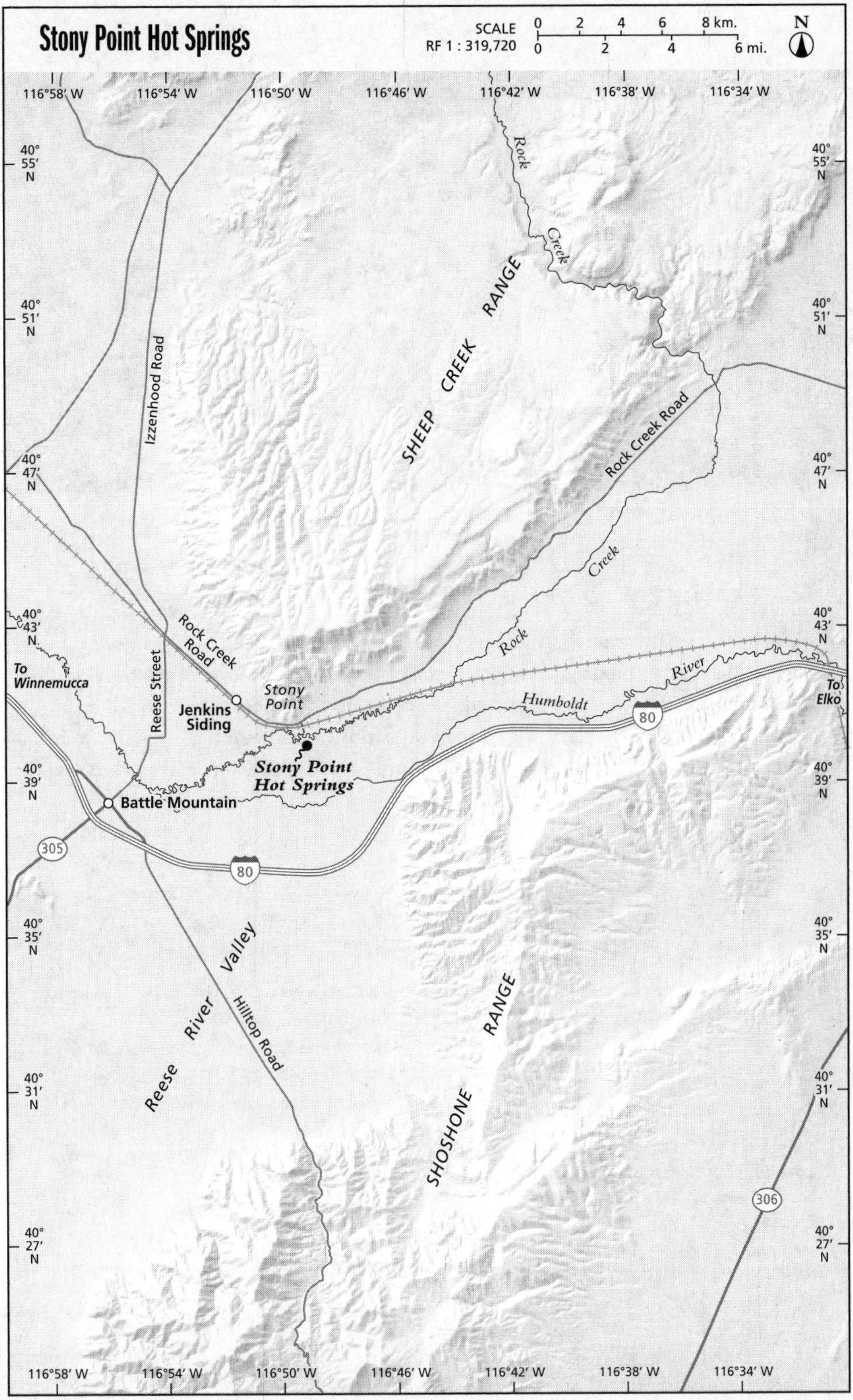

Stony Point Hot Springs
SCALE
RF 1 : 319,720
0 2 4 6 8 km.
0 2 4 6 mi.
N
116°58′ W
116°54′ W
116°50′ W
116°46′ W
116°42′ W
116°38′ W
116°34′ W
40° 55′ N
40° 51′ N
40° 47′ N
40° 43′ N
40° 39′ N
40° 35′ N
40° 31′ N
40° 27′ N
Rock Creek
SHEEP CREEK RANGE
Izzenhood Road
Rock Creek Road
Rock Creek
Rock Creek Road
Reese Street
To Winnemucca
Jenkins Siding
Stony Point
Stony Point Hot Springs
Humboldt River
80
To Elko
Battle Mountain
305
Reese River Valley
Hilltop Road
SHOSHONE RANGE
306

Stony Point Hot Springs

The Hot Springs

Named for the large rocky prominence nearby, Stony Point Hot Springs were described by many pioneers along this part of the California Trail. They provide a substantial amount of water that feeds an idyllic pond in Rock Creek. Wildlife abounds, particularly waterfowl. Though no bathing opportunities exist, this is an interesting and not heavily visited area. The water in this otherwise dry desert will surprise you when you first arrive.

77 Greenhorn (Hot Sulphur, Dry Susie) Hot Springs

General description: Several hot springs flowing out of a small hillside in a dry portion of north-central Nevada. Though currently too hot for bathing, this could change with a little work. Located a few miles off the interstate, the springs are a little tricky to find but worth a visit when in the area.

Location: North-central Nevada, approximately 5 miles north of Carlin and 28 miles east of Elko.

Primitive/developed: Primitive, except for the diversion of water to the plastic tub.

Best time of year: Fall and spring. Summer can be hot, and roads can be muddy in winter.

Restrictions: None; just stay on established roads, and close cattle gates behind you.

Access: High-clearance vehicle recommended, though sturdier passenger cars can make the trip. During wet weather four-wheel drive may be necessary.

Water temperature: 147 degrees F at the source, 110 degrees F or more in the tub.

Nearby attractions: Elko, Tuscarora.

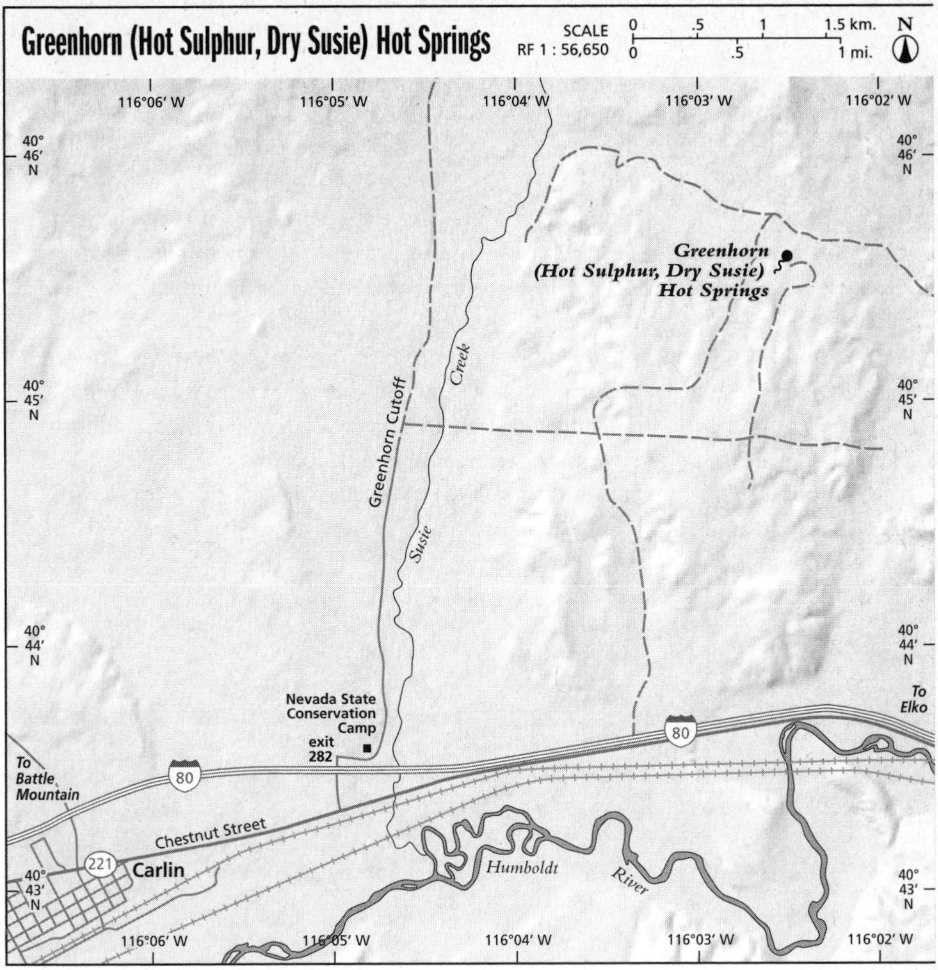

Services: None; nearest gasoline, food, and lodging can be found in Carlin, approximately 5 miles away. The larger town of Elko is about 28 miles away, with several hotels, casinos, gasoline, and food.

Camping: There do not appear to be any restrictions against camping near the springs. This will again be undeveloped camping. Just remember to stay on established roads, and close all cattle gates.

Maps: USGS topographic, Battle Mountain, NV, quadrangle, 1:100,000 scale; Huntsman Ranch, 1: 24,000 scale.

Finding the springs: From Carlin, travel east on Interstate 80 to exit 282, East Carlin. Exit the freeway and head north (crossing the freeway if you are coming from the west). Shortly after crossing over the freeway, turn right immediately before the Nevada State Conservation Camp. Follow this gravel and old paved road as it curves around to the left, staying on it for approximately 1.6 miles. Turn right on a smaller dirt road that follows a buried pipeline. Drive on this dirt road, crossing through a small creek, for approximately 1.5 miles up and over a few hills to the top of another hill, where you will come to a four-way intersection. Turn left here and follow this small dirt road for 0.8 mile to a fence that encompasses the hot springs. Follow the fence line to the right for about 0.5 mile to a gate in the fence. Go through the gate (closing it behind you), and drive a short distance to the springs themselves.

The Hot Springs

Set in dry cattle-grazing country, Greenhorn Hot Springs, also known as Dry Susie (for the nearby creek) and Hot Sulphur, provide a welcome source of vibrant color to the area. There are several springs, but only one has been diverted down the hill into a plastic tub, or watering trough. People have attempted different methods of trapping the water, most of which have failed. Currently the only tub that holds water is too hot for bathing in. Another tub was broken apart recently. There could easily be bathing opportunities here in the future, however.

While not the best bathing opportunity in the book, Greenhorn Hot Springs is a good diversion from a trip along I–80. The hot springs are also located on one of several cutoffs from the California Trail. This one was known as the Greenhorn Cutoff, as it ended up taking many more miles than the original. This particular segment of the Greenhorn Cutoff was known as the Dry Susie fork, for the largely dry creek that runs through the area.

REGION SOUTH OF INTERSTATE 80

Another largely empty portion of the state, the land immediately south of Interstate 80, in the central portion of Nevada, provides ample exploration opportunities. The region is also largely controlled by the Bureau of Land Management, but has a higher percentage of mines than the regions previously described. All of the hot springs described in this subregion are located on the floors of the valleys, between the high mountain ranges. For this reason most are relatively easy to access with a standard vehicle. These hot springs are also located in primarily dry settings, and their waters often give an oasis-like feel to the area. Because of their dry settings, these springs are often used in the watering of stock. In most cases the cattle have been kept out of the springs' sources, maintaining their relatively pristine character. Although the towns of Winnemucca and Battle Mountain are close to some of these springs, they are all still relatively isolated. A private experience can generally be had, but travelers are warned to come prepared. High clearance is recommended, and as always, let someone know where you're going and when you're expected back.

78 Hand-Me-Down Creek Hot Springs

General description: A single hot spring feeding a watering trough that provides for a very nice hot bath in the Crescent Valley.

Location: North-central Nevada, approximately 5 miles east of Crescent Valley and 48 miles southeast of Battle Mountain.

Primitive/developed: Primitive.

Best time of year: Year-round. Summer can be hot, however. The road to the springs may be difficult to impassable in wet weather.

Restrictions: Signs indicate that the hot springs are on Native American reservation land, with particular spiritual significance. Please respect this by obeying all posted signs.

Access: A high-clearance vehicle is recommended for the last mile. Four-wheel drive will be needed in wet weather.

Water temperature: 186 degrees F at the source, cooling off to about 104 degrees F in the watering trough/bathing location.

Nearby attractions: Ghost towns of Tenabo, Gold Acres, and Cortez.

Services: None; nearest gasoline, food, and lodging can be found in Battle Mountain, approximately 48 miles away.

Camping: There does not appear to be any restrictions against camping near the springs. Keep in mind that the springs are right off the road and adjacent to private property and residences, so this may not be the best place to camp. There are no developed campgrounds in the area, but plenty of public land in the surrounding vicinity. Just be sure to obey any NO TRESPASSING signs.

Maps: USGS topographic, Crescent Valley, NV, quadrangle, 1:100,000 scale; Hand-Me-Down Creek, 1:24,000 scale.

Finding the springs: From Battle Mountain, travel east on Interstate 80 for 30 miles to Nevada Highway 306. Turn south onto NV 306 and travel approximately 18.2 miles (passing through the hamlet of Beowawe). Turn left (east) on McDaniel Street, which is a paved road but soon turns to a graded dirt road. Travel on McDaniel Street for approximately 3.8 miles, bearing right on the main road. You will pass a couple of houses. From the bend, continue 6.9 miles, where you bear right. Go another 0.4 mile to a four-way intersection. Turn left here, crossing over a cattle guard (this is about 7.2 miles from the bend in the road, or 11 miles from NV 306). Travel on this graded dirt road for 1.3 miles, and look for a small dirt road on your right, just before you reach a ranch. Turn right on this small dirt road, and go approximately 1.1 miles to a gate with a sign asking you to respect this area. Go through the gate (closing it behind you), and the hot springs are visible on the other side of the gulch. You can park right next to it.

The Hot Springs

Set in a beautiful location, Hand-Me-Down Creek Hot Springs provide for a wonderful soak as well as view. The spring itself is quite hot (186 degrees F at the source), but the water is diverted into a watering trough where it is cool enough for a nice bath. Water in the trough is roughly 104 degrees F. The road to the springs is normally pretty good, but it can be difficult in wet weather. Please respect the wishes of the posted signs, as this is a place of spiritual significance to the local Native Americans.

Cortez, Tenabo, and Gold Acres: Crescent Valley, as is plain to the traveler, is cattle country and has been for over a century, its products serving the mining communities in the surrounding areas. The trio of ghost towns Cortez, Tenabo, and Gold Acres, which at one time were supplied by Crescent Valley, make an interesting side trip. Each were gold-mining towns originally, but quickly declined like so many other boom towns in Nevada. Mining has recently been undertaken

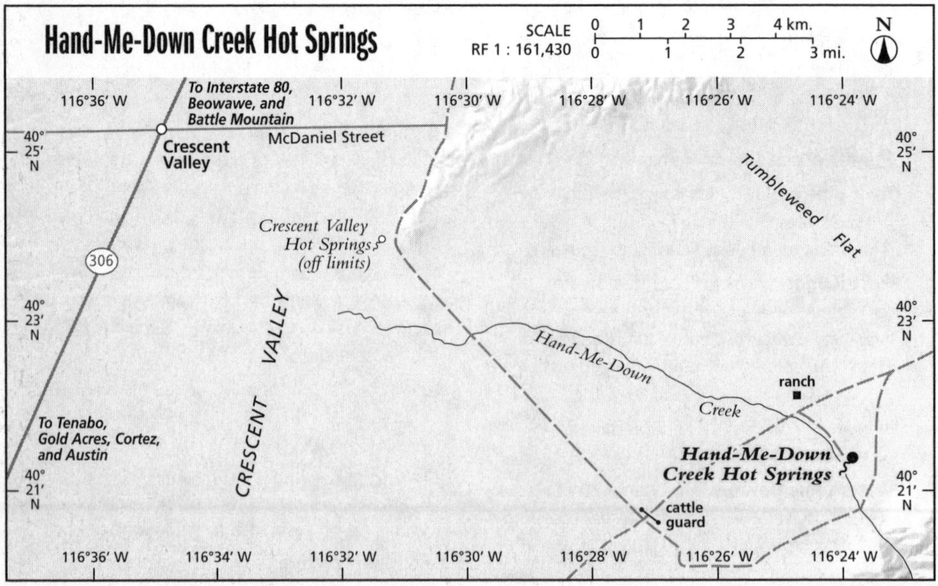

Hand-Me-Down Creek Hot Springs

again in the area (particularly at Gold Acres), and a few people live in and around the old town sites. To reach Cortez, simply continue south on NV 306 out of Crescent Valley, staying on the main road as it enters the mountains. There will generally be a sign for this town on the road, though vandals have been known to remove it or damage it sufficiently so that it cannot be read. To reach Tenabo and Gold Acres, follow NV 306 south out of Crescent Valley, turning right approximately 6 miles out of town. This road should also be marked with a sign to Tenabo and Gold Acres, but occasionally it is also missing.

79 Reese River Valley Hot Springs (North)

General description: A large hot spring source emanating from a small travertine hill, diverted to a makeshift pond, perfect for a hot bath. Located adjacent to an abandoned farmstead in an isolated part of northern Nevada, it is also known as Hot Springs Ranch.

Location: North-central Nevada, approximately 35 miles south of Battle Mountain and 53 miles north of Austin.

Primitive/developed: Primitive, except for the diversion of water to the concrete-lined pond.

Best time of year: Fall, winter, and spring. Summer can hot.

Restrictions: None; just close all cattle gates.

Access: Most passenger cars can make the trip.

Water temperature: 130 degrees F at the source, 100 degrees F in the pond.

Nearby attractions: Historic town of Austin.

Services: None; nearest gasoline, food, and lodging can be found in Battle Mountain, approximately 35 miles away to the north, or in Austin, 53 miles to the south.

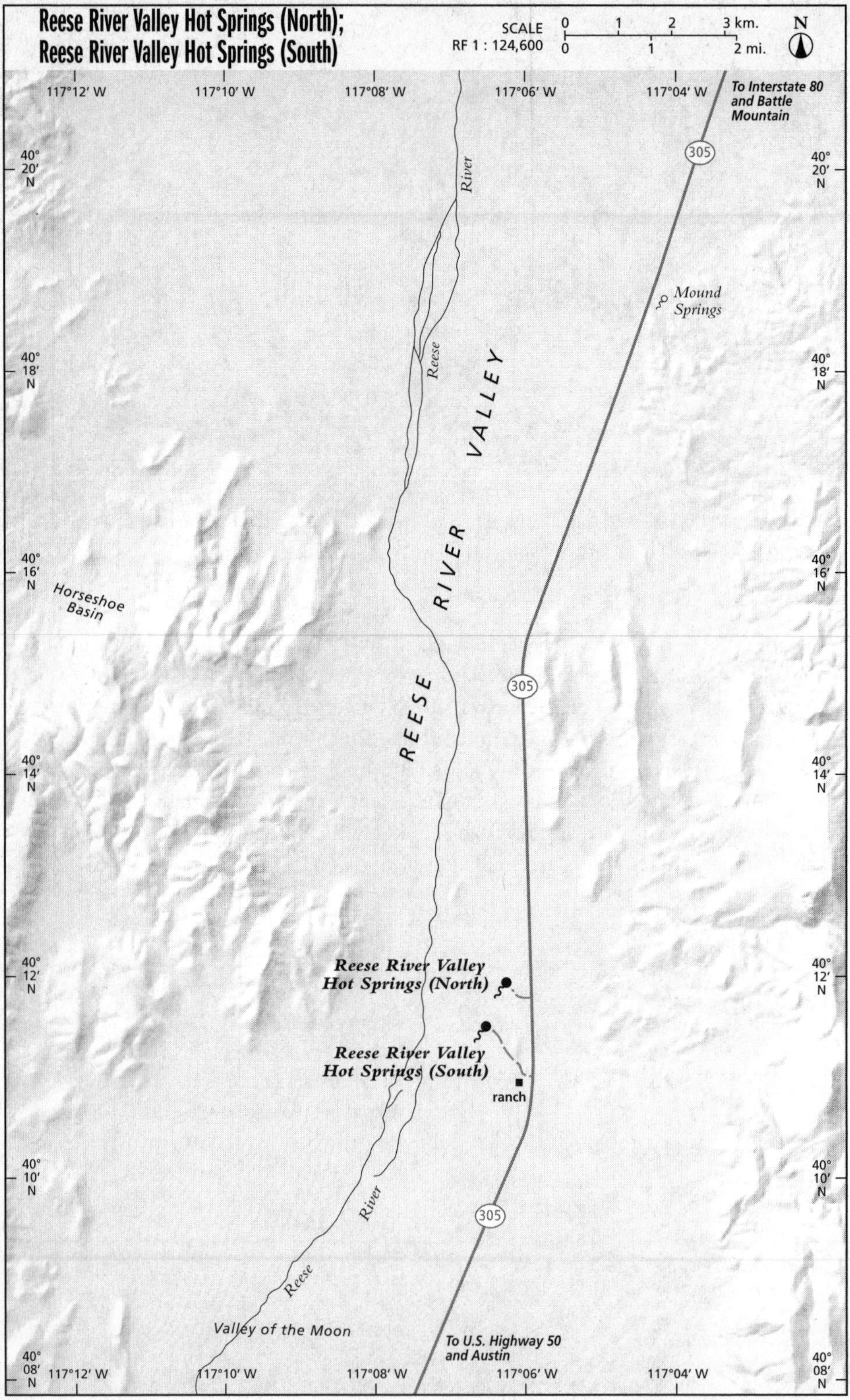

Reese River Valley Hot Springs (North);
Reese River Valley Hot Springs (South)
SCALE
RF 1 : 124,600
0 1 2 3 km.
0 1 2 mi.
N
117°12′ W
117°10′ W
117°08′ W
117°06′ W
117°04′ W
To Interstate 80 and Battle Mountain
305
40° 20′ N
40° 18′ N
40° 16′ N
40° 14′ N
40° 12′ N
40° 10′ N
40° 08′ N
River
Mound Springs
Reese
REESE RIVER VALLEY
Horseshoe Basin
Reese River Valley Hot Springs (North)
Reese River Valley Hot Springs (South)
ranch
Valley of the Moon
To U.S. Highway 50 and Austin

Reese River Valley Hot Springs (North)

Camping: There does not appear to be any restrictions against camping at the site. The hot springs, however, are close to the highway and may not be the most serene camping spot. There are no developed camping sites in the immediate area.

Map: USGS topographic, Fish Creek Mountains, NV, quadrangle, 1:100,000 scale.

Finding the springs: From Battle Mountain, travel south out of town on Nevada Highway 305 for approximately 35 miles. Keep an eye out for a small road on your right with a cattle gate. Turn right (west) onto this road (close the cattle gate behind you), and keep right at a Y in the road. Drive approximately 0.25 mile to the spring.

The Hot Springs

Located in the dry Reese River Valley, the hot spring is a half-hour drive from Battle Mountain and a little more than an hour from Austin. The general area is dotted with abandoned farmsteads, though most of the country is still used for growing alfalfa and raising cattle. Although there are several other hot spring sources to the south, the most productive is on a small hillside comprised almost completely of travertine. There is a small pond from which the hot water emerges at approximately 130 degrees F (far too hot to bathe in). The water is clear and gives off a turquoise color. This hot water flows down a narrow travertine-lined creek, and some of it is diverted into a concrete-lined pond, which makes for a great bath. Water temperature in the pond is approximately 102 degrees F. Be very careful, as the bottom can be quite slippery. The bathing pond is enclosed by a fence, keeping the cattle out. Be sure to close the gate behind you when you leave.

Although close to the road, the spring does not appear to be heavily visited, and little trash has been left behind. The other springs in the area are much smaller and are pretty much seeps, with no pools to speak of. Like so many other springs listed in this part of Nevada, the Reese River Hot Springs are located in a broad and scenic valley between two prominent ridges.

80 Reese River Valley Hot Springs (South)

See map on page 182.

General description: A series of hot springs located immediately south of the springs described above. Although fewer bathing opportunities exist here, these springs are worth visiting while at those located a short distance to the north.

Location: North-central Nevada, approximately 35 miles south of Battle Mountain and 53 miles north of Austin.

Primitive/developed: Primitive; there has been no diversion of hot water for bathing.

Best time of year: Fall, winter, and spring. Summer can hot.

Restrictions: None; just close all cattle gates.

Access: Most passenger cars can make the trip.

Water temperature: Varies, though most springs are in the 110 degrees F range.

Nearby attractions: Historic town of Austin.

Building at Reese River Valley Hot Springs (South)

Services: None; nearest gasoline, food, and lodging can be found in Battle Mountain, approximately 35 miles away to the north, or in Austin, 53 miles to the south.

Camping: There does not appear to be any restrictions against camping at the site. The hot springs, however, are close to the highway and may not be the most serene camping spot. There are no developed camping sites in the immediate area.

Map: USGS topographic, Fish Creek Mountains, NV, quadrangle, 1:100,000 scale.

Finding the springs: From Battle Mountain, travel south on Nevada Highway 305 for approximately 36 miles past a small dirt road for Reese River Valley Hot Springs (North). Turn right on a small dirt road to an abandoned homestead and ranch. Keep right on this road, passing by the abandoned buildings and going through a cattle gate (close it behind you). Continue for approximately 0.5 mile, where you veer to the right and go to the top of a small ridge. Park here. There are several hot spring sources in this area.

The Hot Springs

This second collection of hot springs provides less in the way of bathing, though it contains more springs. Many of the springs have dried up in the recent past. Most of those remaining form small pools in craters of travertine, too shallow to bathe in. Their flow likely varies depending upon the year. A collection of abandoned buildings is located nearby, including a well-built stone structure below the hot springs.

Other springs are located near the Reese River Hot Springs, but do not provide bathing opportunities. Two collections of springs are located immediately north, known as Mound Springs for the hill upon which they emerge. Some of these springs have virtually dried up.

81 Leach Hot Springs

General description: Several extremely hot sources of water emerging out of the ground immediately off a major graded dirt road in an isolated portion of northern Nevada.

Location: North-central Nevada, approximately 26 miles south of Winnemucca.

Primitive/developed: Primitive, except for the diversion of water into a holding pond.

Best time of year: Fall, winter, and spring. Summer can be hot.

Restrictions: There is private property nearby, so be sure to obey all NO TRESPASSING signs.

Access: Most passenger cars can make the trip.

Water temperature: 140 degrees F at the source, with varying temperatures in other pools depending upon distance from the source.

Nearby attractions: Winnemucca, Jersey Valley Hot Springs, Hyder Hot Springs.

Services: None; nearest gasoline, food, and lodging can be found in Winnemucca, approximately 26 miles away.

Camping: There do not appear to be any restrictions against camping near the springs. There is private property close by, so be sure to obey all NO TRESPASSING signs. The springs are immediately off the road, so this may not be the best place to camp, however. There is also plenty of undeveloped space in the immediate vicinity.

Map: USGS topographic, Winnemucca, NV, quadrangle, 1:100,000 scale.

Leach Hot Springs

Finding the springs: From Winnemucca, travel south out of town on Grass Valley Road. This paved road becomes Nevada Highway 294. Travel south for approximately 26 miles. The road turns to dirt a few miles out of town, but it is a graded surface, so most passenger cars should have no problem. Shortly before the road makes a hard left turn, the hot springs are immediately to your left (east). The springs flow under the road in a small iron culvert, into a small creek. A small, faint dirt road follows this creek to the east (or right when facing south). Take this dirt road for approximately 0.5 mile, where the road turns left and reaches a stock pond. There are several places along the creek where bathing is possible.

The Hot Springs

The hot springs on the east (left, coming from Winnemucca) side of the road are small but extremely hot sources of water bubbling up from the ground beneath a small hillside. These sources are not the place to bathe. The hot spring water flows across the road and eventually coalesces into a small creek. Part of this creek has been diverted so that all the water flows into a small stock pond farther downhill, and eventually to a working ranch. Although this pond is rather muddy and uninviting, there are potentially places along the creek where bathing could be possible. Choose the spot that's right for you, provided it's not on private property. Be sure to check the water temperature before getting in.

It is possible to reach Jersey Valley Hot Springs and Hyder Hot Springs from this road, but it is a long drive on a dirt road, far from any towns. To reach these other hot springs, continue south on NV 294 beyond Leach Hot Springs, staying on the main road. This road will continue south into Buffalo Valley, and eventually into Jersey Valley. Follow all signs to Jersey Valley, and refer to the entry and map for Jersey Valley and Hyder Hot Springs. Be sure you have enough gas before departing on this extended trip.

82 Kyle Hot Springs

General description: A fairly large hot spring source that at one time sustained a small resort. A little cement pool has been built around the source, and water is also diverted into a few watering troughs. Located in an isolated part of Nevada, this is an interesting spring, as well as an excellent place to bathe.

Location: Northern Nevada, approximately 56 miles southwest of Winnemucca and 68 miles northeast of Lovelock.

Primitive/developed: This used to be a small resort with a hot pool, steam shacks, and several other buildings. Because of its disuse, however, this spring is rather primitive at present.

Best time of year: Year-round.

Restrictions: None.

Access: Most passenger cars can make the trip.

Water temperature: Approximately 110 degrees F at the cement pool, 90 degrees F at the watering trough.

Nearby attractions: Ghost town of Unionville.

Services: None; nearest gasoline, food, and lodging can be found in Winnemucca, approximately 56 miles away. Do not count on getting supplies at the smaller hamlets along Interstate 80 such as Imlay, Mill City, and Oreana.

Camping: There does not appear to be any restrictions against camping. Keep in mind, however, that this will be undeveloped camping, as there are no developed sites in the immediate vicinity. If you do camp at Kyle Hot Springs, please pack out all your trash, and respect other people's privacy. There are developed campgrounds (public and private) at the Rye Patch Reservoir Recreation Area, approximately 42 miles away, off I–80.

Map: USGS topographic, Fish Creek Mountains, NV, quadrangle, 1:100,000 scale.

Finding the springs: From Winnemucca, travel west on I–80 for 29 miles to Mill City and Nevada Highway 400. Travel south on NV 400 for approximately 16 miles until you see a graded dirt road on your left. This road may or may not have a sign indicating Kyle Hot Springs (and to Gokey Ranch). Either way, turn left on this road and drive 9.3 miles to a fork in the road where you stay left. This road continues up a small hill and less than 1.3 miles to the hot spring.

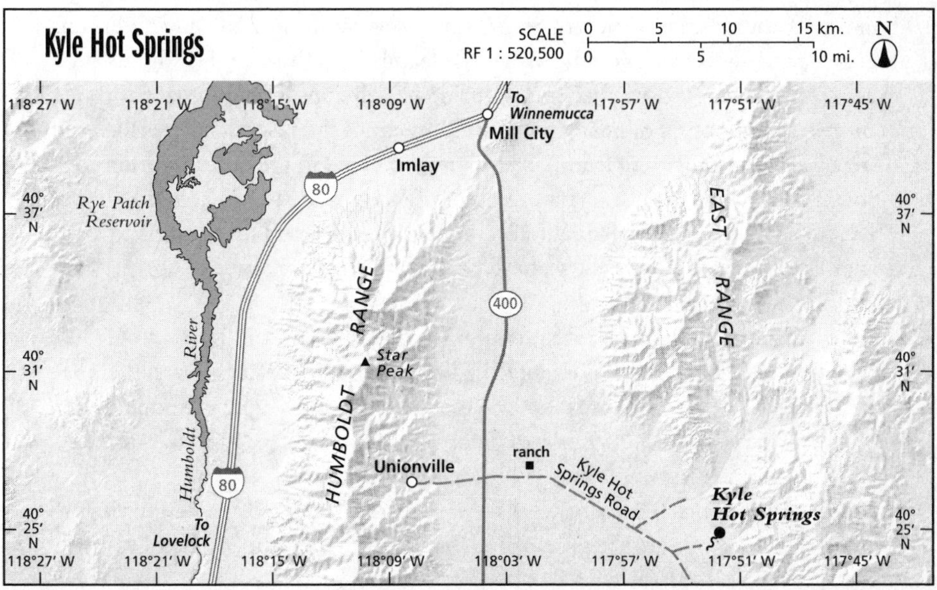

Kyle Hot Springs

The Hot Springs

Kyle Hot Springs was once a mineral bath resort offering lodging, hot baths, and steam treatment. Long since abandoned, vestiges of the resort can still be seen. Across the road from the main source of water are the ruins of a small adobe building. Another small structure remains over several steam vents downhill from the hot spring, which at one time provided steambaths. Although it is unknown exactly when this resort was active, the spring has obviously been utilized for countless generations. Following the abandonment of the resort, the baths fell into disrepair. A local cattleman from Lovelock re-cemented in the hot spring to provide bathing opportunities, and subsequently fenced in the tub to keep cows out. This cement tub is largely stagnant now, but water is diverted to a watering trough downhill a few yards, where the water is pleasantly warm and much cleaner. The view from the trough is beautiful.

The hot spring is better known than most described for this portion of Nevada, and seclusion is not guaranteed when visiting Kyle. Recent partygoers have continued to trash the area, leaving garbage and vandalizing the remains of the structures. Please respect this area before someone feels the need to bulldoze the spring and its surroundings.

Unionville: Once the county seat for Humboldt, Unionville was a thriving town with several hundred people, a large bank, and a newspaper. The town was established following the discovery of silver in the nearby mountains in 1861 by two Frenchmen who maintained a trading post on the emigrant trail along the Humboldt River. Following a veritable rush to the region, two prospectors, Hugo Pfersdorff and J. C. Hannan, found silver in abundance in Buena Vista Canyon. The town grew rapidly, like its sister town Star City, located in Star Canyon near Buena Vista.

Unionville's greatest production came in the years between 1863 and 1870, with a population reaching 1,500 at one point. The intensive mining activity led directly to the settlement of Paradise Valley in 1864, where crops were grown and cattle raised to support the many people at Unionville. Unionville's townspeople were in a virtual panic over the Paradise Valley War of 1865 (see Paradise Valley Hot Spring), their newspaper, the *Humboldt Register,* discussing the events with great concern. By 1870, however, the mines at Unionville had declined considerably in production, and with the completion of the Central Pacific Railroad along the Humboldt River, Winnemucca emerged as the region's commercial center. It is indeed hard to imagine this bustling community, one of the largest towns in Nevada at the time, existing in this now-empty portion of the state.

Much remains of the old town of Unionville, including several houses and portions of the old bank building. Like many Nevada ghost towns, Unionville is still occupied by a few hearty souls. To reach the town site, travel south on NV 400. Before (north of) the turnoff for Kyle Hot Springs, you will see a sign for Unionville on the right. Take this well-maintained dirt road to the west toward the mountains. The road will lead you directly to the town site, which is located in a canyon immediately below the mountains.

DIXIE VALLEY AREA

The Dixie Valley contains a large number of hot springs, hot seeps, and geothermal wells. Fumaroles have also been discovered in the area, particularly around the Senator Mine, near Boyer Ranch. Though no hot springs are associated with these fumaroles, a great deal of siliceous sinter is found in the area. The largest geothermal energy plant in Nevada is located in the northern portion of Dixie Valley. Several geothermal wells have been dug in various parts of the valley, beginning in the 1980s. Despite the large amount of geothermal activity in Dixie Valley, only a few bathing opportunities exist, and they are highlighted below.

83 Jersey Valley Hot Springs

General description: A large hot spring pool with a strong sulfurous smell flowing into a smaller pool in an isolated portion of northern Nevada. The hot spring water runoff is used for watering cattle and produces lush vegetation.

Location: Northern Nevada, approximately 62 miles east of Lovelock.

Primitive/developed: Primitive.

Best time of year: Spring and fall. Roads may be muddy in winter, and summer can be hot.

Restrictions: None.

Access: A high-clearance vehicle is recommended, but most sturdy passenger cars can make the trip.

Water temperature: Approximately 130 degrees F at the source, and 110 degrees F in the lower pool.

Nearby attractions: Hyder Hot Springs, Dixie Valley Hot Springs.

Services: None; nearest gasoline, food, and lodging can be found in Lovelock, approximately 62 miles away. Plan well when visiting this spring.

Camping: There does not appear to be any restrictions against camping at this spring. There are no developed campsites in the area, except for those at Rye Patch Reservoir approximately 85 miles away, off Interstate 80.

Map: USGS topographic, Fish Creek Mountains, NV, quadrangle, 1:100,000 scale.

Finding the springs: From Lovelock, travel east on I–80 for 5.3 miles to Coal Canyon Road, exit 112. Exit the freeway to the right (east) and travel 13 miles on this paved road until you reach a sign for Dixie Valley. Turn left here and travel another 31 miles to a Y in the road with another sign to Dixie Valley. Stay right at this intersection, following the sign to Dixie Valley. Follow this road for another 8 miles to another Y in the road with several small wooden road markers. Stay left at this intersection, following the sign to Jersey Valley. Go another 2.5 miles to a T intersection, turning left along a power line road. Stay on this main road for approximately 10.5 miles to the hot springs immediately off the road to the left.

The Hot Springs

Located in a dry cattle-ranching valley, Jersey Valley Hot Springs is a long drive on a dirt road from any of the closest towns. The hot springs are interesting and are near several other springs, so it's worth a trip. The green vegetation and sulfurous

Jersey Valley Hot Springs

smell will give away the location, and the source itself is an ominous-looking pit with steaming water and muddy bottom and sides. DO NOT BATHE HERE! This hot spring water flows downhill slightly along a small creek and along the way is diverted into a small pool, approximately 4 by 2 feet and 3 feet deep. The water in this smaller pool is approximately 110 degrees F. Because the flow of the main hot spring varies, sometimes this small pool is shallower, stagnant, and unappealing. It can make a nice bath at times, however. This area is cattle-grazing country, and a large ranch is a few miles down the road. Although the evidence of cattle is present, they have not completely trampled the small pool and vegetation created by the spring. Be sure to watch for cattle on the road on your way to this spring, as there are likely to be many in the immediate vicinity.

84 Hyder Hot Springs

General description: A large, colorful hot spring source on an isolated hillside in a remote portion of Nevada. Water from a smaller hot spring is trapped in a small, shallow pool that is bathable.

Location: Northern Nevada, approximately 62 miles from Lovelock.

Primitive/developed: Primitive.

Best time of year: Spring and fall. Roads can be muddy in winter, and summer can be hot.

Restrictions: None.

Access: A high-clearance vehicle is recommended, but many sturdy passenger cars can

Hyder Hot Springs

make the trip. During wet periods four-wheel drive may be required.

Water temperature: 130 degrees F at the source, approximately 95 degrees F in the shallow pool.

Nearby attractions: Jersey Valley Hot Springs, Dixie Valley Hot Springs, Leach Hot Springs.

Services: None; nearest gasoline, food, and lodging can be found in Lovelock, approximately 65 miles away on mostly dirt roads. Plan well when traveling to these hot springs.

Camping: There do not appear to be any restrictions against camping at the hot springs, and although it is undeveloped, this makes an excellent place to spend the night.

Map: USGS topographic, Fish Creek Mountains, NV, quadrangle, 1:100,000 scale.

Finding the springs: From Lovelock, travel east on Interstate 80 for 5.3 miles to Coal Canyon Road, exit 112. Exit the freeway to the right (east) and travel 13 miles on this paved road until you reach a sign for Dixie Valley. Turn left here and travel another 31 miles to a Y in the road with another sign to Dixie Valley. Follow this road for another 8 miles to another Y in the road with several small wooden road markers. Stay left at this intersection, following the sign to Jersey Valley. Go another 2.5 miles to a T intersection, turning left along a power line road. Stay on this road for approximately 7.7 miles to an intersection with a smaller road and turn right. Jersey Valley Hot Springs is another 2.8 miles on the dirt road you turned off. Travel 9.1 miles to another intersection, this time a T. Turn right here (to your left you will see a large ranch) and look for the first road on your left after about 0.2 mile. Take this lesser dirt road for approximately 6.2 miles until the road reaches a small hill/mound. On the other side of this mound, near the top, is where the main hot spring source is located. The smaller source and the small bathing pool is around the other side of the hill, near the base.

The Hot Springs

Hyder Hot Springs rests on a small hill in an isolated portion of northern Nevada. The source itself is a large brown-colored mound, formed by mineral particles from the hot spring and by algae living off the hot water. This hot spring water flows downhill, where green grasses and reeds grow in an area frequently visited by local cattle. Another smaller and less obvious source of hot water is farther down the hill, where it bubbles up out of the ground, eventually flowing into a small dammed-up pool. This pool presents the only bathing opportunity at Hyder Hot Springs and is about 5 by 3 feet, 1 foot deep, and approximately 95 degrees F. The hill on which Hyder rests presents a nice vantage point on a clear day from which most of Jersey Valley and Dixie Valley can be seen.

Another hot spring, Seven Devils, also lies in the same valley as Hyder, but it is on private property. The spring is conspicuous because of its location on a small hill marked with a single tree. Barbed-wire fences and NO TRESPASSING signs surround the spring, however, and it should not be visited for this reason. At one time there was public access to the spring, but recently it was closed off. Perhaps one day the public will be able to enjoy Seven Devils Hot Spring, but until then, respect the landowner's wishes.

85 Dixie Valley Hot Springs

General description: Numerous difficult-to-spot hot spring seeps in an isolated portion of northern Nevada. Although there are few well-defined bathing spots, there are ample places that allow for the creation of small tubs of appropriate temperatures.

Location: Northern Nevada, approximately 75 miles northeast of Fallon.

Primitive/developed: Primitive.

Best time of year: Fall, winter, and spring. Summer can be hot.

Restrictions: Many of the springs are on the other side of a barbed-wire fence, though there do not appear to be any NO TRESPASSING signs.

Access: Most passenger cars can make the trip.

Water temperature: Varies; 130 degrees F at most sources, decreasing in temperature as the water flows away from the source.

Nearby attractions: Ghost town of Wonder, remains of Pony Express station, Sand Hill.

Services: None; nearest gasoline, food, and lodging can be found in Fallon, approximately 75 miles away. There are no services in Dixie Valley.

Camping: This is not the best camping spot, as the springs are all immediately off the road and on the other side of a barbed-wire fence. There is plenty of undeveloped space in the immediate vicinity, however.

Map: USGS topographic, Carson Sink, NV, quadrangle, 1:100,000 scale.

Finding the springs: From Fallon, travel east on U.S. Highway 50 for 38 miles. Turn north (left) onto Nevada Highway 121 and continue for approximately 37.5 miles to the hot springs. This paved road will turn into a graded dirt road. Keep an eye out for darker vegetation off to your right. Also keep an eye out for another dirt road on the right; the hot springs begin immediately after this road meets the main graded road. The springs are immediately off the road, extending for approximately 0.25 mile.

Dixie Valley Hot Springs

The Hot Springs

Consisting of several separate clusters of springs, the Dixie Valley Hot Springs present a marked contrast to a dry desert valley. The series of hot spring seeps extends for approximately 0.25 mile. Though the springs vary in temperature, they are all extremely hot at their sources (130 to 150 degrees F). Do not bathe near the sources! Almost all of the springs run in small creeks for varying distances up to a few hundred yards. As the water cools as it flows from the source, there could potentially be bathing opportunities. There is, however, a substantial amount of brush, limiting access. If you are going to attempt to bathe in these springs, be sure to let any diverted water cool down sufficiently, and always check the temperature before getting in. This is an interesting area, offering several hot springs to explore on your own. It's also an isolated part of Nevada, with few people passing through.

NORTHEASTERN NEVADA

In northeastern Nevada, various attractions await. For those who love the outdoors, this is close to paradise. There are many scenic wonders to explore, not least of which being the Ruby Mountains. These high mountains provide alpine conditions, including dramatic scenery, beautiful lakes, abundant creeks, and forests of numerous species. There are also many points of historical interest, such as ghost towns, emigrant trails, and railroads. There are few modern towns in this region, though Elko provides just about everything the traveler could need. Smaller towns such as Wells also provide many visitor services.

Geothermally active, this portion of Nevada provides some of the hottest hot springs in the state. They are spread out across the region, though many are not accessible to the public. Those that are include a grouping of high temperature springs immediately outside of Elko, as well as another collection spread out for several miles north of Wells.

Twelve-Mile Hot Springs

ELKO REGION

This area is centered around the town of Elko, which makes for a great base for your explorations. The town contains numerous hotels, restaurants, stores, and gas stations. The territory surrounding the town contains fantastic, largely undeveloped country. Some of the least traveled roads are found in this part of the state. Historic sights, mountains, creeks, and, of course, plentiful hot springs make this area great fun for those who appreciate the outdoors.

86 Elko Hot Springs

General description: A collection of three very high-temperature hot springs along the Humboldt River immediately outside of the town of Elko. Though no soaking is provided by these springs, they are of historical and geological interest.

Location: Northeastern Nevada, just outside of the town of Elko.

Primitive/developed: Primitive.

Best time of year: Year-round.

Restrictions: None currently. The larger hot spring, known as the Hot Hole, is fenced to keep people out, as are the Elko Hot Springs. Access to the Humboldt River Hot Springs has been restricted by private property in the past. Obey all posted signs.

Access: Standard vehicles can make the trip, except when the road is wet. You can walk from a paved road in this case.

Water temperature: 133 degrees F in the Hot Hole, 190 degrees F in the Elko Hot Springs, 205 degrees F in Humboldt River Hot Springs.

Nearby attractions: Town of Elko, Ruby Mountains

Services: All services are available in Elko.

Camping: There is no camping available at the springs, but there are plenty of campgrounds in the public lands around Elko.

Maps: USGS topographic, Elko, NV, quadrangle, 1:100,000 scale; Elko, 1:24,000 scale.

Finding the springs: From Elko on the main drag through town (Idaho Street), go south on Fifth Street across the railroad tracks and the Humboldt River. Turn right on Wilson Street after crossing the bridge. Go about 1.2 miles on Wilson (which turns into Bullion Road). On your right you will see a large mound with a fence around it. Pull off here. This is the Hot Hole. The Humboldt River Hot Springs are down the hill alongside the river. A small road leads to a broad parking area near the springs. The third set, the Elko Hot Springs, can be reached from the Catlin Oil Shale Plant road, and by foot from there.

The Hot Springs

There are three clusters of hot springs at this location:

The Hot Hole consists of a huge travertine dome (approximately 50 feet across) with hot water inside. It was a stopping point along the California Trail and later provided water for a municipal swimming pool. At that time a slot was cut into the side of the dome to drain the pool inside and to provide water for the pool. Sometime in the early 1950s, this pool was closed and filled in, and a new

Elko Hot Springs

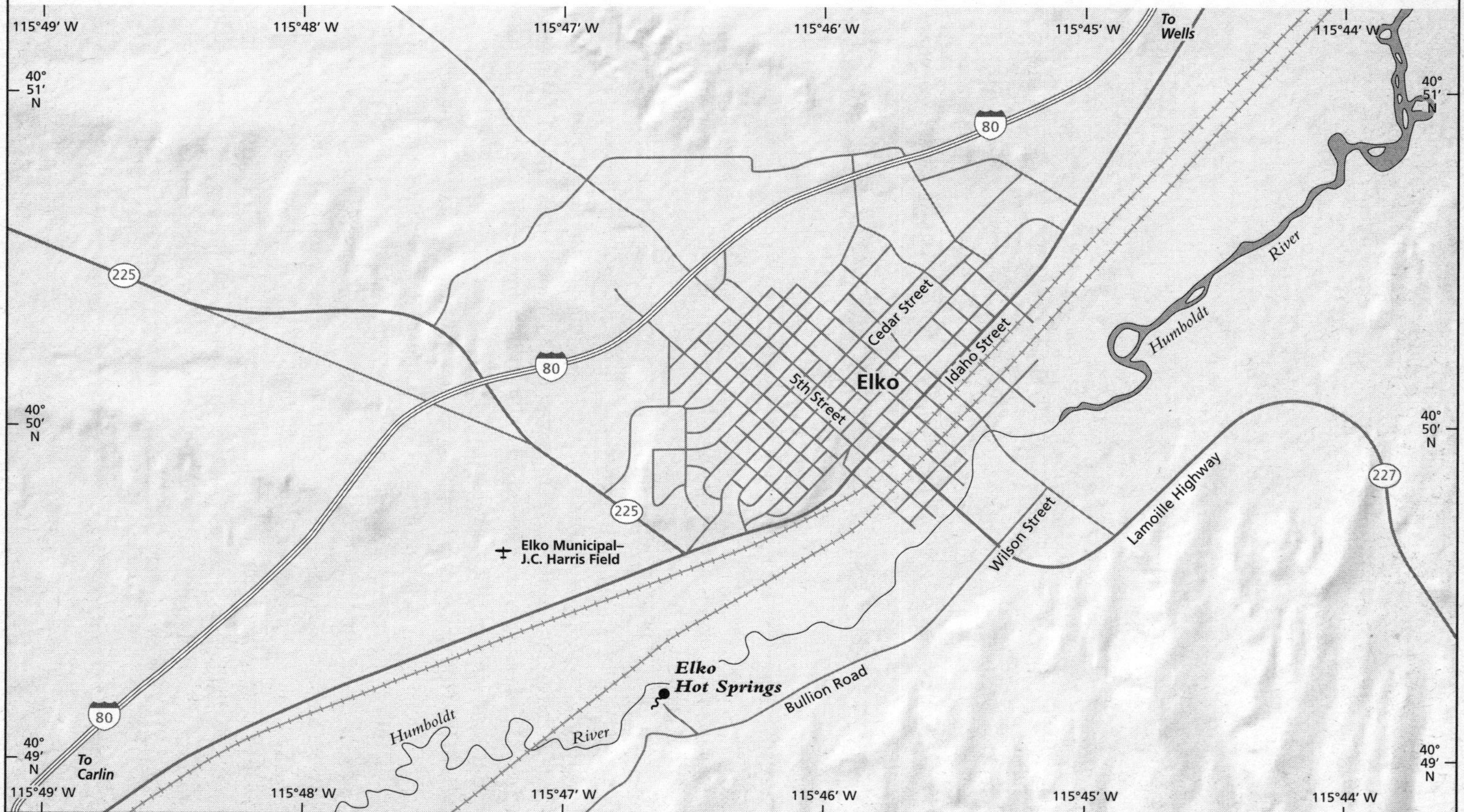

Hot Hole, Elko

pool was built near the modern municipal swimming pool. The Hot Hill is fenced; do not enter.

Humboldt River Hot Springs, downhill from the Hot Hole, are actually hotter in temperature and consist of several clusters of springs emerging on the banks of the Humboldt. Steam gives away their location. The site was at one time used by James Patton for raising bees. The remaining buildings on the site are from this period and served as a beekeeping facility until Patton's death in 1964. Obey signs in this area that indicate private property.

Elko Hot Springs are located to the south, up the hill. These springs were a well-known landmark for those on the California Trail. In 1868 a small bathhouse was built at the springs, and soon a doctor employed there was seeing patients seeking the curative effects of the hot water. By 1869 this facility was known as White Sulphur Springs Hotel. It burned down in 1882 and was subsequently rebuilt, only to burn down again in 1899. Eventually a brick hotel building was constructed, which later stood abandoned for many years. The City of Elko began utilizing the hot water for a variety of purposes, including heating for two schools, a municipal swimming pool, and many other facilities. Today, however, the hot spring itself is completely fenced off, and there are ruins scattered about the site.

87 Twelve-Mile (Bishop Creek) Hot Springs

General description: Hot springs emerging from the side of a creek in an isolated portion of northeastern Nevada. The hot springs at one time filled a large swimming pool, which subsequently broke apart. Today, the foundations from the pool provide a great place for a soak.

Location: Northeastern Nevada, approximately 11 miles north of Wells.

Primitive/developed: Primitive.

Best time of year: Spring, summer, and fall. Roads become very muddy in wet weather.

Restrictions: Access to the hot springs is through a private ranch. Obey all posted signs.

Access: High-clearance vehicle required. Four-wheel drive will be needed when ground is wet.

Water temperature: 102 degrees F at the source. Water temperature in the pool is about 99 degrees F, though it varies.

Nearby attractions: Ghost town of Metropolis, Three-Mile (Sulphur) Hot Springs, Lower Oxley Peak Hot Springs.

Services: None; nearest gasoline, food, and lodging can be found in Wells, approximately 11 miles away.

Camping: There are no campgrounds in the immediate area around the hot springs, though there are signs that people do camp there at times.

Map: USGS topographic, Wells, NV, quadrangle, 1:100,000 scale.

Finding the springs: From Interstate 80, take the West Wells exit (exit 351). Follow this road (Humboldt Avenue) to Sixth Street, which is the main drag through town, and turn right. Travel on Sixth Street through town to Lake Street, where you make a left turn. Cross the railroad tracks and turn left on Eighth Street. Cross Wells Avenue, staying on Eighth Street as it curves past several old buildings and houses. Stay on this paved road out of town for approximately 9.1 miles. Look for a dirt road on your right about 0.5 mile after passing a collection of ranch houses and as the paved road makes a broad turn to the left. Turn right on this small dirt road (notice the small sign for the California Trail). Travel on this dirt road for approximately 2 miles to the hot springs. You will cross the creek, then pass by a large dam (no longer in use); the hot springs will be about 0.1 mile beyond. The springs are at the edge of the creek (on the right side) as the road makes a second crossing.

The Hot Springs

Twelve-Mile Hot Springs, or Bishop Creek Hot Springs, consist of a small collection of hot springs flowing out into Bishop Creek in northeastern Nevada, not far from the town of Wells. The foundation for a swimming pool provides a great place for a warm bath. The road from Wells is paved for most of the way, but the last 2 miles is on a poor dirt road that crosses through Bishop Creek. You will need a high-clearance vehicle and preferably four-wheel drive to make this trip. The hot springs are located in the canyon of Bishop Creek, a beautiful setting. Be sure to obey all signs, as access to the springs goes through a private ranch. Several smaller warm springs emanate from the side of the dirt road but do not provide any bathing opportunities.

Metropolis: This ghost town is a short drive from Twelve-Mile Hot Springs and is worth a visit. Continue on the paved road as it makes its broad turn to the left for approximately 4 miles to get to the ghost town.

Twelve-Mile (Bishop Creek) Hot Springs; Lower Oxley Peak Hot Springs; Three-Mile (Sulphur) Hot Springs

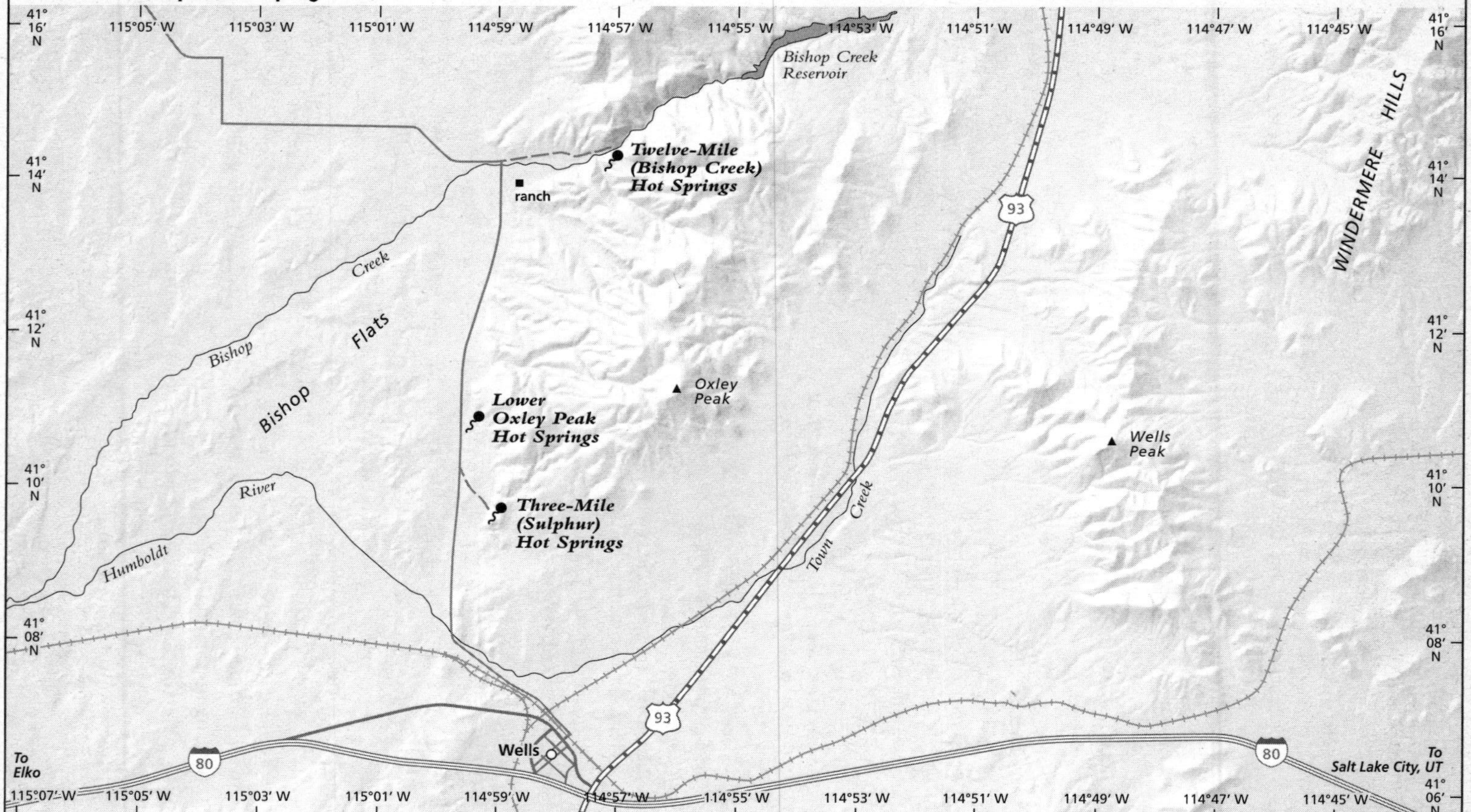

The dam below Twelve-Mile (Bishop Creek) Hot Springs

During the early nineteenth century, much of the Great Basin experienced a great deal of homesteading, as hopeful settlers were gripped with the so-called back-to-the-land movement. The lure of open spaces and private land ownership and a chance to make a living on one's own were powerful draws to those living in the cities. Much of this movement was fed by the railroads, who hoped to sell off their extensive landholdings at top dollar. The homesteading fervor particularly gripped western Utah, but also spilled over into northeastern Nevada, creating towns such as Metropolis, Afton, Tobar Flat, Ruby Valley, and Independence Valley. Metropolis itself was formed in 1911 by the Pacific Reclamation Company, which promised hopeful settlers land, water, and success. A large and elaborate school, hotel, and other town services were constructed to assure homesteaders of the future success of the town. Like other such towns in northeastern Nevada, however, Metropolis also failed by the early 1920s. The climate, soils, repeated crop damage caused by pests such as jackrabbits, and isolation all contributed. Today, the foundations of the school, hotel, and a few homes can still be visited.

88 Lower Oxley Peak Hot Springs

See map on page 200.

General description: A collection of several hot springs on the side of a hill, at one time providing water to a large pool. Today, no bathing opportunities exist.

Location: Northeastern Nevada, approximately 6 miles north of Wells.

Primitive/developed: Primitive.

Best time of year: Spring, summer, and fall. Roads become very muddy in wet weather.

Restrictions: The hot springs are used to provide water for cattle and may be located on private property. Be sure to obey all signs.

Access: High-clearance vehicle required. Four-wheel drive will be needed when ground is wet.

Water temperature: 142 degrees F at the source.

Nearby attractions: Ghost town of Metropolis, Twelve-Mile (Bishop Creek) Hot Springs, Three-Mile (Sulphur) Hot Springs.

Services: None; nearest gasoline, food, and lodging can be found in Wells, approximately 6 miles away.

Camping: This is not a good place for camping.

Maps: USGS topographic, Wells, NV, quadrangle, 1:100,000 scale; Oxley Peak, 1:24,000 scale.

Finding the springs: From Interstate 80, take the West Wells exit (exit 351). Follow this road (Humboldt Avenue) to Sixth Street, which is the main drag through town, and turn right. Travel on Sixth Street through town to Lake Street, where you make a left turn. Cross the railroad tracks and turn left on Eighth Street. Cross Wells Avenue, staying on Eighth Street as it curves past several old buildings and houses. Stay on this paved road out of town for approximately 5.5 miles. Look for a very small dirt road on your right leading to a small hill. Turn right on this small dirt road, and go about 0.25 mile up the hill to the hot springs.

Lower Oxley Peak Hot Springs

The Hot Springs

Located immediately off the paved road to Twelve-Mile (Bishop Creek) Hot Springs, Lower Oxley Peak Hot Springs is worth a visit on your way to the former. They consist of a collection of hot springs flowing out of travertine mounds on a hillside. The water at one time was diverted into a pool or reservoir of some kind. Today, however, this pool is empty and abandoned, and the water serves a cattle herd. There are no bathing opportunities. The travertine formations are interesting, however, and the hillside provides a nice view of the surrounding countryside.

89 Three-Mile (Sulphur) Hot Springs

See map on page 200.

General description: A small pool formed by several hot springs at the base of a mountain in an isolated portion of northeastern Nevada.

Location: Northeastern Nevada, approximately 5.5 miles north of Wells.

Primitive/developed: Primitive.

Best time of year: Spring, summer, and fall. Roads become very muddy in wet weather.

Restrictions: None currently. Be sure to obey all signs.

Access: High-clearance vehicle required. Four-wheel drive will be needed when ground is wet.

Water temperature: 122 degrees F at the source, approximately 95 degrees F in the pool.

Three-Mile (Sulphur) Hot Springs

Nearby attractions: Ghost town of Metropolis, Twelve-Mile (Bishop Creek) Hot Springs, Lower Oxley Peak Hot Springs.

Services: None; nearest gasoline, food, and lodging can be found in Wells, approximately 5.5 miles away.

Camping: This is not a good place for camping.

Map: USGS topographic, Wells, NV, quadrangle, 1:100,000 scale.

Finding the springs: From Interstate 80, take the West Wells exit (exit 351). Follow this road (Humboldt Avenue) to Sixth Street, which is the main drag through town, and turn right. Travel on Sixth Street through town to Lake Street, where you make a left turn. Cross the railroad tracks and turn left on Eighth Street. Cross Wells Avenue, staying on Eighth Street as it curves past several old buildings and houses. Stay on this paved road out of town for approximately 4.6 miles. Look for a small, unutilized dirt road on your right. Turn right on this small dirt road, and go about 0.8 mile, bearing left at a Y in the road. Park when the road comes to a small creek, as it may be too muddy to cross. Instead, cross the creek on foot and walk the short distance (100 yards) to the hot springs at the base of the mountain.

The Hot Springs

Located a short distance off the paved road to Twelve-Mile (Bishop Creek) Hot Springs, Three-Mile (Sulphur) Hot Springs is also worth a visit on your way to the former. The springs consist of a small pool at the base of a mountain, overflowing to form a small creek and marshy area. At one time the water was diverted into a swimming pool, only the foundations of which remain today. The small pool at the base of the mountain provides for a nice, warm soak (about 95 degrees F).

CENTRAL NEVADA

Central Nevada, like the northern part of the state, possesses thousands of acres of public land. The boundaries for the central portion of the state have been arbitrarily drawn for the organization of this book. Anchored in the west by the state capital of Carson City, central Nevada provides a wealth of tourist activities. Even less populated than the northern portion, central Nevada offers ample outdoor recreational opportunities. The region also contains several large mining districts, particularly in the eastern portion. Several high mountain ranges break up the country. Many of the higher reaches of these ranges are controlled by the Toyaibe National Forest, with hiking trails, campgrounds, and places of historical and archaeological interest abounding.

Walley's Hot Springs Resort

GARDNERVILLE, MINDEN, AND THE CARSON VALLEY

Immediately south of Reno and Carson City lie the beautiful communities of Minden and Gardnerville. These small, primarily ranching towns sit at the base of the majestic Sierra Nevada and are well watered by snowmelt. The area contains the oldest settlement in Nevada, the community of Genoa, established by Mormon pioneers in the 1850s. Minden and Gardnerville are situated at the confluence of several major roads, taking you to myriad points beyond. The three resorts listed below are located close to Carson City and Reno and make for easy day trips from either location.

90 Bowers Mansion

General description: A swimming pool fed by hot well water adjacent to a historic mansion in a county park, between Reno and Carson City.

Location: Northern Nevada, approximately 10 miles north of Carson City.

Primitive/developed: Developed.

Best time of year: Pool is only open Memorial Day to Labor Day.

Restrictions: This is a county park, and there is a fee for usage.

Access: Immediately off a main road.

Water temperature: 133 degrees F at the source. The pool is approximately 80 degrees F.

Nearby attractions: Carson City.

Services: None; nearest gasoline, food, and lodging can be found in Carson City, 10 miles

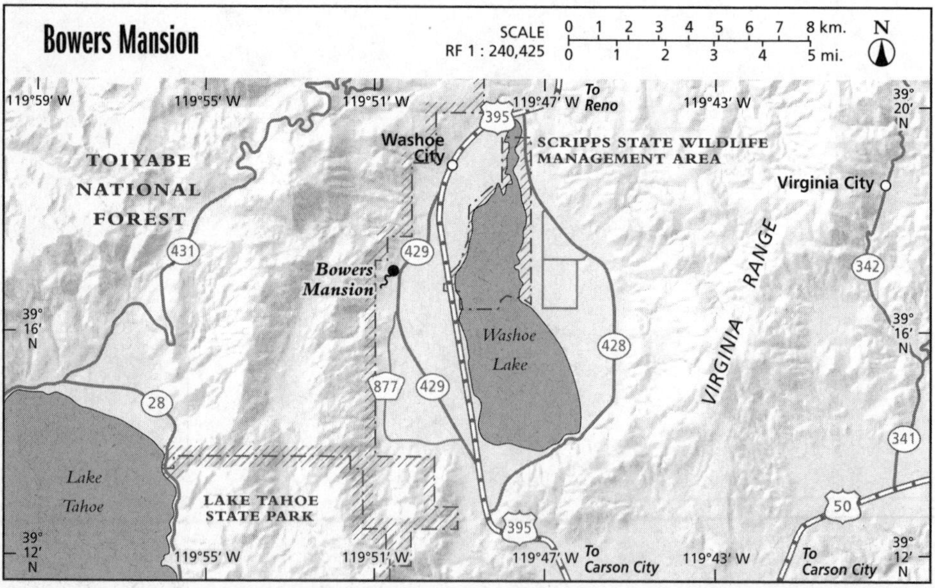

Bowers Mansion

away, as well as other nearby services approximately 4 miles away.

Camping: There is no camping at the county park, but there are campgrounds in the area.

Map: Nevada Highway Map.

Finding the spring: From Reno, travel south on U.S. Highway 395 through Washoe City and turn right on Nevada Highway 429, with signs for Davis Creek County Park. Follow this road past Davis Creek Park to the Bowers Mansion; park on your right. From Carson City, travel north on US 395 for approximately 10 miles. Turn left at signs for Bowers Mansion, and drive approximately 1.5 miles to the park.

The Hot Spring

Adjacent to the historic Bowers Mansion, a Washoe County park, is a large swimming pool fed by a hot well, dug in the 1960s. Originally a pool was fed by the adjacent hot spring, but now that water is used for irrigation. The spring was also known as Franktown Corners Hot Springs in the past. The pool is only open from Memorial Day to Labor Day, and it can become quite busy on weekends. There is a fee for use of the pool. There are also picnic grounds and playgrounds. Bowers Mansion, built in 1864 by wealthy Comstock miner Sandy Bowers, is also worth viewing, and tours are available. Contact the park at (702) 849–1825.

91 Carson Hot Springs

General description: A historic hot spring resort with a swimming pool and several private rooms.

Location: In Carson City.

Primitive/developed: Developed.

Best time of year: Year-round. Summer can be hot.

Restrictions: This is a private establishment, open to the public. There are fees for usage.

Access: In Carson City, on a paved road.

Water temperature: The source is approximately 120 degrees F. The swimming pool is approximately 98 degrees F, and the private rooms range in temperature (generally between 98 and 110 degrees F).

Nearby attractions: Bowers Mansion, Genoa, Walley's Hot Springs Resort.

Services: There is a restaurant next door, as well as a small motel. All services are located in Carson City.

Camping: Not permitted.

Map: Carson City map.

Finding the springs: As of 2005, a new highway was under construction near the hot springs, so these directions may change in the near future. Contact the resort for the latest directions. From the north on U.S. Highway 395 south, turn left on Hot Springs Road. Follow this road to its intersection with College Parkway, where you make a right. Turn left on Goni Road, and then left again on Hot Springs Road. The address is 1500 Hot Springs Road.

The Hot Springs

The Carson Hot Springs have been utilized for centuries, and in 1894 they became a resort known as Shaw's Hot Springs. Countless people visited the springs over the years, many traveling great distances to do so. In the 1910s the name was changed to Carson Hot Springs. The buildings have changed over the years, but the water remains the same. Today, a medium-size swimming pool is maintained at approximately 98 degrees F. Individual private rooms are also fed with hot spring water, with temperatures varying between 95 and 110 degrees F. The water in the private rooms can also be adjusted by adding cold tap water. Carson Hot Springs has been a favorite among locals for years and is increasingly being discovered by travelers. A fee is charged for a day pass to use the pool, and two hours in a private room is a little more expensive. Massage is also available. For more information, contact Carson Hot Springs at (775) 885–8844, or visit their Web site at www.carsonhotspringsresort.com.

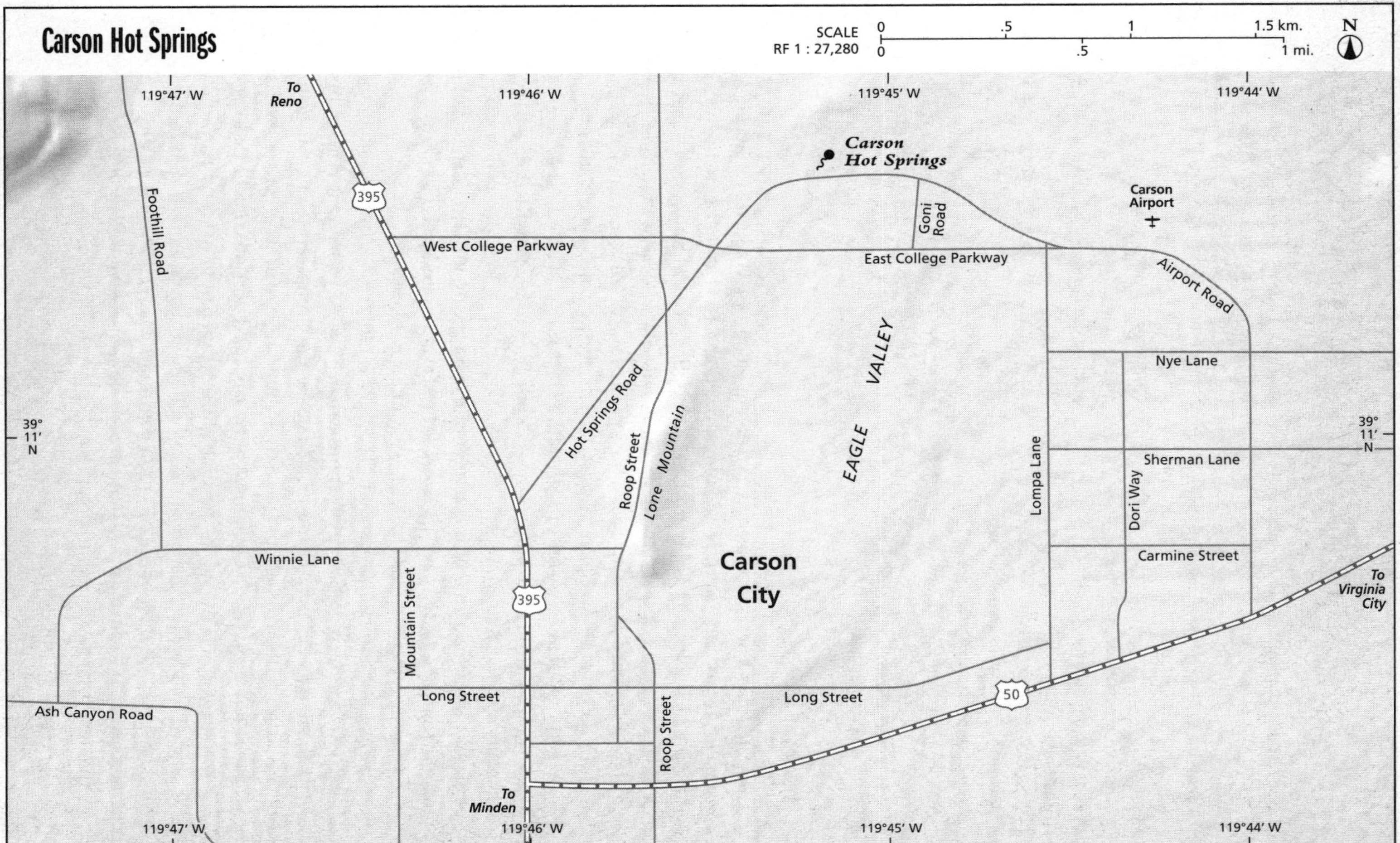
Carson Hot Springs
SCALE
RF 1 : 27,280
0
.5
1
1.5 km.
0
.5
1 mi.
N
119°47′ W
119°46′ W
119°45′ W
119°44′ W
39° 11′ N
To Reno
To Minden
To Virginia City
395
50
Carson Hot Springs
Carson Airport
Foothill Road
West College Parkway
East College Parkway
Goni Road
Airport Road
Hot Springs Road
Roop Street
Lone Mountain
EAGLE VALLEY
Nye Lane
Sherman Lane
Dori Way
Carmine Street
Lompa Lane
Winnie Lane
Mountain Street
Carson City
Long Street
Ash Canyon Road

92 Walley's Hot Springs Resort

General description: An increasingly popular, historic hot spring resort in the beautiful Carson Valley.

Location: Northern Nevada, south of Carson City and 1.7 miles outside the small town of Genoa.

Primitive/developed: Developed.

Best time of year: Year-round.

Restrictions: This is a private resort, open to the public. Fees are charged for usage.

Access: Immediately off a major road.

Water temperature: The source is 160 degrees F. Temperatures vary in the pools and tubs.

Nearby attractions: Carson Hot Springs, Genoa, Mormon Station.

Services: Lodging is available at the resort, and there are two restaurants. Other services are available in Genoa, 1.7 miles away. Additional services, including gas, can be found in Carson City and Minden.

Camping: Not permitted.

Map: Nevada Highway Map.

Finding the springs: From Carson City, drive south on U.S. Highway 395 to Nevada Highway 206 north of Genoa. Turn right and follow the highway into the town of Genoa. From Minden, travel north on US 395 to Nevada Highway 758 (Genoa Lane) to Genoa. Turn left. (Genoa is located at the intersection of NV 206 and NV 758.) Once in Genoa, travel south on NV 206 for 1.7 miles to the resort on your left.

The Hot Springs

A popular resort, with increasing services and amenities, Walley's Hot Springs has been a landmark in western Nevada for more than 150 years. Originally opened in 1862, the resort was a favorite among travelers and Nevadans alike. Several of the facilities from the original resort remain, though a great deal of modernization and upgrades have occurred. Today, the upscale resort is officially known as David Walley's Resort and Hot Springs Spa. There are six hot spring pools and one "relaxation" pool. A full array of spa treatments is also available. The pools range in temperature from 98 to 104 degrees F, while the relaxation pool is 85 degrees F. There are also men's and women's steam rooms, a dry sauna, locker rooms, a workout room, and two tennis courts. A cafe is on the premises, as is a formal dining room and lodge. Contact the resort for reservations and prices at (775) 782–8155 or (800) 628–7831, or visit www.quintusresorts.com.

Mormon Station: Established in 1850 as a trading post along the emigrant trail to California, the small cabin at present-day Genoa was at that time within Utah Territory. The territory was created under the Compromise of 1850, giving the Mormon settlement at Salt Lake City, led by Brigham Young, control over an area covering present-day Utah, most of Nevada, and portions of Colorado. As the Mormons sought to spread their settlements beyond Salt Lake City, members of the church were sent to distant lands, including the eastern slope of the Sierra Nevada. Although there was a Mormon community at Genoa, the majority of the settlers were non-Mormon, or Gentiles, who desired a government of their own. As the territorial government in Salt Lake City treated the Carson Valley settlement

Walley's Hot Springs Resort

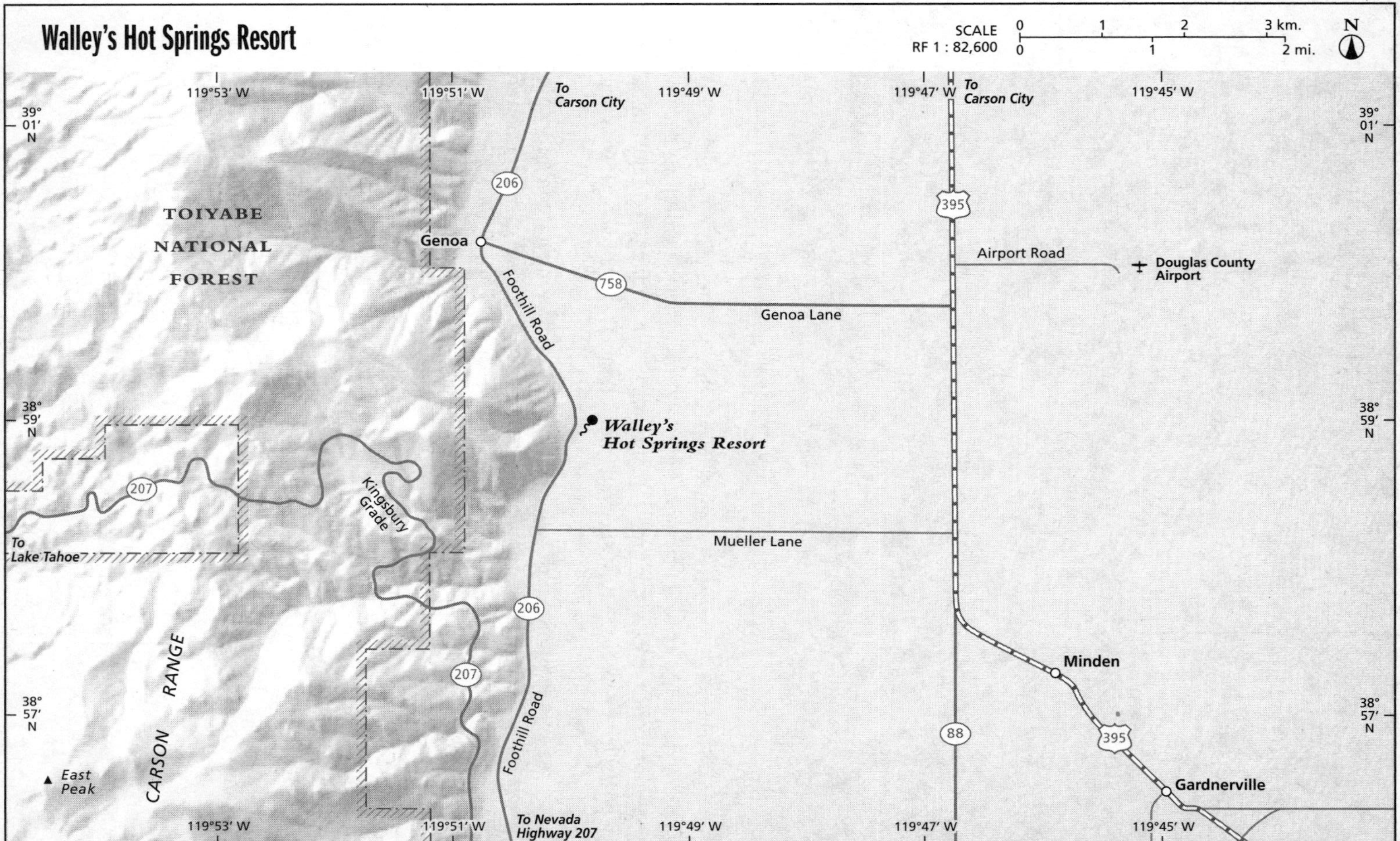

Walley's Hot Springs Resort

with disinterest, the settlers eventually wrote their own constitution, proposing that a new territory be carved out of portions of the state of California and the territory of Utah. Many of these early meetings were held in this original trading post. Despite its changing ownership several times, the post remains (with many renovations, of course) to the present day.

As a result of this constitutional convention, however, Mormon leadership in Salt Lake City was aroused sufficiently to dispatch a large group of Mormon settlers to the Carson Valley in 1855. Because of friction between the federal government and the Mormon territory of Utah, Brigham Young recalled all outlying settlers back to Salt Lake City in 1857, fearing the approach of warfare. This Mormon exodus left the Gentiles in firm control of the Carson Valley once again. Despite several political meetings held by the settlers to establish some form of local government, little was accomplished. The discovery of gold (and later silver in much higher quantities) in the mountains to the north and east did not improve this political inactivity. The Comstock Lode, as this deposit became known, brought about the establishment of Virginia City, the largest town in Nevada for the next fifty years. A population shift occurred due to this fabulous mineral discovery, bringing settlers up into the mountains, taking the focus away from the Carson Valley. From 1859 through the end of the century, Virginia City would become the center of activity in the state. At the onset of the Civil War, the settlements in western Utah were finally organized as a distinct territory in 1861.

FALLON AND THE CARSON SINK

Although there is only one hot spring you can bathe in described in this section, the Fallon region deserves some mention and is worth visiting, especially if you enjoy desert solitude and interesting archaeology. Located at the edge of the Carson Sink, where the Carson River disappears into the desert, Fallon has long been an agricultural center. Irrigated by water from the man-made Lake Lahonton, the town grew up from one of the first reclamation projects in the country. The presence of the Fallon Naval Air Station, and with it the transfer of the U.S. Navy's TOPGUN fighter weapons training program, the town has benefited from a variety of economic pursuits.

Extending east out of Fallon is U.S. Highway 50, the path of the old Pony Express and now called the "Loneliest Road in America." Two spectacular archaeological sites also exist within close range of Fallon. Grimes Point, a self-guided trail along the edges of a prehistoric lake, contains boulders and rocks replete with petroglyphs. The site is located approximately 12 miles east of Fallon on US 50. Further information can be obtained from the Bureau of Land Management at (702) 885–6000. Hidden Cave, another spectacular archaeological site in the area, allows visitors to see a prehistoric storage site and can be accessed by guided tour. For information call (702) 423–3677.

93 Lee Hot Springs

General description: An extremely high-temperature hot spring in central Nevada that was dry until recently. The hot water now flows into a small pond.

Location: Central Nevada, approximately 19 miles south of Fallon.

Primitive/developed: Primitive, except for diversion of water into a small pond and cattle-watering area.

Best time of year: Winter, spring, and fall. Summer can be too hot.

Restrictions: None.

Access: Most passenger cars can make the trip.

Water temperature: 190 degrees F at the source. The water cools off to approximately 105 degrees F in the small pond.

Nearby attractions: Grimes Point Archaeological Site, Hidden Cave, Soda Lake.

Services: None; nearest gasoline, food, and lodging can be found in Fallon, approximately 19 miles away.

Camping: Camping appears to be permitted in the vicinity of the spring, though this will be undeveloped camping if you do. The surrounding area also has plenty of public land where camping is allowed.

Map: USGS topographic, Fallon, NV, quadrangle, 1:100,000 scale.

Finding the springs: From Fallon, travel south out of town on U.S. Highway 95 for approximately 18.5 miles. Turn left onto a dirt road shortly after going over Russell Pass, 1.3 miles past a landfill. Once on this dirt road, bear left immediately and travel for about 1 mile to the spring, bearing right at 0.5 mile.

Lee Hot Springs

The Hot Springs

The extremely hot water bubbles out of the ground on a small hill on the other side of a cattle fence. If the air temperature is low enough, it will have steam emerging from it. A fence and warning signs were placed around the source. The hot water trickles down a small channel into a little pond and eventually out into a cattle pasture. The pond provides for a very shallow but hot bath. At times this hot spring has been dry, but it was flowing at the time of this writing. The setting for the spring is picturesque, although it is dry. Evidence of prehistoric inhabitants is also present. This spring is definitely worth a stopover if you are traveling in the vicinity of Fallon. The archaeological sites in the area are worth a visit, and Walker Lake is approximately 35 miles south on US 95, offering excellent fishing, boating, and general sightseeing.

94 Soda Lake

General description: A large lake in a volcano outside the town of Fallon.

Location: Central Nevada, a few miles outside Fallon.

Primitive/developed: Primitive.

Best time of year: Winter, spring, and fall. Summer can be too hot.

Restrictions: None.

Access: Most passenger cars can make the trip, though the dirt road is a little rough in places.

Soda Lake

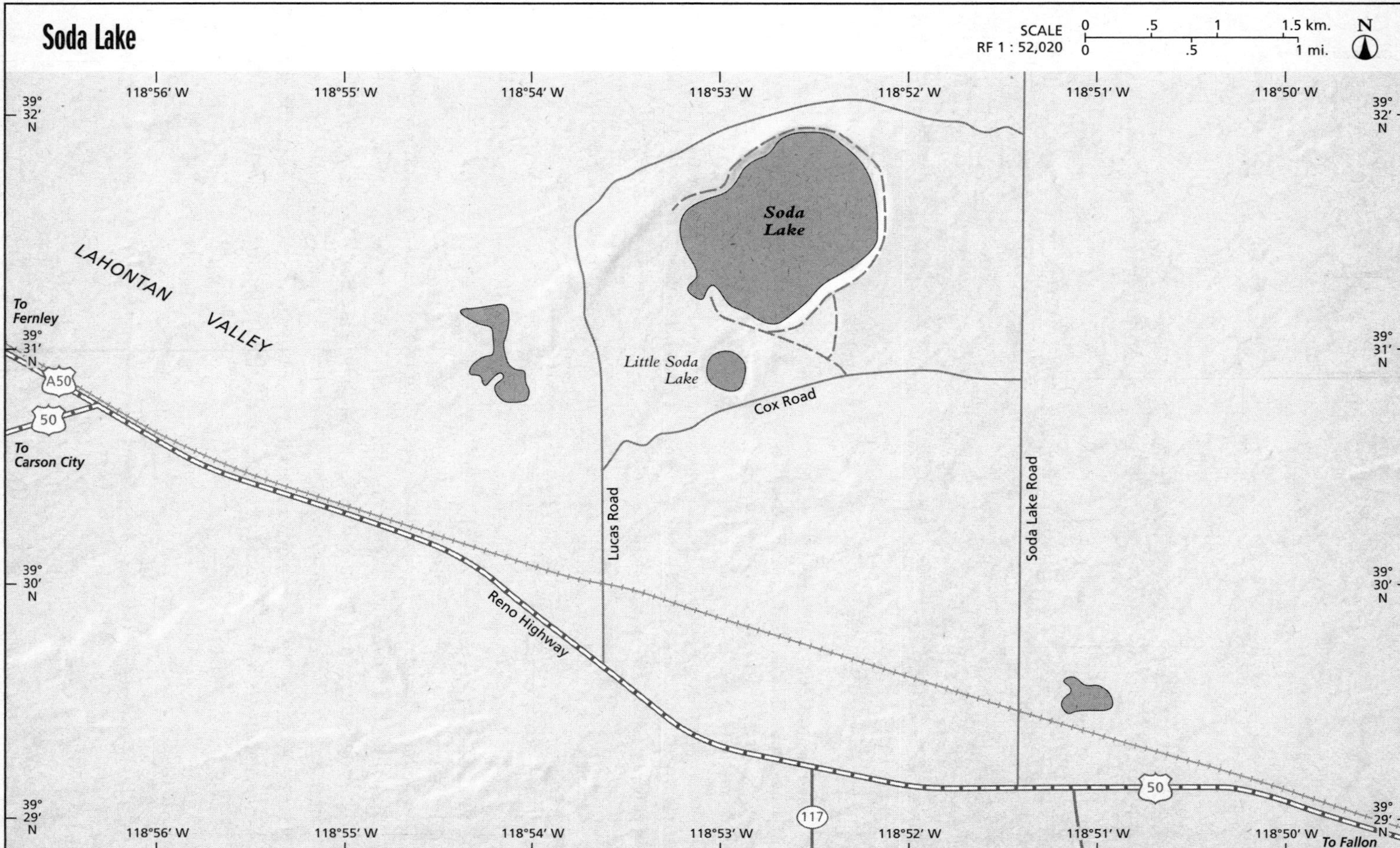
SCALE
RF 1 : 52,020
0 .5 1 1.5 km.
0 .5 1 mi.
N
118°56′ W
118°55′ W
118°54′ W
118°53′ W
118°52′ W
118°51′ W
118°50′ W
39° 32′ N
39° 31′ N
39° 30′ N
39° 29′ N
LAHONTAN VALLEY
To Fernley
A50
50
To Carson City
Soda Lake
Little Soda Lake
Cox Road
Lucas Road
Soda Lake Road
Reno Highway
117
To Fallon

Soda Lake

Water temperature: The springs that feed the lake are approximately 85 degrees F. Other hot spring sources in the area are upwards of 210 degrees F.

Nearby attractions: Grimes Point Archaeological Site, Hidden Cave, Lee Hot Springs.

Services: Gasoline, food, and lodging can be found in Fallon, a few miles away.

Camping: Camping appears to be permitted in the vicinity of the lake, though this will be undeveloped camping if you do.

Map: USGS topographic, Carson Sink, NV, quadrangle, 1:100,000 scale.

Finding the springs: From Fallon, travel west out of town on U.S. Highway 50 to Soda Lake Road, where you turn right. Travel on Soda Lake Road for 2 miles to Cox Road. Turn left on Cox Road and travel approximately 0.7 mile to a dirt road on your right. Continue on this unimproved road uphill to Soda Lake. A road traverses the rim of the lake.

The Hot Springs

Soda Lake consists of a large body of water in a relatively young volcano, fed by numerous hot springs. Although no bathing opportunities exist, the lake is an amazing feature in the area and worth a visit. There are numerous hot water sources in the general area, many of very high temperature. Geologically, the area is known as the Stillwater–Soda Lake Known Geothermal Resource Area, and several shallow wells have located hot water. A geothermal plant is located a short distance to the north.

MONITOR VALLEY AND THE TOYAIBE NATIONAL FOREST

One of the most scenic parts of central Nevada, the mountains and valleys east of Austin offer much. Austin itself is a living ghost town, surviving from its former glory days in the early 1860s. Several other less lived-in ghost towns dot the landscape, including Belmont, Berlin, and Ione. The Toyaibe Range south of Austin contains peaks as high as 11,773 feet and is bordered on the east and west by other ranges almost as high. The roads into these mountains are few and generally poor, but there are many other ways to escape the summer heat of the valleys below. Between the Toyaibe and Monitor ranges lies the well-watered Monitor Valley, where several hot springs are located. The Monitor Valley is largely cattle-ranching country, but also contains ghost towns (including Belmont), abundant wildlife, and beautiful scenery.

Be aware that most of the springs described in this region are well off the beaten track and require preparation. If you plan to travel into the high country, be prepared for colder and possibly wetter conditions than those in the valleys. As usual, stay away from dirt roads when they're wet, and be wary of changing weather patterns.

95 Spencer Hot Springs

General description: A series of hot springs on the site of an old resort in an isolated part of central Nevada, with both natural hot spring pools and a watering trough that has hot spring water diverted into it. Bathing opportunities are some of the best in the area. This is a relatively well-known hot spring, but definitely worth a visit.

Location: Central Nevada, approximately 20 miles southeast of Austin.

Primitive/developed: Primitive, except for the diversion of hot spring water into a tub.

Best time of year: Spring, summer, and fall. Roads can be quite muddy in wet winter months.

Restrictions: None.

Access: Most passenger cars can make the trip. Four-wheel drive will be needed in extremely wet weather.

Water temperature: Varies depending on pool chosen: 110 degrees F in one, 105 degrees F in the others. Temperature also varies in natural pond depending upon where you sit.

Nearby attractions: Historic town of Austin, Toyaibe National Forest.

Services: None; nearest gasoline, food, and lodging can be found in Austin, approximately 20 miles away.

Camping: There is plenty of camping space near the hot springs. You may have to share the area with others, however. Be sure to camp away from the springs themselves, and respect other people's privacy. There are also plenty of camping sites in the Toyaibe National Forest to the east. These campsites are at higher elevations and will be substantially cooler, with snow in the winter.

Map: USGS topographic, Summit Mountains, NV, quadrangle, 1:100,000 scale.

Finding the springs: From Austin, travel east on U.S. Highway 50 for 12 miles. Turn right (south) onto Nevada Highway 376 for approximately 100 yards. Turn left (east) onto a wide, graded dirt road with Forest Service signs to Toquime Cave. Travel on this graded dirt road for approximately 5.5 miles to a Y in the road. Turn left and travel another 1.6 miles uphill to the springs.

The Hot Springs

Spencer Hot Springs basically consist of three springs. The lower hot spring is adjacent to an abandoned swimming pool that has since been bulldozed. The spring is diverted through a metal pipe to a round watering trough. This trough makes an excellent bath, as the water is kept relatively clean by its constant flow into and out of the tub. The temperature also remains relatively constant at 105 degrees F. The other two springs are up the hill and consist of natural pools formed by hot spring water. One of the springs is about 7 by 5 feet, and approximately 3 feet deep. This spring is also excellent for bathing, as the temperature hovers around 110 degrees F and is just deep enough to provide a good soak. A small wooden deck has been built adjacent to the pool. The other upper spring is less desirable, as it is shallower and much cooler. I have yet to see anyone bathe in this one. All three springs are far enough away from each other to provide privacy and a sense of solitude.

Spencer Hot Springs

Austin: The third mineral-rich region in Nevada to be discovered after the Comstock, Austin (or the Reese River District) became one of the most celebrated. Lying along the old Pony Express route, a former express rider discovered silver in Pony Canyon in 1862. News of the discovery spread quickly, and soon people flocked to the area to get rich. Soon after Lander County was created, the growing hamlet of Austin was selected as its seat in 1863. Inhabitants of the neighboring communities of Houston and Jacob's Well soon thereafter relocated to Austin.

With a lull in the activity in the Virginia City mines, and with increased attention from the California press, Austin's population swelled. Because the mineral discovery at Austin was overhyped, capital from all over the country streamed into the town. Elaborate stone, brick, and wood buildings were constructed, including schools, churches, hotels, and saloons, along with several expensive mills to process the ore on-site. Although its mines' production was relatively low, Austin served as a base of operation from which prospectors discovered countless other strikes. These strikes, in turn, brought about the creation of new towns and in some cases whole new counties, including Nye, White Pine, and Eureka.

The town today is a shadow of its lively self of 140 years ago, but many of Austin's original buildings still stand. The more transient buildings are decaying rapidly and may not survive many more years if left to continued neglect, but some of the more substantial stone buildings are still standing in fine shape today.

96 Monitor Valley (Potts) Hot Spring

General description: Several hot springs in an isolated valley in central Nevada. The hot spring with the largest discharge is piped into a circular watering trough, providing a nice bath. This is another scenic valley, and once again the view from the spring is fantastic.

Location: Central Nevada, approximately 45 miles southeast of Austin and 86 miles northeast of Tonopah.

Primitive/developed: Primitive, except for the diversion of the hot spring water into the watering trough.

Best time of year: Year-round.

Restrictions: None.

Access: Most passenger cars can make the trip. The last few miles are on a lesser developed road, but most sturdy cars with sufficient clearance should do fine.

Water temperature: 130 degrees F at the source, 105 degrees F in the tub.

Nearby attractions: Ghost town of Belmont, Toyaibe National Forest.

Services: None; nearest gasoline, food, and lodging can be found in Austin, approximately 45 miles away, or in Tonopah, 86 miles away. There are no services in Belmont.

Camping: There does not appear to be any restrictions against camping at this spot. Understand, however, that this is undeveloped camping. There are several campgrounds in the Toyaibe National Forest to the west, though these are also undeveloped sites.

Map: USGS topographic, Summit Mountains, NV, quadrangle, 1:100,000 scale.

Finding the spring: From Austin, travel east on U.S. Highway 50 for 12 miles. Turn right

Monitor Valley (Potts) Hot Spring

(south) onto Nevada Highway 376 for approximately 100 yards. Turn left on a large, graded dirt road with Forest Service signs to Toquime Cave. Travel on this road, past the turnoff to Spencer Hot Springs, continuing on the main graded dirt road. This Forest Service road takes you up into the mountains and into the Toyaibe National Forest. Travel on this road for approximately 28 miles into the next valley to the east, Monitor Valley. At approximately 28 miles from NV 376, you will reach Monitor Valley Road; turn right (south) here. Travel on this equally well-maintained road for 3.8 miles to a Y in the road, where you stay left. From the Y, travel another 2.1 miles to Forest Service Road 25, which you take and soon thereafter cross a creek and pass an abandoned farmhouse. Travel another 1 mile to another dirt road on your right, which takes you directly to the spring.

The Hot Spring

Like many other hot springs in northern and central Nevada, Monitor Valley Hot Spring is one of several springs flowing into a broad valley used for grazing. These springs are also isolated but unlike some of the others, not well-known. You should have no problem with privacy here. The largest flowing spring is diverted into a circular watering trough, where the water cools from 130 degrees F at source to approximately 105 degrees F in the trough. The water in the trough is kept relatively uniform in temperature and also stays fairly clean due to the constant inflow and outflow of water. The trough is approximately 6 feet across and 3 feet deep. Cattle utilize this area, but the trough is generally clean and provides a great bath in a great location.

97 Diana's Punch Bowl

General description: An absolutely amazing geologic feature in an isolated valley in central Nevada. The spring consists of an immense travertine hill with a pit in the middle, approximately 50 feet across, with hot spring water in the bottom. The hill is visible from miles away and truly awe-inspiring upon inspection. Though it is impossible to bathe at the main source, there are other smaller sources at the base of the hill.

Location: Central Nevada, approximately 50 miles southeast of Austin and 80 miles northeast of Tonopah.

Primitive/developed: Primitive.

Best time of year: Year-round.

Restrictions: Be extremely careful if driving up the travertine hill. Do not try it at night! Be sure to close any cattle gates.

Access: Most passenger cars can make the trip to the hill. I don't recommend driving up the travertine hill, but if you are going to, you may want a car with decent clearance and power.

Water temperature: 190 degrees F at the source, 110 degrees F in the tubs on the margin of the hill.

Nearby attractions: Ghost town of Belmont, Toyaibe National Forest.

Services: None; nearest gasoline, food, and lodging can be found in Winnemucca, approximately 50 miles away, or in Tonopah, about 80 miles away. There are no services in Belmont.

Camping: There do not appear to be any restrictions against camping here, but I would not recommend camping on the travertine hill. There is plenty of space at the base of the hill, where there are other hot springs. There are also campgrounds in the Toyaibe National Forest, though these are also undeveloped spaces.

Map: USGS topographic, Summit Mountains, NV, quadrangle, 1:100,000 scale.

Finding the spring: From Austin, travel east on U.S. Highway 50 for 12 miles. Turn right (south) onto Nevada Highway 376 for approximately 100 yards. Turn left on a large, graded dirt road with Forest Service signs to Toquime Cave. Travel on this road, past the turnoff to Spencer Hot Springs, for approximately 28 miles into the Monitor Valley, turning right on Monitor Valley Road (approximately 28 miles from NV 376). Travel on this road as if you were going to Monitor Valley Hot Spring, bearing left at the Y in the road after 3.8 miles. Continue on the main road, passing Forest Service Road 25 to the Monitor Valley Hot Spring, and travel approximately 2.3 miles past that intersection until you reach another intersection, where you turn left. After another 2.1 miles, turn left on a fairly well-maintained road. By this time you will definitely see the large white travertine hill. Travel for approximately 1.3 miles to the hill, passing through a cattle gate, which must be closed behind you.

The Hot Spring

One of the most amazing geologic features in the state, Diana's Punch Bowl is aptly titled. In the middle of the massive travertine hill is a large cavern that drops almost 30 feet to a big pool of hot water below. The cavern is approximately 50 feet across, and its walls are completely vertical. BE EXTREMELY CAREFUL HERE! If you fall in, there is a good chance you won't be coming out in one piece. Keep a tight hold on pets. Again, I do not recommend driving onto the hill, as it is only a short walk from the base. This caution applies particularly during the night, when you could easily not see the cavern and drive right into it. After staring in amazement at this creation, drive to the far side of the hill where there is a small creek fed by several hot springs. This creek is about 110 degrees F but is quite a nice spot for a break or for camping. The scenery is once again spectacular. The green valley and high mountains in the distance provide an excellent backdrop for Diana's Punch Bowl.

The founder of the town of Tonopah, J. L. Butler, apparently knew about Diana's Punch Bowl, visiting it frequently. Butler claimed that the water level in the spring dropped considerably, indicating that the level fluctuates occasionally. He also mentioned that gas was emitted from the spring, and even claims to have seen flames emerge from the pit on occasion.

Belmont: Perhaps one of the best ghost towns in Nevada, Belmont is worth a special trip in and of itself. Located on the main road from Monitor Valley to Tonopah, Belmont sits on either side of a low divide separating two valleys. The mine itself, mill remains, and smelter are all on the Monitor Valley side, while the town site lies to the west at the north end of NV 376. Founded in 1865, Belmont is one of the oldest and most genuine ghost towns in the state. The high points of the town include a cemetery with original hand-carved wood grave markers, a row of original storefronts, and the magnificent Belmont courthouse, which has had substantial restoration and renovation work. Because of the number of people living in Belmont and the intensive mining activity, the town served as the Nye County seat from 1876 to 1905, when it was supplanted by Tonopah.

The stately two-story walls of the Highbridge ore mill still stand just south of the smelter, illustrating just how much money was invested into this location years ago. With the decreasing production of Belmont's mines by the turn of the century and the rise of mining at Goldfield and Tonopah, Belmont was all but abandoned by 1910. It is hard to imagine this small remnant of a town with the amount and type of activity that must have occurred there at one time. The Belmont saloon is still open today, containing countless relics of the Belmont of old.

To reach Belmont, continue south on Monitor Valley Road past Diana's Punch Bowl, following signs to Belmont and Tonopah. You will soon see the large smokestack to the west, at the base of the mountains. Follow the main road as it approaches the smokestack and over the hill into the town itself. This same road will take you to NV 376, which eventually becomes a paved road, and which in turn will take you to U.S. Highway 6 after approximately 40 miles. Turn right (west) on US 6 and travel 5 miles to Tonopah.

WARM SPRING REGION

The least populated portion of the state so far discussed, this region provides some of the most unanticipated contrasts in the book. The lower, dry desert region surrounding Warm Spring can seem truly desolate and empty, until one makes the drive into magnificent Hot Creek Valley, where towering granite walls meet you and lush green vegetation is watered by a year-round creek. This area also lies to the north of the immense Nellis Air Force Base, the Nevada Test Site (location of nuclear weapons testing), and the mysterious Area 51 and Groom Lake. The Groom Lake region, the most isolated and highly secure portion of Nellis Air Force Base, has been referred to as "Dreamland," as for years the Air Force would not acknowledge its very existence. The small town of Rachel is known by many as the UFO-spotting capital of the country, owing to the large number of sightings reported in the area every year. Nevada Highway 375 (on which Rachel lies) was recently renamed the Extra Terrestrial Highway.

Owing to its lack of population, traveling in this portion of Nevada requires extra preparation, as there are few towns with any services. There are no services at Warm Springs, for example, and Rachel, 62 miles away, provides only the most basic of services (though there is one motel). Alamo and Ash Springs are also very small, though they do provide basic services.

98 Warm Springs

General description: A one-time active hot spring resort in an isolated part of central Nevada, at the intersection of two highways. Although the bathhouse is closed, the hot spring itself can still be visited, and there are portions of the creek that have been dammed up to provide bathing opportunities.

Location: Central Nevada, approximately 50 miles from Tonopah.

Primitive/developed: The developed portions are all closed and fenced off. There are other more primitive pools along the source creek, however.

Best time of year: Spring, fall, and winter. Summer can be too hot.

Restrictions: Keep out of the old pool grounds and the abandoned restaurant. There is also private property just beyond the hot spring source.

Access: As it is immediately off the highway, any car can make the trip. To drive the few hundred yards to the source, you will need a high-clearance vehicle and possibly four-wheel drive. You can always walk if you have neither of these.

Water temperature: 140 degrees F at the source, gradually cooling as it flows downhill. By the time the water reaches the old resort, it is approximately 105 degrees F.

Nearby attractions: Hot Creek Canyon.

Services: None; nearest gasoline, food, and lodging can be found in Tonopah, approximately 50 miles away. At one time there was a bar and restaurant at Warm Springs, but it is now closed.

The source of Warm Springs

Camping: Much of the area around the spring is private property. I do not recommend camping here anyway, as it is immediately off the highway, and there is plenty of interesting country nearby where undeveloped camping abounds.

Map: USGS topographic, Warm Springs, NV, quadrangle, 1:100,000 scale.

Finding the springs: From Tonopah, travel east on U.S. Highway 6 for 50 miles to the abandoned bar and restaurant. You will see the closed pool, and if you go to the back, you will see the diverted creek of water flowing into the pool. To see the source, follow the small road leading up to the travertine hill behind the resort site. After approximately 200 yards, this road climbs to the top of the travertine hill—don't try this with a regular passenger car. Either park and walk the last 50 to 100 yards, or drive up if you can. The cooler pools are adjacent to the closed restaurant and bar, under a few small trees.

The Hot Springs

Also known as Nanny Goat Hot Spring, Warm Springs was quite a resort at one time, boasting a substantial pool and bathhouse. Aside from the hot spring resort, a restaurant and gas station were also once open at Warm Springs but are now closed. The only contact with the outside world here nowadays is a pay phone.

The hot spring source on top of the large travertine hill is another interesting geologic feature. The water emerging from the ground is crystal clear and extremely hot, and the travertine is strikingly white, in direct contrast to the more subdued colors of the surrounding desert. Apparently, the hot spring lies on a major geological fault, with several recently reported earthquakes attributed to it.

Do not bathe at the source, but return to the abandoned resort and find a few small pools dammed up in the creek on the east side of the restaurant. You can also follow the water on the other side of the highway, where it is cooler and the pools are smaller. Although this is an isolated part of the state, do not expect to have the area to yourself. Often, there is someone camped in an RV adjacent to the dammed-up pools, and a surprising number of people pass through this region, usually stopping off at Warm Springs.

99 Ash Meadows

General description: A collection of natural hot and warm springs located within a wildlife refuge in southwestern Nevada. Bathing is not allowed in any of the springs, except for a large reservoir.

Location: Southwest Nevada, approximately 90 miles northwest of Las Vegas.

Primitive/developed: Primitive.

Best time of year: Spring, fall, and winter. Summer can be hot.

Restrictions: The springs are within the Ash Meadows National Wildlife Refuge. The refuge is open for day use only. Vehicles must remain on established roads.

Access: The main roads within the refuge are well-maintained graded dirt roads and accessible by most vehicles. The secondary roads (leading to several of the hot springs) may be impassable in wet weather.

Water temperature: Varies among the several springs. The hottest is Devil's Hole at 92 degrees F. Most of the rest of the springs are in the low 80 degree F range.

Nearby attractions: Death Valley.

Services: There are no services at the refuge. Nearest services are 22 miles away in Pahrump, and limited services (lodging) are found in Death Valley Junction, 7 miles away.

Camping: Camping is not permitted in the wildlife refuge. The nearest camping is in Death Valley.

Maps: Nevada Highway Map; USGS topographic, Death Valley Junction, NV, quadrangle, 1:100,000 scale.

Finding the springs: From Death Valley Junction, travel north on California Highway 127. Shortly after crossing into Nevada, look for a sign for the wildlife refuge on your right. Turn on this paved road (approximately 7 miles from Death Valley Junction), and drive approximately 5 miles to the refuge headquarters. From Pahrump, travel north on Nevada Highway 160, and look for the signs for the refuge on your left. Turn left on the paved road, and travel approximately 20 miles to the refuge. From Las Vegas, travel north on U.S. Highway 95 for approximately 69 miles to NV 160. Turn south and look for the signs for the Ash Meadows National Wildlife Refuge. Turn right on the graded dirt road, and drive approximately 12 miles to the refuge. Once at the refuge, head to the headquarters to pick up a map and information on Ash Meadows.

The Hot Springs

A collection of hot and warm springs feed Ash Meadows, which in 1984 became a national wildlife refuge. Prior to that time, the well-watered valley was used for farming and ranching. There are several hot and warm springs to visit while at Ash

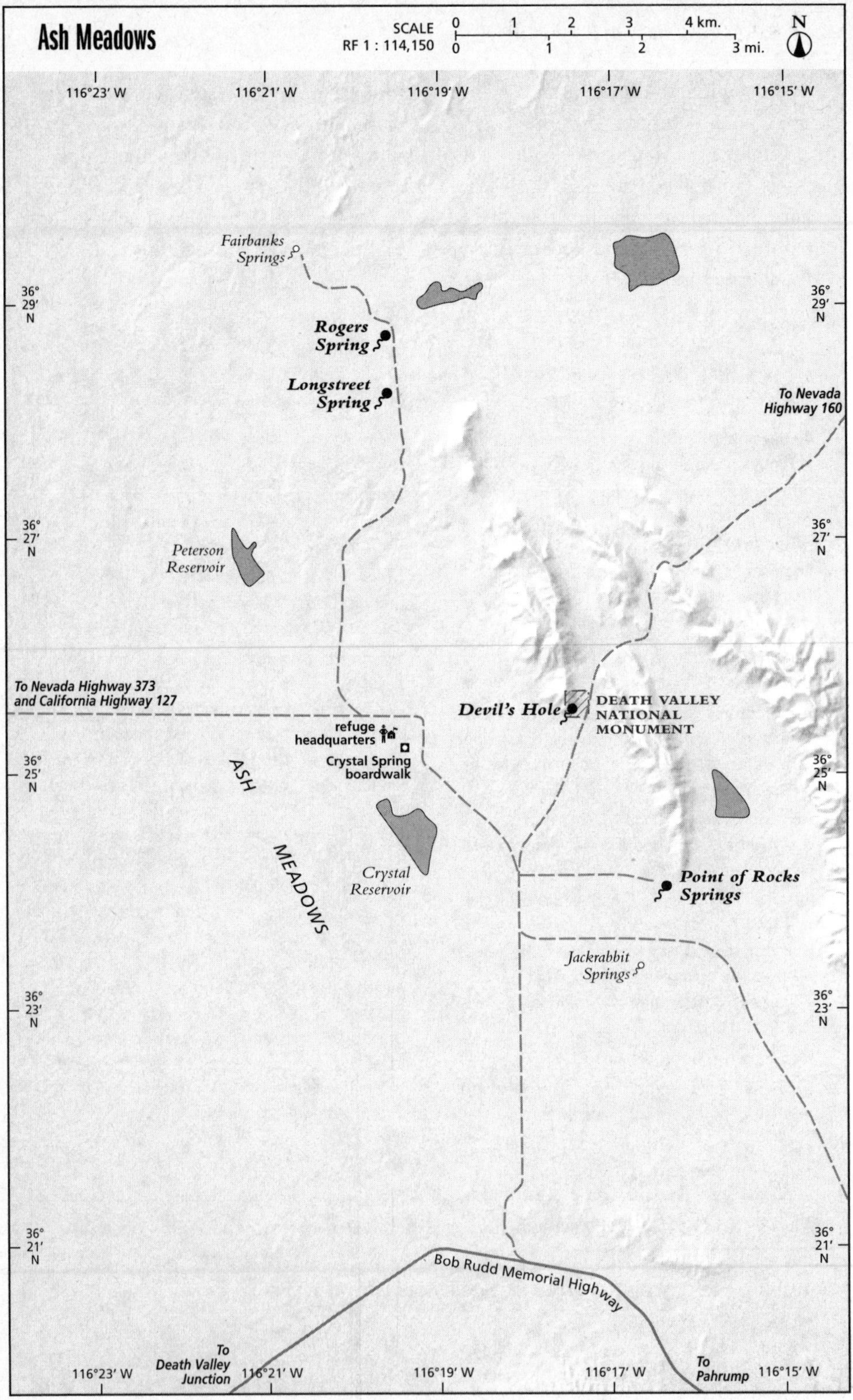
Ash Meadows
SCALE
RF 1 : 114,150
0 1 2 3 4 km.
0 1 2 3 mi.
N
116°23′ W
116°21′ W
116°19′ W
116°17′ W
116°15′ W
36° 29′ N
36° 27′ N
36° 25′ N
36° 23′ N
36° 21′ N
Fairbanks Springs
Rogers Spring
Longstreet Spring
To Nevada Highway 160
Peterson Reservoir
To Nevada Highway 373 and California Highway 127
refuge headquarters
Crystal Spring boardwalk
Devil's Hole
DEATH VALLEY NATIONAL MONUMENT
ASH MEADOWS
Crystal Reservoir
Point of Rocks Springs
Jackrabbit Springs
Bob Rudd Memorial Highway
To Death Valley Junction
To Pahrump

Longstreet Spring, Ash Meadows

Meadows. The first, and most significant, is Devil's Hole, which is actually operated by the National Park Service. Though completely fenced, Devil's Hole can be peered into via a short walk from a parking area. It is worth the stop. Another spring in the area worth a special trip is Point of Rocks Springs. A 91 degree F hot spring feeds a small pond, with the overflow water going into a small creek. Previously this water was channeled into a canal that was utilized for crop irrigation. Today, the water is permitted to follow a natural channel. The area is quite idyllic. This spring is located on a well-graded dirt road, a few miles southwest of the refuge headquarters. Also worth a stop are Rogers and Longstreet Springs (both 82 degrees F) at the north end of the refuge, also located along a secondary dirt road. This road may be impassable during wet weather. The springs both form beautiful pools of clear warm water at their sources. From these pools the water flows out over a broad area, supporting many trees and plants, not to mention a variety of wildlife.

Ash Meadows National Wildlife Refuge is home to numerous threatened and endangered species, including the desert pupfish, who survive in the waters of the many warm springs. Though the area was used for farming for years, it is currently in the process of being "restored" to a more natural state. Many channels of water are being returned to their natural courses. There are no services at the refuge itself, except for portable toilets at the headquarters and a few other locations. Swimming and bathing are allowed only in the Crystal Reservoir, adjacent to the refuge headquarters. An interpretive boardwalk trail leads from the headquarters to Crystal Spring (91 degrees F), pointing out many aspects of the flora and fauna of the refuge. Bird-watching opportunities abound here. Hunting is permitted at certain times and in certain places in the refuge. Call ahead for further information at (775) 372–5435.

100 Ash Springs

General description: A series of natural hot springs and one beautiful bathing pool, surrounded by several large trees in a picnic spot in an isolated portion of south-central Nevada. Ash Springs is an ideal place for a soak, if you happen to be in this isolated part of the state.

Location: South-central Nevada, approximately 97 miles from Las Vegas.

Primitive/developed: Primitive.

Best time of year: Spring, fall, and winter. Summer can be hot.

Restrictions: The springs and pool are on BLM property. Obey all posted signs.

Access: Only a short distance off the highway, most passenger cars can make the trip.

Water temperature: 97 degrees F at the source, approximately 92 to 95 degrees F in the bathing pool.

Nearby attractions: White River Petroglyphs site, Crystal Springs, Caliente Hot Springs, Panaca Warm Springs.

Services: Limited services can be found at Ash Springs, including gasoline and groceries. For more extensive services, you must go all the way to Las Vegas.

Camping: Camping is not permitted at the springs themselves. There is plenty of BLM

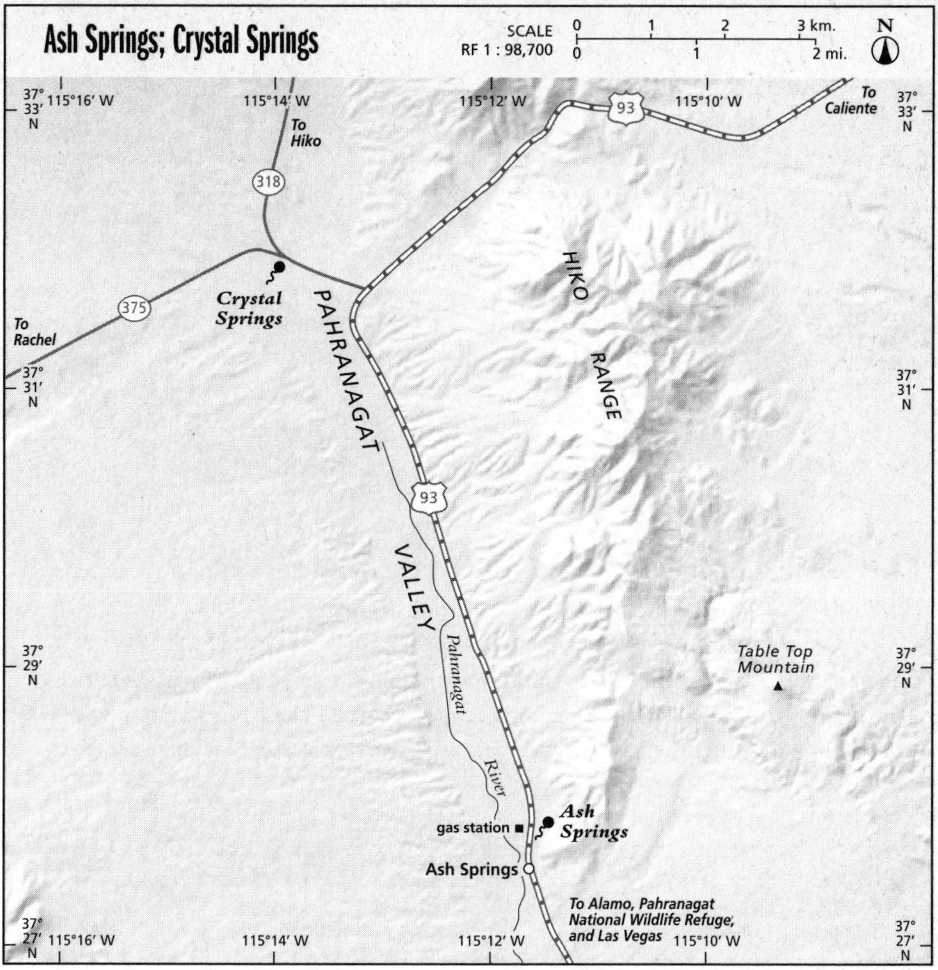

land in the surrounding countryside where undeveloped camping can be had.

Maps: Nevada Highway Map; USGS topographic, Hiko, NV, quadrangle, 1:24,000 scale.

Finding the springs: From Las Vegas, travel east on Interstate 15 for 22 miles to Nevada Highway 93. Travel north on NV 93 for 81 miles to the small hamlet of Alamo, then continue north on NV 93 for approximately 5 miles farther to Ash Springs. Continue past a fenced-in area with NO TRESPASSING signs on the right, and turn right at the end of the fence line onto a dirt road. This road is across the highway from a gas station. Drive a short distance (100 yards) to the picnic area with the springs.

The Hot Springs

A pleasant set of hot springs in an isolated part of the state, Ash Springs provide a welcome oasis to the dry desert. One of the springs has been diverted into a beautiful bathing pool, and several springs form a small creek with a few small pools. Although this is an isolated part of the state, the springs are relatively well known

Ash Springs

and easily accessible. Keep this in mind when bathing. A gas station is located across the highway from the springs, providing limited services. There is no camping permitted at the springs themselves, and there are no hotels in the immediate area.

101 Crystal Springs

See map on page 229.

General description: A series of natural warm springs forming several big ponds, surrounded by many large trees in an isolated portion of south-central Nevada. Crystal Springs is a short distance from Ash Springs and is worth a visit when in this part of the state.

Location: South-central Nevada, approximately 100 miles from Las Vegas.

Primitive/developed: Primitive.

Best time of year: Spring, fall, and winter. Summer can be hot.

Restrictions: There are no posted signs, but camping is likely not permitted.

Access: Within walking distance from the highway.

Water temperature: 90 degrees F at the source, cooling rapidly in the ponds. The lower pond is approximately 75 degrees F.

Nearby attractions: White River Petroglyphs site, Ash Springs, Caliente Hot Springs, Panaca Warm Springs.

Services: Limited services can be found at Ash Springs, including gasoline and groceries. For more extensive services, you must go all the way to Las Vegas.

Camping: Camping is not advisable at the springs themselves. There is plenty of BLM land in the surrounding countryside where undeveloped camping can be had.

Maps: Nevada Highway Map; USGS topographic, Hiko, NV, quadrangle, 1:24,000 scale.

Finding the springs: From Las Vegas, travel east on Interstate 15 for 22 miles to Nevada Highway 93. Travel north on NV 93 for 85 miles (3.7 miles from Ash Springs) to Nevada Highway 318, where you turn left. Travel another 0.5 mile to the intersection with Nevada Highway 375, where you bear left.

Immediately after passing this intersection, look for a state historical marker on your left. Pull off the highway here and park. The hot springs are behind this sign, a short walk through a small opening in a barbed-wire fence in a large collection of cottonwood trees.

The Hot Springs

Another pleasant set of hot springs in an isolated part of the state, Crystal Springs sits in a cluster of large cottonwood trees that form an inviting oasis. Two big ponds are formed from a warm spring with a substantial flow. Both ponds are lukewarm. The lower pond is formed from the damming up of the upper one, with water passing through a large culvert into the second. This appears to be the better pool for bathing.

Pahranagat Valley: The Pahranagat Valley was named by the Paiute Indians, for the "place of many waters." The presence of water in this arid part of the country made it an important place to the Paiutes. The valley was also a natural travel route and served as one of the alternate routes for the Mormon Trail. Early settlers recognized the value of the area in cattle ranching. Crystal Springs, believe it or not, was for a short time the county seat for Lincoln County in 1866, prior to its move to Hiko, a short distance to the north. Settlers continued to arrive, and soon

Crystal Springs

many prosperous small ranches emerged. Ranching continues to be the focus of activity in the area today. The valley is also home to a wide variety of migratory birds, and much of it is designated a wildlife refuge. There are several hot and warm springs in the valley, most of which are on private land.

102 Caliente Hot Springs

General description: A small hotel in the town of Caliente, built over a hot spring that feeds three hot tub rooms.

Location: Southeast Nevada, approximately 150 miles northeast of Las Vegas.

Primitive/developed: Developed, though rustic baths and hotel.

Best time of year: Spring, fall, and winter. Summer can be hot.

Restrictions: This is a private establishment.

Access: Within the town of Caliente.

Water temperature: 118 degrees F at the source, 105 degrees F as it comes out of the ground. Water is admitted into the baths and can be mixed with cold water to obtain the desired temperature.

Nearby attractions: Ash Springs, Crystal Springs, Kershaw-Ryan State Park, Cathedral Gorge State Park, Panaca Warm Springs.

Services: The Caliente Hot Springs hotel contains several small rooms with TV and phone, and some with spa tubs and kitchenettes. Other services (gas, food, lodging, etc.) are available in the town of Caliente.

Caliente Hot Springs

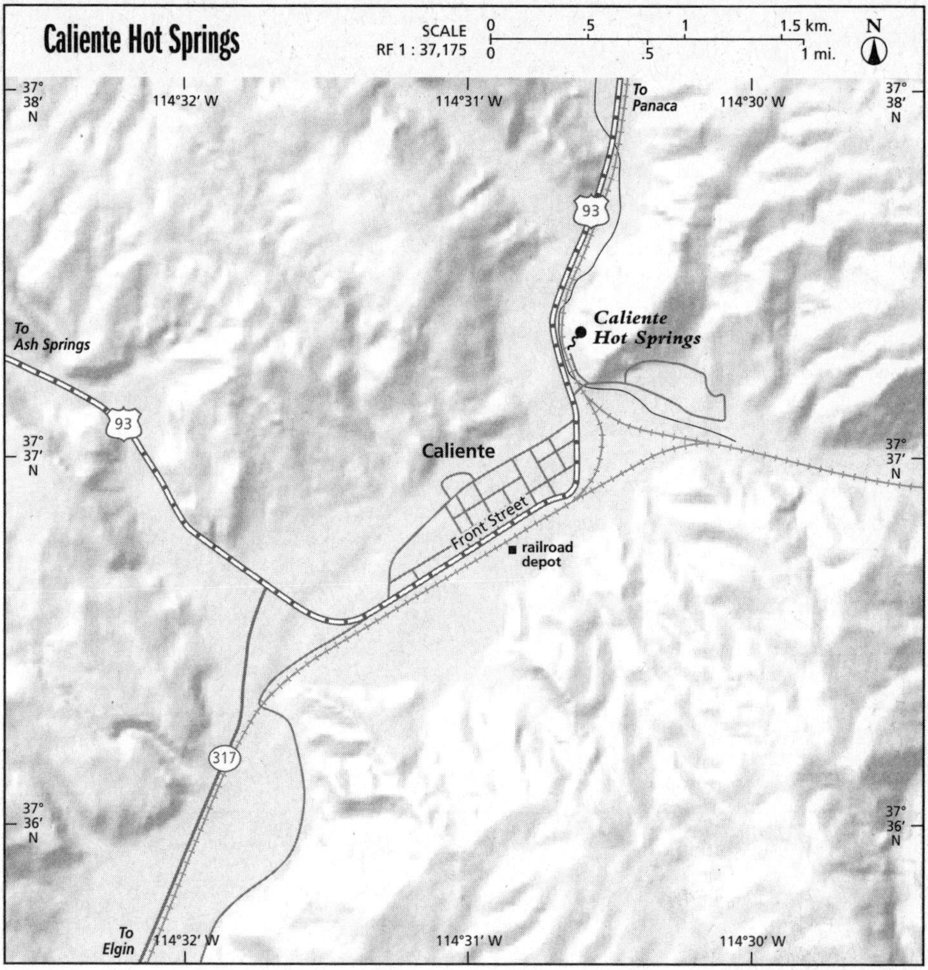

Camping: Several state campgrounds are located nearby.

Map: Nevada Highway Map.

Finding the springs: Located at the north end of the town of Caliente, on U.S. Highway 93. When coming from the south, turn right off US 93 at the sign for the springs, then left after crossing over the creek. The town of Caliente is approximately 150 miles from Las Vegas, 135 miles from Ely, and 110 from St. George, Utah.

The Hot Springs

The small hotel is built adjacent to a large hot spring with an internal temperature of 118 degrees F. The water is piped into three small rooms with large baths. A faucet allows the hot water to fill the baths, and cold water can be added to find the right mixture. For more information call (888) 726–3777, or visit www.calientehotspringsmotel.com.

103 Panaca Warm Springs

General description: Small pond fed by a warm spring outside of the town of Panaca.

Location: Southeast Nevada, 25 miles from Caliente, approximately 175 miles northeast of Las Vegas, and 110 miles south of Ely.

Primitive/developed: Primitive. The only improvements consist of a dam on one side of the pond and a ladder near the source.

Best time of year: Spring, summer, and fall. The dirt road to the spring can be very muddy in wet weather.

Restrictions: The pond is maintained by the town of Panaca, though it rests on BLM land.

Access: A short distance (1 mile) from the small town of Panaca, on a well-maintained dirt road.

Water temperature: 88 degrees F at the source; the pond is cooler.

Nearby attractions: Ash Springs, Crystal Springs, Kershaw-Ryan State Park, Cathedral Gorge State Park, Caliente Hot Springs.

Services: Services (gas, food, lodging, etc.) are available in the town of Panaca, 1 mile away.

Camping: There is no campground at or adjacent to the springs, though there are no posted restrictions against camping. Several state campgrounds are located nearby.

Maps: Nevada Highway Map; USGS topographic, Panaca, NV, quadrangle, 1:24,000 scale.

Finding the springs: From U.S. Highway 93, turn east (right if you are coming from the south from Caliente) on Nevada Highway 319, and drive into the town of Panaca. Turn left on Fifth Street, and drive through the neighborhood for several blocks. Look for a Nevada State historical marker ahead. At the marker (which is in front of a small community park), make a right turn onto a well-graded dirt road. Travel another 0.5 mile on this dirt road to the pond on your right.

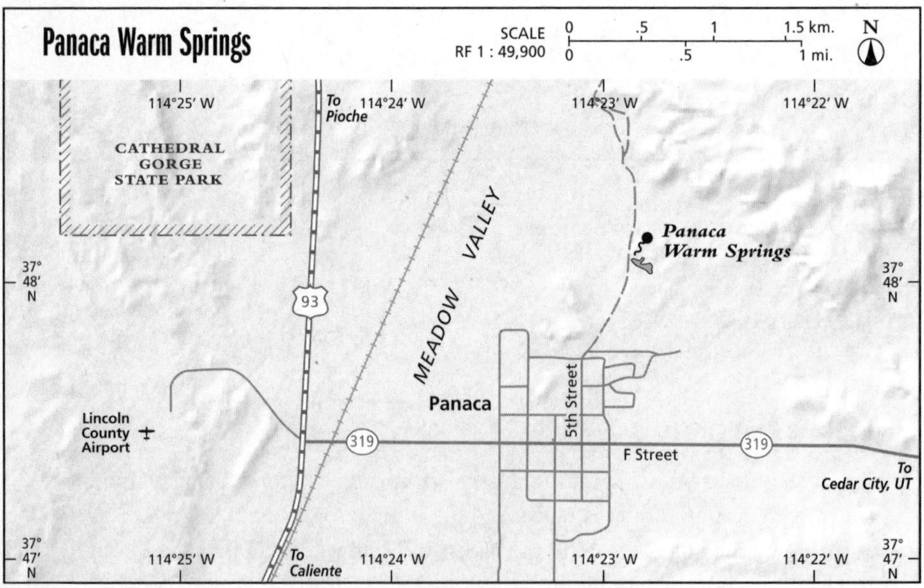

Panaca Warm Springs

The Hot Springs

Panaca Warm Springs emerge out of a small hillside feeding a large shallow pond outside the small town of Panaca. One end of the pond has been dammed up to better control the flow of water. The pond is apparently used by locals during warmer months, as the water is not very hot. A ladder and rope swing are present.

Panaca Warm Springs was a strategic location historically. Forming an important oasis, the springs were visited by the Manley party on their route to California before suffering in Death Valley. The springs form the heart of the Meadow Valley, which was the location of an early Mormon settlement beginning in 1858.

TONOPAH AND GOLDFIELD REGION

Following the demise of the great Comstock Lode in northern Nevada, a second mining boom occurred in the Goldfield-Tonopah region. As with so many mining towns in Nevada, Goldfield grew rapidly once the discovery of its rich ores became known. Beginning in 1900, the Goldfield area yielded silver in abundance. For the next twenty years, until roughly 1920, Goldfield and Tonopah would be the political, economic, and social center of Nevada.

A poor part-time miner by the name of John Butler prospected many portions of Nevada, until in 1900 he came across a rich outcrop in southwestern Nevada, upon which Tonopah would be founded. The ore discovered by Butler, however, required the investment of outside capital. The first to participate was a lawyer named Tasker Oddie. With the help of an assayer and several miners, the partners were able to obtain two tons of ore, for which they received $500. The issuance of this check brought about substantial publicity and another rush, this time to southern Nevada. In 1904 grubstakers hired by Butler and his associates discovered ore approximately 30 miles south of Tonopah. This rich discovery quickly led to the creation of the Goldfield Mining District. As the land on which Tonopah and Goldfield were located was inhospitable, the founders had a difficult time acquiring financial backing. The region was devoid of wood, lacked water, and was far from any settlements or transportation links. Eventually, however, financial backing came, largely from eastern interests, and mines began to be seriously exploited.

Railroads were soon built (including the Tonopah and Goldfield, and the Bullfrog and Goldfield), large mills were constructed, water companies were formed, and more bank money arrived, along with thousands of people. Great advances in mills occurred during this period, as power was brought from miles away and more sophisticated techniques could be experimented with and put to practical use. Transportation saw great improvements as Tonopah and Goldfield were connected to major markets via several small lines to the Carson and Colorado Railroad in 1904. By 1905 the lines were all made standard gauge and were consolidated under the Tonopah and Goldfield Railroad.

By consolidating many of these interests, two men, George Nixon and George Wingfield, were able to gain almost complete control over the towns and, to a large extent, the whole state. The ascendancy of Wingfield and Nixon exemplified the fact that Nevada was truly a mining state during the first two decades of the twentieth century. By 1913 Tonopah and Goldfield were experiencing another new advance, the automobile. Because of their isolated locations and because roads in and out of the mining towns were poor, the automobile did not become a major source of transportation in Tonopah and Goldfield until well after the towns' declines. By the late 1910s the boom days were over, and the population declined rapidly after 1920. Many other towns sprung up in the deserts adjacent to Goldfield and Tonopah, including Bullfrog and Rhyolite, all of which withered away as fast as they developed. Although a small population exists in Goldfield today, the largest town in the area is Tonopah. Tonopah still subsists to a large part on mining, followed by tourism and the military.

104 Alkali Hot Spring

General description: Two hot springs in a small oasis setting in the middle of a dry portion of central Nevada. One of the springs is diverted into a makeshift tub, making for a nice bath.

Location: Central Nevada, approximately 11 miles west of Goldfield and 27 miles southwest of Tonopah.

Primitive/developed: Primitive, except for the creation of the tub and the diversion of water into it.

Best time of year: Fall, winter, and spring. Summer can be hot.

Restrictions: There are NO TRESPASSING signs in the area.

Access: Most passenger cars can make the trip, as the springs are immediately off a paved highway.

Water temperature: Approximately 120 degrees F at the source, 110 degrees F in the tub.

Nearby attractions: Historic mining town of Goldfield.

Services: None; nearest gasoline, food, and lodging can be found in Tonopah, approximately 27 miles away, and Goldfield, 11 miles away. There are few services in Goldfield, which is all but a ghost of its boisterous self in the early 1900s.

Camping: This is not the most ideal place to camp, as it is immediately off the road. There are also many NO TRESPASSING signs in the vicinity. There is plenty of undeveloped space in the surrounding area, however.

Map: USGS topographic, Goldfield, NV, quadrangle, 1:100,000 scale.

Finding the spring: From Tonopah, travel south on U.S. Highway 95 for 21 miles, and turn right (west) on the road to Silverpeak and Alkali. From Goldfield, travel north on US 95 for 4 miles, turning left on the same road. Travel on this paved road for approximately 6.8 miles. After rounding a curve, you will see the remains of a building on your left, which lies adjacent to the hot springs. Pull off the road here in the broad flat area, and look for the hot springs on the side of the hill.

The Hot Spring

Hot water emerges from the side of a small hill in a dry desert area. A few trees and an empty pool mark what was at one time a hot spring resort. The hot water is trapped in two separate pools. A small concrete deck has been built adjacent to the pools to make getting in and out easier. The pools are big enough for three or four people and are approximately 3 feet deep. The water temperature varies depending upon the time of year visited, but averages about 108 degrees F in one pool and 100 degrees F in the other. The water is a little murky, but it's still a pleasant bath. Although the road passing by the springs is lightly traveled, the pools are only a short distance from it and within sight. Use appropriate decorum. This can be a rather popular place with locals on weekend nights, but there generally won't be anyone around on weekdays.

The Giusti Resort: Like so many other hot springs described in this book, Alkali was also a hot spring resort. Originally, the hot springs consisted of only a few seeps, with little surface manifestation. In 1900, however, the Combination Mines Company drilled a substantial hole into the side of the hill to draw out more of the water. The water was concentrated into a channel and piped all the way to Goldfield to be utilized in the company's mill. During the early 1900s, during Goldfield's heyday, the springs were developed into a thriving resort. The spa contained a big swimming pool (which lies in ruins today), a large bathhouse, and several outbuildings. The spa was mostly patronized by folks from Goldfield, though travelers from other areas were also known to visit the spring. If you look closely, you can see many hints of this long-deserted resort.

Other hot springs in the area: There are several other hot springs in the general vicinity of Alkali. The nearby town of Silver Peak, approximately 18 miles from Alkali Hot Spring, contains one small hot spring on the north side of town, immediately off Nevada Highway 265. The hot springs were reportedly used for the town's original water supply. The Waterworks Hot Spring (as Silver Peak's springs were once known) are quite radioactive, and perhaps for this reason are not a source of the town's water today. The community of Silver Peak supports the large lithium mine in the adjacent Clayton Valley. Clayton Valley, in fact, is one of the world's principal sources of lithium.

On the east side of the Clayton Valley, between Silver Peak and Alkali Hot Spring, hot springs have been reported at different times. Labeled Pearl Hot Springs on the USGS topographic map, these hot springs are largely below the surface but have surface manifestation during certain times of the year. No water could be found at this location on three separate visits in the 1990s.

105 Fish Lake Valley

General description: A large geothermal well piped into a big concrete pool, overflowing into several warm ponds in an isolated portion of central Nevada. Owned by Esmerelda County, the hot spring has been improved over the years but has also seen substantially increased use and, with it, damage.

Location: Central Nevada, approximately 70 miles southwest of Tonopah.

Primitive/developed: Primitive in location only. The hot spring water has been piped into a fancy, brand-new pool.

Best time of year: Fall and spring. Summer can be hot, and the road to the spring can be wet and impassable at times during winter.

Restrictions: Please help to keep this place from being bulldozed by removing trash and refraining from vandalism.

Access: Most sturdy passenger cars can make the trip. Four-wheel drive may be required in

Fish Lake Valley

wet periods, and the road can become completely washed out in flash floods.

Water temperature: Approximately 105 degrees F in the tub, overflowing into several lukewarm ponds.

Nearby attractions: Ghost towns of Candelaria and Basalt.

Services: None; nearest gasoline, food, and lodging can be found in Tonopah, approximately 70 miles away. You can also drive to Bishop, approximately 80 miles west along U.S. Highway 6.

Camping: There is plenty of undeveloped space at the hot spring where camping is permitted. Keep in mind that there is no water or toilets here, however, and you may be sharing the area with others.

Map: USGS topographic, Davis Mountain, NV, quadrangle, 7.5-minute scale.

Finding the spring: From Tonopah, travel west on US 6 for 41 miles to Coaldale Junction. Stay on US 6 for another 6 miles to Nevada Highway 773, where you turn left (south). Drive south on NV 773 for 9 miles, connecting with Nevada Highway 264, on which you continue south. Travel approximately 5.7 miles from the intersection of NV 773 and NV 264, at which point you turn left onto a graded dirt road (immediately before a small house). Drive on this graded road for approximately 5.8 miles, where you bear left at a Y in the road, and continue another 1.2 miles to the spring.

The Hot Spring

Discovered in 1970 by an oil-exploration well, the hot water at Fish Lake Valley has been an excellent place to bathe ever since. The high-volume hot well is piped into a big concrete pool complete with wooden benches and a large concrete patio. The pool is approximately 7 by 2 feet and about 3 feet deep. The water overflows into two warm ponds (which now contain goldfish), keeping the pool's water clean and very appealing. The pool has been improved over the years by the county, with fences, barbecues, and trash cans all put in.

A few years ago this spring was not widely known, and due to its rather isolated location, a pleasant, private desert hot spring experience could be had. The increase in the use of the spring has brought along the usual ramifications, including trash, vandalism, alcohol abuse, and other assorted problems. Several signs remind visitors that if these types of problems do not cease, the area will be closed (which probably means bulldozing). Generally, however, this is still a pleasant place to visit and is certainly a great place for a hot bath. There are other hot wells reported in the Fish Lake Valley, but none of these have any bathing opportunities at present. The area does seem to have substantial geothermal potential, though most of it is below the surface.

SOUTHERN NEVADA

Dominated by Las Vegas in the south, southern Nevada possesses some of the most beautiful and desolate country in the state. Although the military owns and operates a large portion of the region, there is ample space to explore and experience. As with other portions of Nevada, much of the land is owned by the Bureau of Land Management. There are few towns once you get away from Las Vegas, so plan ahead if you're going to venture out. Also be aware that this part of the state can be significantly hotter than the other regions discussed. You may want to avoid this area during the heat of summer.

Many of the springs described for this region are a short trip from Las Vegas and are worth visiting if you're staying in the big city. Four of the hot springs profiled are within the Lake Mead National Recreation Area and tend to see more visitors than others described in the book. To reach the three hot springs located below the Hoover Dam, a boat trip is recommended. Though two of the springs can be hiked to, one of the hikes is difficult, and the other is even worse. By renting a boat at Willow Beach, however, the springs can be accessed relatively easily by water.

Bailey's Hot Spring

DEATH VALLEY REGION

Located a few hours from Las Vegas, this area is bordered on the west by Death Valley National Monument and on the east by Nellis Air Force Base. The region is bisected by U.S. Highway 95, connecting it to Tonopah to the north and Las Vegas to the south. The mostly dry Amargosa River runs from mountains within Nellis Air Force Base, through Beatty, and eventually into Badwater, the lowest spot in the United States at 282 feet below sea level, in Death Valley National Monument. Numerous ghost towns dot the area, including Rhyolite, Bullfrog, Amargosa, Chloride Cliff, and Leadfield, to name only a few.

There is an amazing number of hot and warm springs in the Death Valley region. Several within Death Valley National Park itself have been harnessed for various purposes. Nevares Springs, for example, provides water for the service area immediately north of Furnace Creek. Travertine Warm Springs provides water for the Furnace Creek Inn. There are several other springs that can be visited in a more natural state. Distances in this area can be long and towns few. The semi–resort town of Tecopa is approximately 80 miles to the southeast, and the hot springs in the Saline Valley can be reached via a long drive on paved highway, then a longer drive on dirt roads. Dirty Socks Hot Spring is farther west beyond the turnoff for the Saline Valley, on California Highway 190, approximately 105 miles from Beatty.

106 Bailey's Hot Spring

General description: A very rustic hot spring resort with three separate gravel-bottom pools, outside a small town in southern Nevada.

Location: Immediately north of the town of Beatty, in southwestern Nevada, approximately 115 miles northwest of Las Vegas.

Primitive/developed: Developed, though certainly not fancy.

Best time of year: Fall, winter, and spring. Summer is hot, and bathing even in an indoor hot spring may not be appealing.

Restrictions: This is a private resort; the tubs must be rented to use.

Access: As the resort is immediately off the highway, any car can make the trip.

Water temperature: Varies from 100 to 108 degrees F, depending upon the pool chosen.

Nearby attractions: Ghost towns of Rhyolite and Bullfrog, Death Valley, Keane Wonder Springs.

Services: There are no services at the resort but 5 miles away in Beatty.

Camping: Spaces can be rented for tents or RVs. Pool use is free to those camping at the resort.

Map: Nevada Highway Map.

Finding the spring: From Las Vegas, travel north on U.S. Highway 95 for approximately 115 miles to the town of Beatty. Continue north out of town for about 5 miles to the resort on the right side of the highway. From Tonopah, travel south on US 95 for approximately 87 miles to the resort on the left side of the highway. From Death Valley, drive east on California Highway 190, which becomes Nevada Highway 374, to the town of Beatty, where you will turn left on US 95, and travel 5 miles to the resort.

Bailey's Hot Spring

The Hot Spring

This simple, unadorned hot spring facility is supplied by several natural hot springs, each with substantial flow and temperature. The hot spring water is diverted into three pools at Bailey's, each covered and private. The water comes from a large natural hot spring and is piped into each room, where it is kept clean by a sufficient flow. The pools are all large, with sandy bottoms. The pool use is free to campers and open to the public for a small fee.

There are several other hot springs in the area surrounding Beatty. One of these springs supplies water for part of the town of Beatty. Others are on private property. With the discovery of gold in the early 1900s in the mountains to the southwest, Beatty emerged as a kind of transportation center. A rush to the area occurred following the discovery of gold in 1904 at Bullfrog, and prospecting occurred throughout the region immediately thereafter. One of the towns to emerge during this period was Lee, located near the state line. There were actually two towns known as Lee, one on each side of the state line. Because they were located in such an isolated, dry area, water had to be hauled to the towns. This was done by Adolph Nevares, for whom Nevares Springs in Death Valley are named. Between 1906 and 1907 a total of three railroads were constructed through Beatty to service the new mines of Rhyolite and Bullfrog, connecting them with Tonopah, Goldfield, and Las Vegas. Rhyolite and Bullfrog are ghost towns today and worth a visit. They are located immediately west of Beatty, off NV 374. Follow signs from town, on a dirt road, for approximately 3 miles from the highway. Beyond, on NV 374, is Death Valley National Monument, via Hell's Gate. Keane Wonder Springs is located a short distance away, off of the Beatty Cutoff (Daylight Pass Cutoff) Road.

LOWER COLORADO RIVER REGION

The narrow Black Canyon below the mighty Boulder Dam is home to three delightful hot springs. All of the springs are excellent for bathing, and all can be reached relatively easily by boat. Two of the springs are located in Nevada, and the third is in Arizona. Since they are all in the same vicinity, they are included in this section of the book for ease in trip planning. As these springs are located within the Lake Mead National Recreation Area, stop in at one of the ranger stations for further information, including up-to-date weather information, access issues, and regulations. The most convenient station to visit is the Alan Bible Visitor Center, (702) 293–8906, located at the intersection of U.S. Highway 93 and Nevada Highway 147, outside of Boulder City. The visitor center is open daily from 8:30 A.M. to 4:30 P.M.; closed on Thanksgiving, Christmas, and New Year's Day. From the hot springs in the Lower Colorado River, an easy trip can be made to Rogers Warm Spring, on the west shore of Lake Mead.

Traveling in this region requires extra care and preparation. Thunderstorms can be particularly sudden and dangerous, and flash floods can strike with little warning. Be sure to check local weather forecasts, and stay out when storms threaten. Bring plenty of water, and do not attempt to make shortcuts from any of the hikes described. Always register at the visitor center, and never hike alone.

107 Gold Strike Hot Spring

General description: A picturesque hot spring in a fabulous narrow valley near the Colorado River. The spring can only be reached by a rather technically difficult hike or by boat and a shorter hike.

Location: Southern Nevada, approximately 7 miles southeast of Boulder City.

Primitive/developed: Primitive.

Best time of year: Fall, winter, and spring. Summer is too hot.

Restrictions: Check in with the visitor center for information on trail condition, flash floods, and inclement weather.

Access: The hot spring requires a 2-mile hike, which involves some boulder climbing. The trailhead can be reached by any vehicle. By boat, the hike is approximately 100 yards.

Water temperature: 110 degrees F at the source, varying depending on pool chosen. The largest pool is approximately 100 degrees F.

Nearby attractions: Boulder Dam, Lake Mead.

Services: None; nearest gasoline, food, and lodging can be found in Boulder City, approximately 7 miles away.

Camping: Camping is permitted in the canyon, but because the spring cannot be reached by car, all equipment must be packed in. Do not camp in the canyon if rain is approaching, as flash floods can be deadly. Check in with the Alan Bible Visitor Center for latest camping information and requirements.

Map: USGS topographic, Boulder City, NV, quadrangle, 1:100,000 scale.

Gold Strike Hot Spring canyon

Finding the spring: From Boulder City, travel on U.S. Highway 93 for approximately 3 miles to the Alan Bible Visitor Center at the intersection with Nevada Highway 166. Stop in here to check with the rangers regarding latest access information and to pick up a map. Continue on US 93 for 1.2 miles past the Gold Strike Inn and Casino to a paved turnoff on the right. This paved road is rather steep, and if you don't think your vehicle can take it, park on the other side of the highway. Approximately 30 feet down this paved road is the trailhead to the spring. The trail is not well marked, but just follow the wash downstream. The trail is approximately 2 miles to the spring. By boat, travel up the Colorado River (north) from Willow Beach toward Boulder Dam until you reach mile marker 62. Keep an eye out for a pit toilet on the left, which marks the entrance to the canyon with the hot spring. You will also be able to see the warning cable across the river from the mouth of the canyon.

The Hot Spring

Once you make it the 2 miles down the canyon, you will begin to see water in the canyon. The last half of the hike is the most difficult, requiring some boulder scrambling, with substantial drop-offs. You will eventually come to the hot spring sources. Continue down the canyon until you find a large pool, which is ideal for bathing. There are also small waterfalls of hot water in this area and several other smaller pools to choose from. If you wish, you can hike down to the river, but be careful, as there are many difficult parts to this trek, with steep drop-offs.

108 Boy Scout Hot Spring

General description: A spectacular hot spring in a narrow canyon, accessible only by boat. A short hike is required from the beach at the mouth of the canyon.

Location: Southern Nevada, on the Colorado River, approximately 10 miles from Willow Beach.

Primitive/developed: Primitive.

Best time of year: Year-round. Summer can be hot.

Restrictions: None.

Access: By boat only, along with a short hike.

Water temperature: Varying depending upon pool chosen. Most are approximately 105 degrees F.

Nearby attractions: Boulder Dam, Lake Mead.

Services: None; nearest gasoline, food, and lodging can be found in Boulder City, approximately 20 miles away. Willow Beach has boat ramps, a store, and gasoline.

Camping: You can camp at the mouth of the canyon, but there is limited space. The river level also fluctuates widely, depending upon water released from the dam. Keep this in mind when securing your watercraft, and it pays to check in with the Bureau of Reclamation for more details, (702) 293–8415 or (702) 293–8000.

Map: USGS topographic, Boulder City, NV, quadrangle, 1:100,000 scale.

Finding the spring: To reach Willow Beach, travel east on U.S. Highway 93 from Boulder City. After crossing Boulder Dam, travel approximately 13 miles south to the access road to Willow Beach, on the right. It is a short drive to the beach and marina. From Willow Beach (by boat), travel upstream for approximately 9 miles. The canyon containing Boy Scout Hot Spring is a little over 0.5 mile from mile marker 61. The canyon is on the left, immediately before the river makes a bend to the right. After securing your watercraft (again, keep in mind changing water levels), hike up the canyon for a few hundred yards to the first spring.

The Hot Spring

Located in another narrow canyon, Boy Scout Hot Spring is an excellent adventure when boating the Colorado River. It is an unusual feeling to arrive at a hot spring accessible only by water. Despite this, however, the hot spring sees a high volume of visitation during the boating season (roughly May to October). Warm water trickles all the way to the river, so you will have to do some hiking in the creek bed to reach the hot spring. As you move farther upstream, the flow increases, along with the temperature. There are several pools ideal for bathing, plus waterfalls larger than those in the Gold Strike Hot Spring canyon. The size of these pools can vary widely, depending upon recent weather activities. As with the other canyons, be aware of flash floods, and stay out if rain threatens.

109 Arizona Hot Spring

General description: The third hot spring in the cluster along the Colorado River below Hoover Dam. Arizona Hot Spring contains a waterfall and an excellent pool for bathing, and can be reached by boat or a 3.25-mile hike.

Location: Southern Nevada, approximately 12 miles southeast of Boulder City.

Primitive/developed: Primitive.

Best time of year: Year-round, if coming by boat. Avoid the hike in the summer, as air temperatures can exceed 110 degrees F.

Restrictions: None.

Access: This spring requires a boat ride and a small hike, or a 3.25-mile hike from the highway.

Water temperature: 110 degrees F at the source, decreasing as it flows down the canyon. At the waterfall the water is approximately 95 degrees F.

Nearby attractions: Boulder Dam, Lake Mead.

Services: None; nearest gasoline, food, and lodging can be found in Boulder City, approximately 12 miles away. Willow Beach has boat ramps, a store, and gasoline.

Camping: There is plenty of open space at the mouth of the canyon where camping is permitted. There are no developed sites here, however, just lots of sand.

Map: USGS topographic, Boulder Dam, NV, quadrangle, 1:100,000 scale.

Finding the spring: From Boulder City, travel southeast on U.S. Highway 93 to Hoover Dam. Cross the dam and continue on US 93 to mile marker 4.2 and a National Park Service sign. Pull off the highway here, and park in the provided parking area. The hike begins here, at White Rock Canyon. Follow the main wash downstream for approximately 3 miles to the Colorado River. Once you reach the river, turn left (downstream) to the next canyon, approximately 0.25 mile away. Hike the short distance up the canyon to the first pool. If approaching by boat, travel upstream (north) from Willow Beach to mile marker 59. Travel almost another mile until you see warning buoys and a canyon on your right. There may also be a portable toilet at the mouth of the canyon. Secure your watercraft and hike the short distance to the spring.

The Hot Spring

As with the other hot springs in this area, Arizona can be reached by boat, so despite its relative isolation, it receives quite a few visitors. Because the hot spring water does not reach the Colorado on the surface, the first pool you reach is one of the better soaking pools. As you continue up the canyon, you will reach other soaking pools and eventually a large ladder, which takes you up to other pools and waterfalls.

Boulder Dam: Built in 1935, Boulder Dam is one of the engineering marvels of the world. The reason for the dam's construction was threefold: to control the sometimes violent and unpredictable waters of the Colorado River, to provide hydroelectric power to cities in the Southwest, and to put thousands of unemployed Americans to work in the middle of the Great Depression. The construction successfully completed all of these goals. Prior to the placement of the dam, steamboats actually navigated the waters of the Colorado from its mouth in the Gulf of California. The large boats steamed up the river to as far as a tiny hamlet of Mormon settlers at Calville (the creation of the reservoir submerged the remains of the town). To reach Calville, however, the steamboats utilized cable and pulley systems to drag them through the oftentimes treacherous Black Canyon (where the hot springs are located).

The dam construction lasted for over five years and required the labor of over 5,000 men and the capital of several large corporations. The growth of Las Vegas was aided in large part by the dam, particularly from its hydroelectric power, the infusion of money into the area, and the relative ease by which water could be drawn from the reservoir to support the city. Boulder City grew up as a supply center for the massive project and remains as a tourist supply center today. Tours can be taken within the dam itself and are conducted every day from 8:00 A.M. to 4:15 P.M. Memorial Day to Labor Day, 9:00 A.M. to 4:15 P.M. the rest of the year. Admission is $3.00 for adults, $1.50 for seniors, and free for children.

LAKE MEAD REGION

The massive Lake Mead is a boaters' and anglers' paradise. The lake is over 110 miles long, with a shoreline five times that distance. Although Nevada Highway 147 extends along the entire north shore of the lake, most of the rugged shoreline is only accessible by boat. The surrounding countryside is a rugged, dry landscape, offering panoramic vistas at every turn, with the geologic formations providing brilliant colors to the mountainsides. Several recreation areas on the shore offer boat ramps, boat rentals, campgrounds, stores, and restaurants. Boat cruises can also be booked on the *Desert Princess,* a sternwheeler, by contacting Lake Mead Cruises at (702) 293–6180.

For truly spectacular geologic formations and vistas, travel to the Valley of Fire State Park, located on Nevada Highway 169, east of Interstate 15. The park offers several points of interest, displays, and hiking trails. In addition, prehistoric rock art can be found in several locations in the park, including Atlatl Rock and Mouse's Tank. Because of its unusual rock formations and rare beauty, Valley of Fire has been the scene of several movies and television commercials and shows. The visitor center is located immediately off NV 169, midway into the park, and can be reached at (702) 397–2088. The center's hours are daily from 8:30 A.M. to 4:30 P.M., closed Christmas and New Year's Day.

110 Rogers Warm Spring

General description: A large picturesque pond and small creek near Lake Mead. Located in the Lake Mead National Recreation Area, this is a popular picnicking spot and not the place for a private hot spring soak.

Location: Southern Nevada, approximately 50 miles northeast of Las Vegas.

Primitive/developed: There are picnic grounds, a parking lot, and restrooms. The pond itself is natural, though a small concrete dam has been built on one side.

Best time of year: Fall and spring. Summer is too hot, and winter can be too cold for soaking in the warm water.

Restrictions: Rogers Warm Spring is within the Lake Mead National Recreation Area and is operated by the National Park Service. You must obey all the Park Service rules.

Access: Any car can make the trip, as the pond is located off a paved road.

Water temperature: 100 degrees F at the source, varying throughout the pond, which averages approximately 90 degrees F. The water cools quickly as it flows out of the pond into the small creek.

Nearby attractions: Lake Mead, Valley of Fire State Park.

Services: None; nearest gasoline, food, and lodging can be found in Las Vegas or Henderson, both approximately 50 miles away. Some services can be found in Overton and Logandale, although these are primarily small farming communities.

Camping: There is no camping permitted at Rogers Warm Spring. There are several developed and primitive campgrounds nearby, within the Lake Mead National Recreation Area.

Rogers Warm Spring

Map: USGS topographic, Lake Mead, NV, quadrangle, 1:100,000 scale.

Finding the spring: From Las Vegas, travel east on Lake Mead Boulevard. This road becomes Nevada Highway 147. Continue on NV 147 to the Lake Mead National Recreation Area and Nevada Highway 169 (North Shore Drive). Turn left (east) here. Continue on NV 169 for approximately 27 miles to Rogers Warm Spring on your left. There will be a Park Service sign for the picnic area and warm spring shortly before you reach the spring.

The Hot Spring

A natural hot spring forms this large pond in the middle of the dry desert, a few miles from Lake Mead. The water in the pond is pleasantly warm for bathing, although it has a murky and unappealing appearance. The water flows over a small concrete dam with a bridge over it and forms a small creek. The small waterfall produced by this flow out of the pond can be a nice spot for a bath if the weather is nice (i.e., not too hot or cold). Keep in mind that the water is not hot in the pond and is rather lukewarm by the time it flows out into the creek. Keep in mind also that this is a public picnic spot that receives a lot of visitors from Lake Mead—this is not a secluded spring. The Park Service warns you not to allow any of the water to get into your nose, mouth, or ears, as a type of amoeba has been found in the water that can be extremely dangerous. Please follow this advice, and do not put your head under water.

APPENDIX A
Closed, But Not Forgotten

You may have heard about these hot springs, but alas! all are now closed to the public. Do not visit them; do not trespass!

California

Bassett Hot Springs
Crabtree Hot Springs
Democrat Hot Springs: These high-temperature (115 degrees F) springs served a resort built in 1904. The springs were named after the political party that was in power at that time. Now they are on private property; do not trespass!
Gilroy Hot Springs: Once the site of a fantastic mountain resort, these hot springs have been purchased by the State of California to add to Henry Coe State Park, which we hope will reopen the property.
Kelly Hot Spring
San Juan Capistrano Hot Springs: These springs were closed for a road-widening project.
Scovern Hot Springs: Located in Isabella, Scovern Hot Springs are the hottest in the area. Local Native Americans believe spiritual powers are present at the site, preventing it from ever being developed.
Wheeler Hot Springs

Nevada

Brady's Hot Springs: These are some of the hottest springs in the state, with a source temperature of 209 degrees F! Located on private property, they can be viewed *from a distance* as they boil and produce steam off Interstate 80 at the Hot Springs/Nightingale exit east of Fernley.
Crescent Valley Hot Springs
Gerlach Hot Springs
Golconda Hot Springs: These springs are located on private property. If you're near Golconda or Winnemucca in northern Nevada, ask around town for permission to see the springs, but don't make a special trip.
Golconda Hot Springs (South): On the other side of town, this spring is dry, leaving just a shallow pit.
Great Boiling Hot Springs
Hot Creek Canyon
Hot Pot: Also known as Blossom Hot Springs, this spot is now dry.

Howard Hot Spring
Lawton Hot Springs (River Inn Hot Springs)
Moapa Hot Springs: Also known as Iverson's Warm Spring, this scenic resort may reopen.
Monte Neva Hot Springs
Pyramid Lake Hot Springs: Sadly, these hot springs are closed indefinitely because of vandalism.
Saratoga Hot Spring
Tyrol Warm Spring

APPENDIX B
Further Reading

Garside, Larry J., and John H. Schilling. *Thermal Waters of Nevada.* Bulletin 91, Nevada Bureau of Mines and Geology. Mackay School of Mines, University of Nevada, Reno, 1979.

Lund, John W. "Balneological Use of Thermal and Mineral Waters in the U.S.A." *Geothermics* 25, no. 1 (1996): 103–47.

Vredenburgh, Larry M., Gary L. Shumway, and Russell Hartill. *Desert Fever: An Overview of Mining in the California Desert.* Canoga Park, Calif.: Living West Press, 1981.

Wheeler, Sessions. *The Desert Lake: The Story of Nevada's Pyramid Lake.* Caldwell, Idaho: Caxton Printers, 1980.

———. *The Nevada Desert.* Caldwell, Idaho: Caxton Printers, 1982.

INDEX

ABOUT THE AUTHOR

Matt Bischoff lives in the foothills outside Sacramento, California with his wife, Patty, and his son, Luke. He is a professional historian by trade, currently working for California State Parks. One of his greatest enjoyments is exploring God's creation and seeking out new hot springs. Often, the stories surrounding hot springs are just as interesting as the hot springs themselves, as each one has its own unique history. The hot springs listed in this book are some of his favorites for a variety of reasons. His hope is that you will find the same thrill in discovering a new hot springs and learning a little bit more about their stories.